The Oxford Poetry Library

Gerard Manley Hopkins

Edited by
CATHERINE PHILLIPS

Oxford New York
OXFORD UNIVERSITY PRESS
1995

Oxford University Press, Walton Street, Oxford OX2 6DP
Oxford New York
Athens Auckland Bangkok Bombay
Calcutta Cape Town Dar es Salaam Delhi
Florence Hong Kong Istanbul Karachi
Kuala Lumpur Madras Madrid Melbourne
Mexico City Nairobi Paris Singapore
Taipei Tokyo Toronto
and associated companies in
Berlin Ibadan

Oxford is a trade mark of Oxford University Press

This selection first published in the Oxford Poetry Library 1995

British Library Cataloguing in Publication Data
Data available

Library of Congress Cataloging in Publication Data
Data available
ISBN 0-19-282303-5

1 3 5 7 9 10 8 6 4 2

Typeset by J&L Composition Ltd
Filey, North Yorkshire
Printed in Great Britain by
Biddles Ltd
Guildford and King's Lynn

Contents

Abbreviations

EDD English Dialect Dictionary

J. *The Journals and Papers of Gerard Manley Hopkins*, ed. Humphry House and Graham Storey (London, 1959)

L. I *The Letters of Gerard Manley Hopkins to Robert Bridges*, ed. C. C. Abbott (London, 1935, 1955)

L. II *The Correspondence of Gerard Manley Hopkins and Richard Watson Dixon*, ed. C. C. Abbott (London, 1935, 1955)

L. III *The Further Letters of Gerard Manley Hopkins*, ed. C. C. Abbott (London, 2nd edn., 1956)

Poems *The Poems of Gerard Manley Hopkins*, ed. W. H. Gardner and N. H. MacKenzie (4th edn., Oxford, 1967, 1982)

OET *The Poetical Works of Gerard Manley Hopkins*, ed. Norman H. MacKenzie (Oxford English Texts; Oxford, 1990)

S. *The Sermons and Devotional Writings of Gerard Manley Hopkins*, ed. Christopher Devlin, SJ (London, 1959)

For details of critical books mentioned, see Further Reading, pp. 252–5.

Introduction

GERARD MANLEY HOPKINS was born at Stratford near London on 28 July 1844, the first of eight children of Manley and Catherine Hopkins (a ninth died in infancy). Manley was a self-made man, born into a family whose decline in material fortunes meant that he was unable to fulfil his ambition of going to university. He worked as an average adjustor, establishing insurance claims arising from marine disasters, and went on to write the standard handbook on the subject and establish his own successful firm of adjustors into which Cyril, one of his younger sons, entered. There is only one published photograph of Manley and his appearance in it does not suggest his drive, nor the range of his interests. He wrote poetry, a significant amount of which was published in two volumes, and in the journal *Once a Week* under the pseudonym Berni. In many of the poems it is possible to see traits that shaped Gerard's sensibility. There is the protective love of nature, braced by a more scientifically accurate observation than in much nature poetry of the day; there are, too, religious concerns and an amateur's interest in the operation of the mind. Gerard (and his sister Grace) also followed Manley in writing music.

Catherine's strong and pious personality deeply affected Gerard, too. Her handwriting is strikingly aggressive for a woman, with vigorous cross-strokes and scything up-strokes. It was she who often wrote out poems for Gerard's commonplace book, who I think transcribed his prize-winning poem at school, 'The Escorial', and who drafted the incomplete letter of protest at his conversion ending, 'Gerard, my darling boy, are you indeed gone from me.' It was his mother's feelings that Gerard records hurting most often during the difficult period of 1864–6, when he was breaking away from his closely bonded family to go down a religious path whose consequences they dreaded for him. But Gerard Manley Hopkins did not have a personality to which the easy way appealed. He was independent in his thinking from a surprisingly early age, and, as a boy, clever with a tendency to condescension and unkind mimicry, but also gifted with an extraordinary sensitivity to beauty in nature and man. So intense was his appreciation of colour, for example, that he told his friend Richard Watson Dixon that certain shades of blue and red had once been sights to draw tears from him. His special responsiveness to visual and aural impressions prompted him to think at one time that he might make a career as a poet–artist, as Dante Gabriel Rossetti had done. Gerard's brothers Everard and Arthur both made their careers as illustrators and artists and his sister Kate was also artistically talented.

Gerard was sent to Highgate School, where his love of the classics was fostered along with a resentment of its bullying headmaster, the Revd Dr J. B. Dyne. From success there Gerard won a place, although not a college scholarship, at Balliol College, Oxford, where he thrived. The university was in the midst of a number of intellectual movements, among them the rise of science—the famous debate between Bishop Wilberforce and Thomas Huxley had taken place in the new Oxford Museum [of science] just three years before Hopkins became an undergraduate. He was caught up in the second wave of conversions to Roman Catholicism inspired by John Henry Newman and the criticisms of the Anglican Church made by such influential members of the Oxford Movement as Edward Pusey and Henry Parry Liddon, both of whom were Gerard's confessors and counsellors. Poems written while he was an undergraduate show Hopkins working through not only his religious convictions but the philosophical problems of how man's experience of the world is shaped by internal as well as external forces. They show too a self-discontent in his struggle to control his sexual impulses and the rougher edges of his personality. The general stylistic influence of Keats, Tennyson, Spenser, and Christina Rossetti is evident, as well as echoes of Shakespeare and Milton. It was during his undergraduate years, largely through his growing dissatisfaction with Tennyson's poetry, that Hopkins formulated his ideas on poetic quality, distinguishing 'poetry proper', written in an inspired mood by accomplished poets, from 'Parnassian' (poetry written by the accomplished but with less imaginative fire). He applied a third term, 'Delphic', to verse that has the form of poetry rather than prose but has none of the intensity Hopkins associated with poetry proper. Matthew Arnold, Professor of Poetry at Oxford while Hopkins was an undergraduate, was to make similar distinctions.

Hopkins's circle of friends included Robert Bridges, with whom he was later to develop an important correspondence, and William Mowbray Baillie, with whom he exchanged ideas on art and literature and, later, philology. Both were to remain his friends through most of his life. More influential during his undergraduate days were probably the friendships with others who were attracted to Catholicism, such as William Addis, and Digby Mackworth Dolben, a relative of Bridges. Dolben and Hopkins met during a visit Dolben paid to Oxford in February 1865. They discovered that they had much in common—interests in writing poetry, religious inclinations, and probably a certain sexual attraction. Dolben failed to reply to letters Hopkins sent him, and Hopkins's feelings for him seem quite quickly to have grown less intense, so that, when Dolben was drowned in 1867, Hopkins wrote to Bridges: 'I looked forward to meeting Dolben and his being a Catholic more than to anything. At the same time from never having met him but once I find it difficult to realise his death or feel as if it were anything to me' (*L.* I 16).

The most important decision that Hopkins made while he was at Oxford occurred, he said, 'all in a minute': the decision of July 1866 to become a Roman Catholic. Although the actual turning-point may have been sudden and impelled in part by that of a number of his friends, who were all received within a few weeks of each other, the thought leading up to it was careful. Hopkins's diaries show that for some eighteen months he patiently examined what he could of the claims made by Catholicism and the Anglican Church to be the 'true' church. At the time of his conversion Hopkins wrote that not belonging to the true church would lead to eternal damnation, although he later investigated ways in which such a sentence might be averted for people whom he loved and who were not Catholic (see *L.* III 147–8 to his mother, 'Henry Purcell'). But the change of religious affiliation also had worldly consequences. The Catholic hierarchy—its structure of parishes, dioceses, and so on—had been set in place only in 1850 and fear of Catholics, linked to fear of such Catholic countries as France and Spain, was still widespread and adversely affected the professional advancement of many Catholics. Those working within the Catholic hierarchy, on the other hand, worked within a system at full stretch to cover the demands on it from parishes, schools, and seminaries.

Hopkins left Oxford having achieved firsts in Moderations and Greats. He then took a temporary post as a teacher at the Oratory school for Catholic boys in Birmingham, an institution established and then still led by John Henry Newman, who had admitted Hopkins to the Catholic Church. But Hopkins missed the intellectual excitement of his university days, which he had further enhanced by attending art exhibitions in London, reading contemporary literature, and taking advantage of opportunities of meeting such celebrities as the Rossettis and William Butterfield, whose architecture he greatly admired. School teaching, by contrast, he found somewhat dreary and demanding.

The next large decision that he took was to join a religious order. After some hesitation, he chose the Society of Jesus, which he entered on 7 September 1868. The struggle to control his own nature, his keen awareness of how difficult it was to lead a life that followed Christian tenets undeviatingly, would have been strong motives in seeking an outer structure to assist him. He was also caught between strongly individual and independent thought and a desire for the safety of well-established precedent. It was in the novitiate that he began to practise the Spiritual Exercises of St Ignatius, whose pervasive influence on his life can be seen in his constant awareness of the potential religious significance and symbolism of much that he saw and experienced. This systematically Christocentric approach to the world suffuses his mature poetry, setting it apart from the writing of such other close and imaginative observers of nature as John Clare and Francis Kilvert.

After two years spent at Manresa House, the Jesuit novitiate in London, Hopkins was sent to St Mary's Hall at Stonyhurst, Lancashire. It was while he was studying philosophy here that he came across the *Oxford Commentary* on the *Sentences* of Peter Lombard by Duns Scotus. In his Journal Hopkins wrote of the find that he was 'flush with a new stroke of enthusiasm. It may come to nothing or it may be a mercy from God. But just then when I took in any inscape of the sky or sea I thought of Scotus' (*J.* 221). What Hopkins valued in Scotus was in part the authority he gave to what was probably the central experience of Hopkins's life. This experience was of feeling God's presence in nature so that perceiving the essence or 'inscape' of a thing was to perceive some part of God and even to feel at times that it was possible to communicate directly with him through nature (see 'Hurrahing in Harvest'). The idea allowed Hopkins to fuse his intense appreciation of natural beauty with his religious worship. In addition to 'inscape', he invented a second, related term—'instress'—to indicate the force that held the thing or individual together or described a momentary flash of communication between an observer and the thing observed (see 'The Wreck of the Deutschland', stanza 5).

Hopkins's training was interrupted for almost a year from September 1873, when he was sent back to Manresa House to prepare Juniors for examinations in Classics and English for the University of London. Writing his lectures called for the investigation of basic ideas about rhythm and rhyme, an important stage in his technical development as a poet. Although he had made his first experiments in what he later called 'sprung rhythm' while he was an undergraduate (see notes to 'St. Dorothea'), he produced the first of his mature poems in the metre in Wales when he resumed his training. This was 'The Wreck of the Deutschland' (1876), the longest of his complete poems and an ode in which he set out to explain the wreck of a steamer in terms of God's providence. Into it Hopkins poured natural observation, intense religious experience, and doctrinal zeal. The poem was not published during his life but freed him from scruples about spending time on poetry, so that in 1877 he wrote a number of remarkable sonnets, including 'The Windhover' and 'God's Grandeur'. In them, in his efforts to express his emotions and observations, he experimented constantly with rhythm, and rhyme influenced by Greek and Welsh patterns.

During the next six years Hopkins fulfilled a number of roles as priest, preacher, and school teacher within various Catholic communities in mainland Britain from London and Oxford to Liverpool and Glasgow. He was appalled by the poverty of the working classes, by the misery caused by drunkenness, and by the poor physique resulting from urban squalor. His letters to Bridges and Dixon speak of fatigue and suggest the oppression of spirit he felt in trying to fulfil roles that did not come easily to him, though 'Felix Randal' shows the compassion and self-awareness he was capable of in relating to his parishioners. He was generally happier during the year's respite of his tertianship from October 1881, a year of contemplation away from the demands of the everyday industrial world of nineteenth-century Britain.

Then in 1883 he was sent to Dublin to be Professor of Greek and Latin Literature at University College. He wrote to Bridges that, when he thought of the six examinations he would have to mark each year, each with hundreds of candidates, he felt that enough gold to cover Stephen's Green, the ample park over which University College looked, would not pay for it. But examining was not the worst bane of Hopkins's existence during the last five years of his life. He found that in Ireland, although he was surrounded by

Catholics, he was attached to an academically poor institution and was inextricably part of a movement actively working to throw the English out of Ireland. An English patriot at heart, he lamented that his efforts were 'like prisoners made to serve the enemies' gunners'. It may have been for reasons of nationality that Hopkins withdrew from many of the social opportunities available to him in University College. Whatever the reason, loneliness became increasingly evident in his letters and poetry. The Sonnets of Desolation, probably written in 1885–6, contain much of the material mentioned in his letters of the period: feelings of a lack of worldly success, of having wasted his talents, of a loneliness and corrosive self-loathing. Yet these poems are skilfully shaped, suggesting a greater objectivity and control over the emotions they express than their intensity might lead one to expect. There were happier times, too, spent with a colleague Robert Curtis, minor successes in his writing of music, and periods of a serene religious certainty evident in such poems as 'That Nature is a Heraclitean Fire and of the comfort of the Resurrection'.

Throughout his adult life Hopkins expressed guilt over the writing of his poetry, since it did not bring about the conversions to Catholicism that he had hoped and had cost him time and energy which might have been better spent in other ways. However, in retreat notes made in January 1889, he consciously left his poetry to God's care, putting aside frustrations at his lack of worldly recognition and trusting that work so evidently personal would not be used against his name. The note represents at least a temporary truce in the internal debate Hopkins had waged with himself since his undergraduate days over the relation of his vocation and artistic impulses. A few weeks later he contracted typhoid, from which he died on 8 June. His poetry was not published in an edition until 1918 and only slowly met with widespread appreciation.

Although Hopkins bemoaned his fragmentary and slim productivity, his poems have greater originality, intellectual and emotional creativity than can be found in many more prolific writers. Numerous poets have tried to imitate aspects of his work with results that are always ventriloquial, but the experience of studying so exacting a writer has subsequently helped to strengthen the mature work of such poets as David Jones, Robert Lowell, Sylvia Plath, and Seamus Heaney. For the general reader it is probably the music of Hopkins's poetry and his honesty and intelligence that have so much to do with his current and continuing popularity.

Chronology

1844 28 July, born at Stratford, Essex. Gerard was the first of eight children. His father, Manley Hopkins, was a marine adjuster and Consul-General for Hawaii in London.

1854–62 Gerard attends Highgate School. He does well academically, winning five prizes, among them the School Poetry Prize for 'The Escorial' (1860), the Governors' Gold Medal for Latin Verse, and a school Exhibition.

1862 Wins an exhibition to Balliol College, Oxford.

1863 Apr., enters Balliol.

1866 July, decides to join Catholic Church.
21 Oct., received by Newman into the Catholic communion.

1867 June, graduates with first-class degree.
Sept.-Apr. 1868, teaches at the Oratory, Birmingham.

1868 2 May, decides to become a priest, although unsure whether to join the Benedictines or the Jesuits.
11 May, burns copies of his poems, indicating his new, vocational goal.
3 July–1 Aug., walking holiday in Switzerland with Edward Bond.
7 Sept., enters the Jesuit novitiate at Manresa House, Roehampton (London).

1870 9 Sept., begins three years of philosophy at St Mary's Hall, Stonyhurst, Lancashire.

1872 Reads the *Oxford Commentary* of Duns Scotus on the *Sentences* of Peter Lombard.

1873 From September teaches rhetoric at Roehampton.

1874 Aug., begins three years of theology at St Beuno's, Wales.

1875 Dec., begins to write 'The Wreck of the Deutschland'.

1876 Writes 'Silver Jubilee', 'Ad Episcopum', 'Cywydd', and 'Penmaen Pool'.

1877 Feb.–Sept., writes 'God's Grandeur', 'The Starlight Night', 'As kingfishers catch fire', 'Spring', 'The Sea and the Skylark', 'In the Valley of the Elwy', 'The Windhover', 'Pied Beauty', 'Hurrahing in Harvest', and 'The Lantern out of Doors'.
23 Sept., ordained.

Oct., sent to Mount St Mary's College, Chesterfield, where a classical scholar was required as teacher.

1878 Apr., moved to Stonyhurst to prepare students for the University of London examinations. 'The Loss of the Eurydice' and 'The May Magnificat' written here.
July–Nov., acting curate at Mount Street, London.
Dec., becomes curate at St Aloysius' church, Oxford.

1879 Feb.–Oct., writes nine complete poems ('Duns Scotus's Oxford', 'Binsey Poplars', 'Henry Purcell', 'The Candle Indoors', 'The Handsome Heart', 'The Bugler's First Communion', 'Andromeda', 'Morning, Midday, and Evening Sacrifice', and 'Peace') and a number of fragments, and begins to compose music.
Oct.–Dec., curate at St Joseph's, Bedford Leigh, where he writes 'At the Wedding March'.
30 Dec., becomes Select Preacher at St Francis Xavier's, Liverpool.

1880 Writes 'Felix Randal' and 'Spring and Fall'.

1881 Sept., becomes assistant in Glasgow. Visits Loch Lomond and there writes 'Inversnaid'.
Oct., starts tertianship at Roehampton; composes no extant poetry during the year but writes notes towards a commentary on the Spiritual Exercises.

1882 Sept., sent to Stonyhurst College to teach classics. There he completes 'The Leaden Echo and the Golden Echo' and writes 'Ribblesdale'.

1883 Bridges begins his second collection of Hopkins's poems (MS *B*).
Hopkins writes 'The Blessed Virgin compared to the Air we Breathe'.
Aug., meets Coventry Patmore.

1884 Feb., moves to Dublin as Fellow in Classics and Professor of Greek and Latin Literature at the newly formed University College. His duties at first were as examiner in Greek.
Oct.–Apr. 1885, writes most of the extant passages of *St. Winefred's Well.*

1885 May well have written most of the poems called 'The Sonnets of Desolation' as well as 'To what serves Mortal Beauty?', 'The Soldier', 'To his Watch', and 'The times are nightfall'.

1886 May, meets Bridges while on holiday in England.
Completes 'Spelt from Sibyl's Leaves', writes 'On the Portrait

of Two Beautiful Young People', translates 'Songs from Shakespeare'.

1887 Aug., holiday in England.
Writes 'Harry Ploughman', 'Tom's Garland', and, perhaps, 'Ashboughs'.

1888 Begins 'Epithalamion', writes 'That Nature is a Heraclitean Fire . . .', 'What shall I do for the land that bred me', and 'St. Alphonsus Rodriguez'.
Aug., holiday in Scotland.

1889 Jan., retreat at Tullabeg. Writes 'Thou art indeed just, Lord', 'The shepherd's brow', and 'To R. B.'.
8 June, dies of typhoid; buried at Glasnevin, Dublin.

Note on the Text

WHEN, shortly after Hopkins's death, Robert Bridges started to edit his friend's poems, it was the second time that he had contemplated an edition of them. His first attempt to print Hopkins's poetry was with that of four other poets and was begun in 1880. The attempt faltered because the chosen publisher, a friend of Bridges's later to publish a number of volumes of his poetry, was just starting his press and was not confident of being able to carry through the project. Jean-Georges Ritz speculates that Hopkins also raised objections himself. In 1889 the plan failed, in part because Bridges at that time considered a lengthy biographical introduction necessary and he was too upset by Hopkins's depression and his own feeling that his friend's life had been wasted to write it, and partly because he did not consider contemporary poetic taste ready to accept such rhythms and diction.

Between 1889, and 1918, when Bridges prepared the first edition of Hopkins's verse, he published sixteen of Hopkins's poems or parts of them in various collections. In his edition he was less concerned to present an accurate version of the poems as Hopkins had left them than to win acceptance for the poetry. Consequently, he chose those versions or combinations of them that he thought most appealing, even when, as in the case of 'The Handsome Heart', Hopkins had himself cancelled the copy. The introduction was made editorial rather than biographical; in it Bridges was critical of sources of ambiguity, such as the omission of the subjective relative pronoun, 'that', and the use of homophones in grammatically uncertain positions. He also condemned what he saw as faults of taste in rhyme and metaphor which today few people would find objectionable.

The edition of 750 copies sold slowly and it was not until 1930 that Charles Williams, a poet himself and house-editor at Oxford University Press, was asked to produce an enlarged second edition. W. H. Gardner then carried this work further in 1948 and 1956, adding also a biographical introduction. Much of the editing of the early poems was done by Humphry House and published in *The Notebooks and Papers of Gerard Manley Hopkins* (1937). The fourth edition of the poems, edited jointly by W. H. Gardner and N. H.

MacKenzie in 1967, and reprinted with corrections by N. H. MacKenzie a number of times since, caught numerous errors that had crept into the text and restored many of Hopkins's readings in place of those of Bridges.

This selection follows my Oxford Authors edition in discarding the subsections in which the poems had previously been placed and presents them in chronological order. Absolute chronology cannot be achieved. The dates Hopkins assigned were normally those of the poem's inception, but he revised his work and left many of his poems without dates. It is hoped that, despite the imperfections, a rough chronology will give a fuller idea of Hopkins's poetic interests at each stage. The order used here is one to which a number of other critics have also contributed, among them Humphry House and Graham Storey, W. H. Gardner, and, most of all, N. H. MacKenzie. There are, however, disagreements as to the most likely sequence.

This volume takes as text that of my Oxford Authors edition, which was prepared from the manuscripts, with improvements made by N. H. MacKenzie in his Oxford English Texts edition. There remain some differences in our interpretation of the manuscripts. Many of Hopkins's early poems are contained in two tiny diaries, *C* I and *C* II, where pencil drafts are fragmented by prose entries. These, and a number of poems written on loose leaves, are housed in Campion Hall, Oxford. Most of the later manuscripts are in the Bodleian Library. The majority of these belong to the four collections described by Robert Bridges:

A is my own collection, a MS. book made up of autographs—by which word I denote poems in the author's handwriting—pasted into it as they were received from him, and also of contemporary copies of other poems. These autographs and copies date from '67 to '89, the year of his death . . .

B is a MS. book into which, in '83, I copied from *A* certain poems of which the author had kept no copy. He was remiss in making fair copies of his work, and his autograph of *The Deutschland* having been (seemingly) lost, I copied that poem and others from *A* at his request. After that date he entered more poems in this book as he completed them, and he also made both corrections of copy and emendations of the poems which had been copied into it by me. Thus, if a poem occur in both *A* and *B*, then *B* is [generally] the later, and, except for overlooked errors of copyist, the better authority . . .

D is a collection of the author's letters to Canon Dixon . . . they contain autographs of a few poems with late corrections.

H is the bundle of posthumous papers that came into my hands at the author's death. These were at the time examined, sorted, and indexed; and the more important pieces—of which copies were taken—were inserted into a scrap-book. That collection is the source of a series of his most mature sonnets, and of almost all the unfinished poems and fragments. Among these papers were also some early drafts.

Some of these poems have subsequently been bound in other volumes by the staff of the Bodleian; among these are MS *C*, an important and miscellaneous collection of Hopkins's poems, and *F*, a few pages taken from letters to his mother.

There are, in addition, a couple of manuscripts in the British Library and some in private hands.

In general the version which I believe to be that last written has been taken for text. This policy has been followed because Hopkins's poetic powers were far from spent when he died and although questions of the influence of Bridges and Dixon arise, it is clear that Hopkins did not simply follow their advice but considered it and, even when conceding their objections, normally found his own solutions to them.

Editorial intervention could have been still further reduced by showing all uncancelled variants in the text but it has been felt that while this is appropriate for scholars (and has been done by N. H. MacKenzie in the Oxford English Texts edition) it is unnecessary in an introduction to the poetry. Some of the variants can be found in the notes, and in poems where extensive changes have resulted from choosing the final version as text, as for example in 'The Handsome Heart', and 'St. Alphonsus Rodriguez', the earlier but better-known versions are also printed complete. I have not included the poems in Latin, Greek, and Welsh, and have omitted the shorter poetic fragments.

Throughout the edition layout of poems and marks of punctuation have been changed as a result of scrutiny of the manuscripts. In MS *B*, many pages of which contain writing by both Bridges and Hopkins, slight differences in ink-colour and magnification of pen-tracks suggest that some punctuation marks thought in the past to have been introduced by Bridges were in fact made by Hopkins. As in the fourth edition, layout has generally been taken from MS *A* since that used in MS *B* was chosen by Bridges.

The metrical marks that appear in this volume are all Hopkins's own and come for the most part from MS *B*, which was Hopkins's compromise between the more prolific markings of MS *A* and the absence of any guidance. Cost and editorial opinion at Oxford University Press have restricted metrical marks in the text to simple stresses. In some poems written out after 1881 Hopkins introduced a scheme differentiating stress. The full system is marked in the notes but in the text single stresses have been used to show the heaviest accents. The only exception is 'Tom's Garland', where the one double stress marked in MS *B* has been incorporated into the text.

The Escorial

Βάτραχος δὲ ποτ᾽ ἀκρίδας ὥς τις ᾽ερίσδω

1

There is a massy pile above the waste
Amongst Castilian barrens mountain-bound;
A sombre length of grey; four towers placed
At corners flank the stretching compass round;
A pious work with threefold purpose crown'd—
A cloister'd convent first, the proudest home
Of those who strove God's gospel to confound
With barren rigour and a frigid gloom—
Hard by a royal palace, and a royal tomb.

2

They tell its story thus; amidst the heat
Of battle once upon St. Lawrence' day
Philip took oath, while glory or defeat
Hung in the swaying of the fierce melée,
'So I am victor now, I swear to pay
The richest gift St. Lawrence ever bore,
When chiefs and monarchs came their gifts to lay
Upon his altar, and with rarest store
To deck and make most lordly evermore.'

3

For that staunch saint still prais'd his Master's name
While his crack'd flesh lay hissing on the grate;
Then fail'd the tongue; the poor collapsing frame,
Hung like a wreck that flames not billows beat—
So, grown fantastic in his piety,
Philip, supposing that the gift most meet,
The sculptur'd image of such faith would be,
Uprais'd an emblem of that fiery constancy.

St. 2: At the battle of St Quentin, between the French and Spaniards, Philip II vowed the Escorial to St Laurence, the patron saint of the day, if he gained the victory.

St. 3: St Laurence is said to have been roasted to death on a gridiron.

4

He rais'd the convent as a monstrous grate;
The cloisters cross'd with equal courts betwixt
Formed bars of stone; Beyond in stiffen'd state
The stretching palace lay as handle fix'd.
Then laver'd founts and postur'd stone he mix'd.
—Before the sepulchre there stood a gate,
A faithful guard of inner darkness fix'd—
But open'd twice, in life and death, to state,
To newborn prince, and royal corse inanimate.

5

While from the pulpit in a heretic land
Ranters scream'd rank rebellion, this should be
A fortress of true faith, and central stand
Whence with the scourge of ready piety
Legates might rush, zeal-rampant, fiery,
*Upon the stubborn Fleming; and the rod
Of forc'd persuasion issue o'er the free.—
For, where the martyr's bones were thickest trod,
They shrive themselves and cry, 'Good service to our God.'

6

No finish'd proof was this of Gothic grace
With flowing tracery engemming rays
Of colour in high casements face to face;
And foliag'd crownals (pointing how the ways
Of art best follow nature) in a maze
Of finish'd diapers, that fills the eye
And scarcely traces where one beauty strays
And melts amidst another; ciel'd on high
With blazoned groins, and crowned with hues of majesty.

St. 4: The Escorial was built in the form of a gridiron,—the rectangular convent was the grate, the cloisters the bars, the towers the legs inverted, the palace the handle.

The building contained the royal Mausoleum; and a gate which was opened only to the newborn heir apparent, and to the funeral of a monarch.

St. 5: * Philip endeavoured to establish the Inquisition in the Netherlands.

St. 6: Philip did not choose the splendid luxuriance of the Spanish Gothic as the style of architecture fitted for the Escorial.

7

This was no classic temple order'd round
With massy pillars of the Doric mood
Broad-fluted, nor with shafts acanthus-crown'd,
Pourtray'd along the frieze with Titan's brood
That battled Gods for heaven; brilliant hued,*
With golden fillets and rich blazonry,
Wherein beneath the cornice, horsemen rode†
With form divine, a fiery chivalry—
Triumph of airy grace and perfect harmony.

8

*Fair relics too the changeful Moor had left
Splendid with phantasies aerial,
Of mazy shape and hue, but now bereft
By conqu'rors rude of honor; and not all
Unmindful of their grace, the Escorial
Arose in gloom, a solemn mockery
Of those gilt webs that languish'd in a fall.
This to remotest ages was to be
The pride of faith, and home of sternest piety.

9

. . . .

10

He rang'd long corridors and cornic'd halls,
And damasqu'd arms and foliag'd carving piled.—
With painting gleam'd the rich pilaster'd walls—.
*Here play'd the virgin mother with her Child

St. 7: Nor the Classic.
* The Parthenon &c. were magnificently coloured and gilded.
† The horsemen in the Panathenaic processions.
St. 8: * The Alhambra &c.
St. 8: The Architect was Velasquez; the style Italian Classic, partly Ionic partly Doric. The whole is sombre in appearance, but grand, and imposing.
St. 10: The interior was decorated with all the richest productions of art and nature. Pictures, statues, marble, fountains, tapesty, &c. (*He* refers to Philip.)
* In one of Raphael's pictures the Madonna and St Joseph play with their Child in a wide meadow; behind is a palm-tree.

In some broad palmy mead, and saintly smiled,
And held a cross of flowers, in purple bloom;
†He, where the crownals droop'd, himself reviled
And bleeding saw.—Thus hung from room to room
The skill of dreamy Claude, and Titian's mellow gloom.

11

Here in some‡ darken'd landscape Paris fair
Stretches the envied fruit with fatal smile
To golden-girdled Cypris;—Ceres there
Raves through Sicilian pastures many a mile;
¶But, hapless youth, Antinous the while
Gazes aslant his shoulder, viewing nigh
Where Phoebus weeps for him whom Zephyr's guile
‖Chang'd to a flower; and there, with placid eye
§Apollo views the smitten Python writhe and die.

. . . .

12

Then through the afternoon the summer beam
Slop'd on the galleries; upon the wall
Rich Titians faded; in the straying gleam
The motes in ceaseless eddy shine and fall
Into the cooling gloom; till slowly all
Dimm'd in the long accumulated dust;
Pendant in formal line from cornice tall
*Blades of Milan in circles rang'd, grew rust
And silver damasqu'd plates obscur'd in age's crust.

† Alluding to Raphael's 'Lo Spasimo', which is, I believe, in the Escorial.

St. 11: ‡ Alluding to the dark colouring of landscapes to be seen in Rubens, Titian &c.

¶ A beautiful youth drowned in the Nile; the statue has the position described.

‖ Hyacinthus. § The Belvidere Apollo.

St. 12: The Escorial was adorned by succe[e]ding kings, until the Peninsular war, when the French as a piece of revenge for their defeats, sent a body of dragoons under La Houssaye, who entered the Escorial, ravaged and despoiled it of some of its greatest treasures. The monks then left the convent. Since that time it has been left desolate and uninhabited. The 12th stanza describes this.

* Alluding to the practise (*sic*) of arranging swords in circles, radiating from their hilts.

13

†But from the mountain glens in autumn late
Adown the clattering gullies swept the rain;
The driving storm at hour of vespers beat
Upon the mould'ring terraces amain;
The Altar-tapers flar'd in gusts; in vain
Louder the monks dron'd out Gregorians slow;
Afar in corridors with painèd strain
Doors slamm'd to the blasts continuously; more low,
Then pass'd the wind, and sobb'd with mountain-echo'd woe.

14

Next morn a peasant from the mountain side
Came midst the drizzle telling how last night
Two mazèd shepherds perish'd in the tide;
But further down the valley, left and right,
Down-splinter'd rocks crush'd cottages.—Drear sight—
An endless round of dead'ning solitude:
[x]Till, (fearing ravage worse than in his flight,
What time the baffled Frank swept back pursu'd
Fell on the palace, and the lust of rabble rude,)

15

*Since trampled Spain by royal discord torn
Lay bleeding, to Madrid the last they bore,
The choicest remnants thence;—such home forlorn
The monks left long ago: Since which no more
†Eighth wonder of the earth, in size, in store
And art and beauty: Title now too null—
More wondrous to have borne such hope before
It seems; for grandeur barren left and dull
Than changeful pomp of courts is aye more wonderful.

St. 13: † The Escorial is often exposed to the attacks of the storms which sweep down from the mountains of Guadarrama.

St. 14: [x] Some years ago, fearing that the Carlists would plunder the Escorial, they removed the choicest remaining treasures to Madrid.

St. 15: * The civil wars of late years in Spain.

† The Spaniards call it 8th wonder of the world.

(6)

Aeschylus: Promêtheus Desmotês

Lines 88–100, 114–27

PROMÊTHEUS

Divinity of air, fleet-feather'd gales,
Ye river-heads, thou billowy deep that laugh'st
A countless laughter, Earth mother of all,
Thou sun, allseeing eyeball of the day,
Witness to me! Look you I am a god,
And these are from the gods my penalties.
Look with what unseemliness
I a thousand thousand years
Must watch down with weariness
Fallen from my peers.
The young chief of the bless'd of heaven
Hath devis'd new pains for me
And hath given
This indignity of chains.
What is, and what is to be,
All alike is grief to me;
I look all ways but only see
The drear dull burthen of unending pains.

. . . .

Ah well a day!—
What was that echo caught anigh me,
That scent from breezes breathing by me,
Sped of gods, or mortal sign,
Or half-human half-divine?
To the world's end, to the last hill
Comes one to gaze upon my ill;
Be this thy quest or other, see
A god enchain'd of Destiny:
Foe of Zeus and hate of all
That wont to throng Zeus' banquet-hall,
Sith I loved and loved too well
The race of man; and hence I fell.
Woe is me, what do I hear?

Fledgèd things do rustle near;
Whispers of the mid-air stirring
With light pulse of pinions skirring,
And all that comes is fraught to me with fear.

Il Mystico

Hence sensual gross desires,
Right offspring of your grimy mother Earth!
My Spirit hath a birth
Alien from yours as heaven from Nadir-fires:
You rank and reeking things,
Scoop you from teeming filth some sickly hovel,
And there for ever grovel
'Mid fever'd fumes and slime and cakèd clot:
But foul and cumber not
The shaken plumage of my Spirit's wings.
But come, thou balm to aching soul,
Of pointed wing and silver stole,
With heavenly cithern from high choir,
Tresses dipp'd in rainbow fire,
An olive-branch whence richly reek
Earthless dews on ancles sleek;
Be discover'd to my sight
From a haze of sapphire light,
Let incense hang across the room
And sober lustres take the gloom;
Come when night clings to what is hers
Closer because faint morning stirs;
When chill woods wake and think of morn,
But sleep again ere day be born;
When sick men turn, and lights are low,
And death falls gently as the snow;
When wholesome spirits rustle about,
And the tide of ill is out;
When waking hearts can pardon much
And hard men feel a softening touch;
When strangely loom all shapes that be,
And watches change upon the sea;

Silence holds breath upon her throne,
And the waked stars are all alone.
  Come because then most thinly lies
The veil that covers mysteries;
And soul is subtle and flesh weak
And pride is nerveless and hearts meek.

. . . .

Touch me and purify, and shew
Some of the secrets I would know.

. . . .

Grant that close-folded peace that clad
The seraph brows of Galahad,
Who knew the inner spirit that fills
Questioning winds around the hills;
Who made conjecture nearest far
To what the chords of angels are;
And to the mystery of those Things

. . . .

Shewn to Ezekiel's open'd sight
On Chebar's banks, and why they went
Unswerving through the firmament;
Whose ken through amber of dark eyes
Went forth to compass mysteries;
Who knowing all the sins and sores
That nest within close-barrèd doors,
And that grief masters joy on earth,
Yet found unstinted place for mirth;
Who could forgive without grudge after
Gross mind discharging foulèd laughter;
To whom the common earth and air
Were limn'd about with radiance rare
Most like those hues that in the prism
Melt as from a heavenly chrism;
Who could keep silence, tho' the smart
Yawn'd like long furrow in the heart;

. . . .

Or, like a lark to glide aloof
Under the cloud-festoonèd roof,
That with a turning of the wings
Light and darkness from him flings;
To drift in air, the circled earth
Spreading still its sunnèd girth;
To hear the sheep-bells dimly die
Till the lifted clouds were nigh;
In breezy belts of upper air
Melting into aether rare;
And when the silent height were won,
And all in lone air stood the sun,
To sing scarce heard, and singing fill
The airy empire at his will;
To hear his strain descend less loud
On to ledges of grey cloud;
And fainter, finer, trickle far
To where the listening uplands are;
To pause—then from his gurgling bill
Let the warbled sweetness rill,
And down the welkin, gushing free,
Hark the molten melody;
In fits of music till sunset
Starting the silver rivulet;
Sweetly then and of free act
To quench the fine-drawn cataract;
And in the dews beside his nest
To cool his plumy throbbing breast.
Or, if a sudden silver shower
Has drench'd the molten sunset hour,
And with weeping cloud is spread
All the welkin overhead,
Save where the unvexèd west
Lies divinely still, at rest,
Where liquid heaven sapphire-pale
Does into amber splendours fail,
And fretted clouds with burnish'd rim,
Phoebus' loosen'd tresses, swim;
While the sun streams forth amain
On the tumblings of the rain,
When his mellow smile he sees

Caught on the dark-ytressèd trees,
When the rainbow arching high
Looks from the zenith round the sky,
Lit with exquisite tints seven
Caught from angels' wings in heaven,
Double, and higher than his wont,
The wrought rim of heaven's font,—
Then may I upwards gaze and see
The deepening intensity
Of the air-blended diadem,
All a sevenfold-single gem,
Each hue so rarely wrought that where
It melts, new lights arise as fair,
Sapphire, jacinth, chrysolite,
The rim with ruby fringes dight,
Ending in sweet uncertainty
'Twixt real hue and phantasy.
Then while the rain-born arc glows higher
Westward on his sinking sire;
While the upgazing country seems
Touch'd from heaven in sweet dreams;
While a subtle spirit and rare
Breathes in the mysterious air;
While sheeny tears and sunlit mirth
Mix o'er the not unmovèd earth,—
Then would I fling me up to sip
Sweetness from the hour, and dip
Deeply in the archèd lustres,
And look abroad on sunny clusters
Of wringing tree-tops, chalky lanes,
Wheatfields tumbled with the rains,
Streaks of shadow, thistled leas,
Whence spring the jewell'd harmonies
That meet in mid-air; and be so
Melted in the dizzy bow
That I may drink that ecstacy
Which to pure souls alone may be. . . .

A windy day in summer

The vex'd elm-heads are pale with the view
Of a mastering heaven utterly blue;
Swoll'n is the wind that in argent billows
Rolls across the labouring willows;
The chestnut-fans are loosely flirting,
And bared is the aspen's silky skirting;
The sapphire pools are smit with white
And silver-shot with gusty light;
While the breeze by rank and measure
Paves the clouds on the swept azure.

A fragment of anything you like

Fair, but of fairness as a vision dream'd;
Dry were her sad eyes that would fain have stream'd;
She stood before a light not hers, and seem'd

The lorn Moon, pale with piteous dismay,
Who rising late had miss'd her painful way
In wandering until broad light of day;

Then was discover'd in the pathless sky
White-faced, as one in sad assay to fly
Who asks not life but only place to die.

A Vision of the Mermaids

Rowing, I reach'd a rock—the sea was low—
Which the tides cover in their overflow,
Marking the spot, when they have gurgled o'er,
With a thin floating veil of water hoar.
A mile astern lay the blue shores away;
And it was at the setting of the day.
Plum-purple was the west; but spikes of light

Spear'd open lustrous gashes, crimson-white;
(Where the eye fix'd, fled the encrimsoning spot,
And gathering, floated where the gaze was not;)
And thro' their parting lids there came and went
Keen glimpses of the inner firmament:
Fair beds they seem'd of water-lily flakes
Clustering entrancingly in beryl lakes:
Anon, across their swimming splendour strook,
An intense line of throbbing blood-light shook
A quivering pennon; then, for eye too keen,
Ebb'd back beneath its snowy lids, unseen.
  Now all things rosy turn'd: the west had grown
To an orb'd rose, which, by hot pantings blown
Apart, betwixt ten thousand petall'd lips
By interchange gasp'd splendour and eclipse.
The zenith melted to a rose of air;
The waves were rosy-lipp'd; the crimson glare
Shower'd the cliffs and every fret and spire
With garnet wreaths and blooms of rosy-budded fire.
  Then, looking on the waters, I was ware
Of something drifting thro' delighted air,
—An isle of roses,—and another near;—
And more, on each hand, thicken, and appear
In shoals of bloom; as in unpeopled skies,
Save by two stars, more crowding lights arise,
And planets bud where'er we turn our mazèd eyes.
I gazed unhinder'd: Mermaids six or seven,
Ris'n from the deeps to gaze on sun and heaven,
Cluster'd in troops and halo'd by the light,
Those Cyclads made that thicken'd on my sight.
  This was their manner: one translucent crest
Of tremulous film, more subtle than the vest
Of dewy gorse blurr'd with the gossamer fine,
From crown to tail-fin floating, fringed the spine,
Droop'd o'er the brows like Hector's casque, and sway'd
In silken undulation, spurr'd and ray'd
With spikèd quills all of intensest hue;
And was as tho' some sapphire molten-blue
Were vein'd and streak'd with dusk-deep lazuli,
Or tender pinks with bloody Tyrian dye.
From their white waists a silver skirt was spread

To mantle-o'er the tail, such as is shed
Around the Water-Nymphs in fretted falls,
At red Pompeii on medallion'd walls.
A tinted fin on either shoulder hung;
Their pansy-dark or bronzen locks were strung
With coral, shells, thick-pearlèd cords, whate'er
The abysmal Ocean hoards of strange and rare.
Some trail'd the Nautilus; or on the swell
Tugg'd the boss'd, smooth-lipp'd, giant Strombus-shell.
Some carried the sea-fan; some round the head
With lace of rosy weed were chapleted;
One bound o'er dripping gold a turquoise-gemm'd
Circlet of astral flowerets—diadem'd
Like an Assyrian prince, with buds unsheath'd
From flesh-flowers of the rock; but more were wreath'd
With the dainty-delicate fretted fringe of fingers
Of that jacinthine thing, that, where it lingers,
Broiders the nets with fans of amethyst
And silver films, beneath with pearly mist,
The Glaucus cleped; others small braids encluster'd
Of glassy-clear Aeolis, metal-lustred
With growths of myriad feelers, crystalline
To shew the crimson streams that inward shine,
Which, lightening o'er the body rosy-pale,
Like shiver'd rubies dance or sheen of sapphire hail.
  Then saw I sudden from the waters break
Far off a Nereid company, and shake
From wings swan-fledged a wheel of watery light
Flickering with sunny spokes, and left and right
Plunge orb'd in rainbow arcs, and trample and tread
The satin-purfled smooth to foam, and spread
Slim-pointed sea-gull plumes, and droop behind
One scarlet feather trailing to the wind;
Then, like a flock of sea-fowl mounting higher,
Thro' crimson-golden floods pass swallow'd into fire.
  Soon—as when Summer of his sister Spring
Crushes and tears the rare enjewelling,
And boasting 'I have fairer things than these'
Plashes amidst the billowy apple-trees
His lusty hands, in gusts of scented wind

Swirling out bloom till all the air is blind
With rosy foam and pelting blossom and mists
Of driving vermeil-rain; and, as he lists,
The dainty onyx-coronals deflowers,
A glorious wanton;—all the wrecks in showers
Crowd down upon a stream, and, jostling thick
With bubbles bugle-eyed, struggle and stick
On tangled shoals that bar the brook—a crowd
Of filmy globes and rosy floating cloud:—
So those Mermaidens crowded to my rock,
And thicken'd, like that drifted bloom, the flock
Sun-flush'd, until it seem'd their father Sea
Had gotten him a wreath of sweet Spring-broidery.
   Careless of me they sported: some would plash
The languent smooth with dimpling drops, and flash
Their filmy tails adown whose length there show'd
An azure ridge; or clouds of violet glow'd
On prankèd scale; or threads of carmine, shot
Thro' silver, gloom'd to a blood-vivid clot.
Some, diving merrily, downward drove, and gleam'd
With arm and fin; the argent bubbles stream'd
Airwards, disturb'd; and the scarce troubled sea
Gurgled, where they had sunk, melodiously.
Others with fingers white would comb among
The drenchèd hair of slabby weeds that swung
Swimming, and languish'd green upon the deep
Down that dank rock o'er which their lush long tresses weep.
   But most in a half-circle watch'd the sun;
And a sweet sadness dwelt on everyone;
I knew not why,—but know that sadness dwells
On Mermaids—whether that they ring the knells
Of seamen whelm'd in chasms of the mid-main,
As poets sing; or that it is a pain
To know the dusk depths of the ponderous sea,
The miles profound of solid green, and be
With loath'd cold fishes, far from man—or what;—
I know the sadness but the cause know not.
Then they, thus ranged, 'gan make full plaintively
A piteous Siren sweetness on the sea,
Withouten instrument, or conch, or bell,
Or stretch'd chords tuneable on turtle's shell;

Only with utterance of sweet breath they sung
An antique chaunt and in an unknown tongue.
Now melting upward thro' the sloping scale
Swell'd the sweet strain to a melodious wail;
Now ringing clarion-clear to whence it rose
Slumber'd at last in one sweet, deep, heart-broken close.
  But when the sun had lapsed to ocean, lo
A stealthy wind crept round seeking to blow,
Linger'd, then raised the washing waves and drench'd
The floating blooms and with tide flowing quench'd
The rosy isles: so that I stole away
And gain'd thro' growing dusk the stirless bay;
White loom'd my rock, the water gurgling o'er,
Whence oft I watch but see those Mermaids now no more.

The End.

Winter with the Gulf Stream

The boughs, the boughs are bare enough
But earth has never felt the snow.
Frost-furred our ivies are and rough

With bills of rime the brambles shew.
The hoarse leaves crawl on hissing ground
Because the sighing wind is low.

But if the rain-blasts be unbound
And from dank feathers wring the drops
The clogged brook runs with choking sound

Kneading the mounded mire that stops
His channel under clammy coats
Of foliage fallen in the copse.

A simple passage of weak notes
Is all the winter bird dare try.
The bugle moon by daylight floats

So glassy white about the sky,
So like a berg of hyaline,
And pencilled blue so daintily,

I never saw her so divine.
But through black branches, rarely drest
In scarves of silky shot and shine,

The webbed and the watery west
Where yonder crimson fireball sets
Looks laid for feasting and for rest.

I see long reefs of violets
In beryl-covered fens so dim,
A gold-water Pactolus frets

Its brindled wharves and yellow brim,
The waxen colours weep and run,
And slendering to his burning rim

Into the flat blue mist the sun
Drops out and all our day is done.

Spring and Death

I had a dream. A wondrous thing:
It seem'd an evening in the Spring;
—A little sickness in the air
From too much fragrance everywhere:—
As I walk'd a stilly wood,
Sudden, Death before me stood:
In a hollow lush and damp,
He seem'd a dismal mirky stamp
On the flowers that were seen
His charnelhouse-grate ribs between,
And with coffin-black he barr'd the green.
'Death,' said I, 'what do you here
At this Spring season of the year?'

'I mark the flowers ere the prime
Which I may tell at Autumn-time.'
Ere I had further question made
Death was vanish'd from the glade.
Then I saw that he had bound
Many trees and flowers round
With a subtle web of black,
And that such a sable track
Lay along the grasses green
From the spot where he had been.
 But the Spring-tide pass'd the same;
Summer was as full of flame;
Autumn-time no earlier came.
And the flowers that he had tied,
As I mark'd, not always died
Sooner than their mates; and yet
Their fall was fuller of regret:
It seem'd so hard and dismal thing,
Death, to mark them in the Spring.

Pilate

The pang of Tartarus, Christians hold,
Is this, from Christ to be shut out.
This outer cold, my exile from of old
From Gôd and man, is hell no doubt.
Would I could hear the other Pilates shout.
But yet they say Christ comes at the last day.
Then will he keep in this stay?

2

Unchill'd I handle stinging snow;
The sun whose vast afflictive heat
Does lay men low with one blade's sudden blow
Cleaves not my brain, burns not my feet,
When the fierce skies are blue to black, albeit
The shearing rays contract me with their blaze
Most dead-alive upon those days.

3

Then I seek out the shadow and stones
And to those stones become akin
My several moans come distant in their tones
As though they were not from within
And for that fearful hour life is more thin
And numbs and starves, as between icy wharves
A freezing runnel sobs and dwarfs.

[4]

Sometimes I see the summit stake
High up the balanced stony air
In whose dead lake even a voice may make
The hanging snows rush down and bare
Their rocky lodges. Then the weather rare
Allows the sound of bells in hamlets round
To come to me from the underground.

5

Often when winds impenitent
Beat, heave and the strong mountain tire
I can stand pent in the monstrous element
And feel no blast.—The fretful fire
Breathe o'er my bare nerve rather. I desire
They swathe and lace the shroud-plaits o'er my face,
But to be ransom'd from this place.

6

Whatever time this vapourous roof,
The screen of my captivity,
Folds off aloof, that signal is and proof
Not of clear skies, but storm to be.
But then I make an eager shift to see
Houses that make abode beside the lake,
And then my heart goes near to break.

7

Then clouds come, like ill-balanced crags,
Shouldering. Down valleys smokes the gloom.

The thunder brags. In joints and sparkling jags
    The lightnings leap. The day of doom!
I cry 'O rocks and mountain make me room'
And yet I know it would be better so,
    Ay, sweet to taste beside this woe.

. . . .

    There is a day of all the year
    When life revisits me, nerve and vein.
They all come here and stand before me clear
    I try the Christus o'er again.
Sir! Christ! against this multitude I strain.—
Lord, but they cry so loud. And what am I?
    And all in one say 'Crucify!'

    Before that rock, my seat, He stands;
    And then—I choke to tell this out—
I give commands for water for my hands;
    And some of those who stand about,—
Vespillo my centurion hacks out
Some ice that locks the glacier to the rocks
    And in a bason brings the blocks.

    I choose one; but when I desire
    To wash before the multitude
The vital fire does suddenly retire
    From hands now clammy with strange blood.
My frenzied working is not understood.
Now I grow numb. My tongue strikes on the gum
    And cleaves, I struggle and am dumb.

    I hear the multitude tramp by.
    O here is the most piteous part,
For He whom I send forth to crucify,
    Whispers 'If thou have warmth at heart
Take courage; this shall need no further art.'

. . . .

    But if this overlast the day
    Undone, and I must wait the year,

Yet no delay can serve to grate away
    A purpose desperately dear

. . . .

    I have a hope if so it be,
    A hope of an approved device;
I will break free from the Jews' company,
    And find a flint, a fang of ice,
Or fray a granite from the precipice:
When this is sought trees will be wanting not,
    And I shall shape one to my thought.

    Thus I shall make a cross, and in't
    Will add a footrest there to stand,
And with sharp flint will part my feet and dint
    The point fast in, and my left hand
Lock with my right; then knot a barken band
To hold me quite fix'd in the selfsame plight;
    And thus I will thrust in my right:—

    I'll take in hand the blady stone
    And to my palm the point apply,
And press it down, on either side a bone,
    With hope, with shut eyes, fixedly;
Thus crucified as I did crucify.

. . . .

'She schools the flighty pupils'

She schools the flighty pupils of her eyes,
With levell'd lashes stilling their disquiet;
And puts in leash her pair'd lips lest surprise
Bare the condition of a realm at riot.
If he suspect that she has ought to sigh at
His injury she'll avenge with raging shame.
She kept her love-thoughts on most lenten diet,
And learnt her not to startle at his name.

(21)

A Soliloquy of One of the Spies left in the Wilderness

He feeds me with His manna every day:
My soul does loathe it and my spirit fails.
A press of wingèd things comes down this way:
The gross flock call them quails.
Into my hand he gives a host for prey,
Come up, Arise and slay.

Sicken'd and thicken'd by the glare and sand,
Who would drink water from a stony rock?
Are all the manna-bushes in the land
A shelter for this flock?
Behold at Elim wells on every hand!
And seventy palms there stand.

Egypt, the valley of our pleasance, there!
Most wide ye are who call this gust Simoom.
Your parchèd nostrils snuff Egyptian air.
The comfortable gloom
After the sandfield and the unreinèd glare!
Goshen is green and fair.

Not Goshen. Wasteful wide huge-girthèd Nile
Unbakes my pores, and streams, and makes all fresh.
I gather points of lote-flower from an isle
Of leaves of greenest flesh.
Ye sandblind! Slabs of water many a mile
Blaze on him all this while.

In beds, in gardens, in thick plots I stand.
Handle the fig, suck the full-sapp'd vine-shoot.
From easy runnels the rich-piecèd land
I water with my foot.
Must you be gorged with proof? Did ever sand
So trickle from your hand?

Strike timbrels, sing, eat, drink, be full of mirth.
Forget the waking trumpet, the long law.
Spread o'er the swart face of this prodigal earth.

Bring in the glistery straw.
Here are sweet messes without price or worth,
And never thirst or dearth.

Give us the tale of bricks as heretofore;
To plash with cool feet the clay juicy soil.
Who tread the grapes are splay'd with stripes of gore.
And they who crush the oil
Are spatter'd. We desire the yoke we bore,
The easy burden of yore.

Who is this Moses? Who made him, we say,
To be a judge and ruler over us?
He slew the Egyptian yesterday. To-day
In hot sands perilous
He hides our corpses dropping by the way,
Wherein he makes us stray.

Your hands have borne the tent-poles: on you plod:
The trumpet waxes loud: tired are your feet.
Come by the flesh-pots: you shall sit unshod
And have your fill of meat;
Bring wheat-ears from the loamy stintless sod,
To a more grateful god.

. . . .

Go then: I am contented here to lie.
Take Canaan with your sword and with your bow.
Rise: match your strength with monstrous Talmai
At Kirjath-Arba: go.—
Sure, this is Nile: I sicken, I know not why,
And faint as though to die.

The Lover's Stars

The destined lover, whom his stars
More golden than the world of lights,
O'er passes bleak, o'er perilous bars
Of rivers, lead, thro' storms and nights,

Or if he leave the West behind,
  Or father'd by the sunder'd South,
Shall, when his star is zenith'd, find
  Acceptance round his mistress' mouth:

Altho' unchallenged, where she sits,
  Three rivals throng her garden chair,
And tho' the silver seed that flits
  Above them, down the draught of air,

And keeps the breeze and clears the seas
  And tangles on a down of France,
Yet leaves him in ungirdled ease
  8000 furlongs in advance.

But in the other's horoscope
  Bad Saturn with a swart aspect
Fronts Venus.—His ill-launchèd hope
  In unimperill'd haven is wreck'd.

He meets her, stintless of her smile;
  Her choice in roses knows by heart;
Has danced with her: and all the while
  They are Antipodes apart.

His sick stars falter. More he may
  Not win, if this be not enough.
He meets upon Midsummer day
  The stabbing coldness of rebuff.

The peacock's eye

Mark you how the peacock's eye
Winks away its ring of green,
Barter'd for an azure dye,
And the piece that's like a bean,
The pupil, plays its liquid jet
To win a look of violet.

Love preparing to fly

He play'd his wings as though for flight;
They webb'd the sky with glassy light.
His body sway'd upon tiptoes,
Like a wind-perplexèd rose;
In eddies of the wind he went
At last up the blue element.

Barnfloor and Winepress

And he said, If the Lord do not help thee, whence shall I help thee?
Out of the barnfloor, or out of the winepress?

2 KINGS vi. 27.

Thou that on sin's wages starvest,
Behold we have the joy in harvest:
For us was gather'd the first-fruits,
For us was lifted from the roots,
Sheaved in cruel bands, bruised sore,
Scourged upon the threshing-floor;
Where the upper mill-stone roof'd His head,
At morn we found the heavenly Bread,
And, on a thousand altars laid,
Christ our Sacrifice is made!

Thou whose dry plot for moisture gapes,
We shout with them that tread the grapes:
For us the Vine was fenced with thorn,
Five ways the precious branches torn;
Terrible fruit was on the tree
In the acre of Gethsemane;
For us by Calvary's distress
The wine was rackèd from the press;
Now in our altar-vessels stored
Is the sweet Vintage of our Lord.

In Joseph's garden they threw by
The riv'n Vine, leafless, lifeless, dry:
On Easter morn the Tree was forth,
In forty days reach'd heaven from earth;
Soon the whole world is overspread;
Ye weary, come into the shade.

The field where He has planted us
Shall shake her fruit as Libanus,
When He has sheaved us in His sheaf,
When He has made us bear His leaf.—
We scarcely call that banquet food,
But even our Saviour's and our blood,
We are so grafted on His wood.

New Readings

Although the letter said
On thistles that men look not grapes to gather,
I read the story rather
How soldiers platting thorns around CHRIST'S Head
Grapes grew and drops of wine were shed.

Though when the sower sowed
The wingèd fowls took part, part fell in thorn
And never turned to corn,
Part found no root upon the flinty road,—
CHRIST at all hazards fruit hath shewed.

From wastes of rock He brings
Food for five thousand: on the thorns He shed
Grains from His drooping Head;
And would not have that legion of winged things
Bear Him to heaven on easeful wings.

'He hath abolished the old drouth'

He hath abolished the old drouth,
And rivers run where all was dry,
The field is sopp'd with merciful dew.
He hath put a new song in my mouth,
The words are old, the purport new,
And taught my lips to quote this word
That I shall live, I shall not die,
But I shall when the shooks are stored
See the salvation of the Lord.
We meet together, you and I,
Meet in one acre of one land,
And I will turn my looks to you,
And you shall meet me with reply,
We shall be sheavèd with one band
In harvest and in garnering,
When heavenly vales so thick shall stand
With corn that they shall laugh and sing.

Heaven-Haven

(a nun takes the veil)

I have desired to go
  Where springs not fail,
To fields where flies no sharp and sided hail
  And a few lilies blow.

And I have asked to be
  Where no storms come,
Where the green swell is in the havens dumb,
  And out of the swing of the sea.

'I must hunt down the prize'

I must hunt down the prize
  Where my heart lists.
Must see the eagle's bulk, render'd in mists,
  Hang of a treble size.

Must see the waters roll
  Where the seas set
Towards wastes where round the ice-blocks tilt and fret
  Not so far from the pole.

or

Must see the green seas roll
  Where waters set
Towards those wastes where the ice-blocks tilt and fret,
  Not so far from the pole.

'Why should their foolish bands'

Why should their foolish bands, their hopeless hearses
Blot the perpetual festival of day?
Ravens, for prosperously-boded curses
Returning thanks, might offer such array.
Heaven comfort sends, but harry it away.
Gather the sooty plumage from Death's wings
And the poor corse impale with it and fray
If so it be, an angel's hoverings.
And count the rosy cross with bann'd disastrous things.

'It was a hard thing'

It was a hard thing to undo this knot.
The rainbow shines, but only in the thought
Of him that looks. Yet not in that alone,
For who makes rainbows by invention?

And many standing round a waterfall
See one bow each, yet not the same to all,
But each a hand's breadth further than the next.
The sun on falling waters writes the text
Which yet is in the eye or in the thought.
It was a hard thing to undo this knot.

'Glimmer'd along the square-cut steep'

Glimmer'd along the square-cut steep.
They chew'd the cud in hollows deep;
Their cheeks moved and the bones therein.
The lawless honey eaten of old
Has lost its savour and is roll'd
Into the bitterness of sin.

What would befal the godless flock
Appear'd not for the present, till
A thread of light betray'd the hill
Which with its lined and creased flank
The outgoings of the vale does block.
Death's bones fell in with sudden clank
As wrecks of minèd embers will.

'Miss Story's character'

Miss Story's character! too much you ask,
When 'tis the confidante that sets the task.
How dare I paint Miss Story to Miss May?
And what if she my confidence betray!
What if my Subject, seeing this, resent
What were worth nothing if all compliment!
No: shewn to her it cannot but offend;
But candour never hurt the dearest *friend*.
  Miss Story has a moderate power of will,
But, having that, believes it greater still:
And, hide it though she does, one may divine

She inly nourishes a wish to shine;
Is very capable of strong affection
Tho' apt to throw it in a strange direction;
Is fond of flattery, as any she,
But has not learnt to take it gracefully;
Things that she likes seems often to despise,
And loves—a fatal fault—to patronize;
Has wit enough, if she would make it known
And charms—but they should be more freely shewn.
About herself she is most sensitive,
Talks of self-sacrifice, yet can't forgive;
She's framed to triumph in adversity;
Prudence she has, but wise she'll never be;
And, well supplied with virtues on the whole,
Is slightly selfish in her inmost soul
Her character she does not realize,
And cannot see at all with others' eyes;
Believes herself religious, and is not;
And, thinking that she thinks, has never thought;
Married, will make a sweet and matchless wife,
But single, lead a misdirected life.

(*Epigrams*)

(i)

Of virtues I most warmly bless,
Most rarely see, Unselfishness.
And to put graver sins aside
I own a preference for Pride.

(ii)

You ask why can't Clarissa hold her tongue.
Because she fears her fingers will be stung.

(iii)

On a dunce who had not a word to say for himself

He's all that's bad, I know; a knave, a flat,
But his effrontery's not come to that.

(iv)

By Mrs. Hopley

He's wedded to his theory, they say.
If that were true, it could not live a day.
And did the children of his brains enjoy
But half the pains he spends upon his boy,
You may depend that ere a week was fled,
There would not be a whole place in his head.

On seeing her children say Goodnight to their father.

Bid your Papa Goodnight, Sweet exhibition!
They kiss the Rod with filial submission.

(v)

Modern Poets

Our swans are now of such remorseless quill,
Themselves live singing and their hearers kill.

(vi)

By one of the old school who was bid to follow Mr. Browning's flights

To rise you bid me with the lark
With me 'tis rising in the dark.

(vii)

On a Poetess

Miss M.'s a nightingale. 'Tis well
  Your simile I keep.
It is the way with Philomel
  To sing while others sleep.

(viii)

On one who borrowed his sermons

Herclot's preachings I'll no longer hear:
They're out of date—lent sermons all the year.

Floris in Italy

(i)

Floris, having found by chance that Giulia loves him, reasons with himself (or perhaps with Henry) in defence of his not returning her love. Her beauty is urged.

Beauty it may be is the meet of lines
Or careful-spacèd sequences of sound,
These rather are the arc where beauty shines,
The temper'd soil where only her flower is found.
Allow at least it has one term and part
Beyond, and one within the looker's eye;
And I must have the centre in my heart
To spread the compass on the all-starr'd sky:
For only try by gazing to divide
One star by daylight from the strong blue air,
And find it will not therefore be descried
Because its place is known and charted there.
No, love prescriptive, love with place assign'd,
Love by monition, heritage, or lot,
Love by prenatal serfdom still confined
Even to the tillage of the sweetest spot,—
It is a regimen on the imperfect wind,
Piecing the elements out by plan and plot.
Though self-made bands at last may true love bind,
New love is free love, or true love 'tis not. [*exit*

Henry. Thus he ties spider's web across his sight
And gives for tropes his judgment all away,
Gilds with some sparky fancies his black night
And stumbling swears he walks by light of day.
Blindness! A learnèd fool and well-bred churl
That swinishly refuses such a pearl!

(ii)

Giulia writing. Fool jumps up and seats himself in window.

F. Madam.
G. You startled me.
F. Madam, what are you doing?

G. Fool, writing a letter.

F. I thought it was your will. I approve your care; but indeed it is better to have a lawyer at once. For my part I never send a loveletter without an attorney. I would never bid anyone to dinner without taking legal opinion.

G. This is not a loveletter nor an invitation. It is to my cousin. I can make nothing of it. Dictate to me now, Fool.

F. Truth or untruth?

G. Truth.

F. And will you set down whatever I read you?

G. Why, truth, they say, is not expedient to speak at all times.

F. Do you defend lying, Madam?

G. You know what I mean. It is better to conceal at times.

F. There are some ladies who conceal all things at all times. Crystal sincerity hath found no shelter but in a fool's cap; I have long found it so. It loves the innocent tinkle of the bells, and only speaks by the mouths of men of my profession. But to the letter. Whether when it is set down you will send it or no, you shall decide. If you do not send it, I shall despair of your judgment. But it shall be as you will. Now will you promise to set down what I read you?

G. If it be truth.

F. You must forfeit a gold piece, if you refuse.

G. Very well, I will forfeit a gold piece.

F. Lay it down on the table.

G. Can you not trust me?

F. No, Madam, not a woman; least of all in matters of money.

G. Then you shall not have it at all.

F. I said so. Madam, you stand convicted. You must even pack with your sex.

G. Then there it is (*laying it down.*)

F. A hostage. Now, truth, you say?

G. Why, would you have me write lies?

F. Madam, if you follow me, I will take care it will be nothing but truth. If at any place you refuse to write, you forfeit. Is it agreed?

G. As long as you keep to truth, it is.

F. Thus then. *Cousin,–*

G. Why what a boorish opening is that. Do you suppose I

assail my cousin with such martial peremptory salutations? I say *dearest Cousin* or *dear Cousin.*

F. But she is neither *dearest Cousin* nor *dear Cousin* now. And you have forfeited your gold piece.

G. No, I have put it down. Go on.

F. *Cousin, Neither wish to deceive me, for you shall never put out my eyes; nor*

G. Why,—

F. Madam, beware for your forfeit. *Neither wish to deceive me, for you shall never put out my eyes; nor think that I can be silent on what I see. You are doing that thing a woman can never forgive, and which, in your way of doing it, is a very shame to a woman to do.*

G. What is all this?

F. Madam! *That I love desperately you know well: that you love at all I much doubt: that I am not loved is my misery: that you are loved is the fear that graces my Lent of lovelessness with the diet of gall and the mortifying of tears.* You are not writing.

(iii)

It does amaze me, when the clicking hour
Clings on the stroke of death, that I can smile.
Yet when my unset tresses hung loose-traced
Round this unsexing doublet,—while I set
This downy counterfeit upon my lip,

. . . .

—Lately I fear'd
My signalling tears might ring up Floris; now
Methinks there is more peril from my laughter.
Well, I know not. But all things seem to-night
Double as sharp, meaning and forcible,
With twice as fine a sense to apprehend them,
As ever I remember in my life.
Laughing or tears. I think I could do either—
So strangely elemented is my mind's weather,
That tears and laughter are hung close together.
Comes to the bed.
Sleep Floris while I rob you. Tighten, O sleep,
Thy impalpable oppression. Pin him down,

Ply fold on fold across his dangerous eyes,
Lodge his eyes fast; but yet as easy and light
As the laid gossamers of Michaelmas
Whose silver skins lie level and thick in field,
Hold him.—
I must not turn the lantern on his face.—
No I'll not hazard it. Only his hand,
Turns the lantern on Floris' hand.

. . . .

Trying on the ring.
It is too large for me. What does that mean?
No time to think. I'll knot it on this ribbon,
And wear it thus, a pectoral, by my heart.
—

Did I say but lately
That I was so near laughter? Alas now
I find I am as ready with my tears
As the fine morsels of a dwindling cloud
That piece themselves into a race of drops
To spill o'er fields of lilies. So could I
So waste in tears over this bed of sweetness,
This flower, this Floris, this dear majesty,
This royal manhood.—'Tis in me rebellion
To speak so, yet I'll speak it for this once;
Deep shame it were to be discover'd so,
Worse than when Floris found me in the garden
Weeping,—even now I curse myself remembering;—
No, let that go; I have said Goodnight to shame.
Now let me see you, you large princely hand,
Since on the face it is unsafe to look;
Yet this could be no other's hand than his,
'Tis so conceived in his true lineament.
I have wrong'd it of its coronet, and now
I outrage it with treasonable kissing.
Ah Floris, Floris, let me speak this little

. . . .

What I do now is but the least least thing.
But since I have no scope for benefits

Tho ill-contented, precious precious Floris,
Most ill-content, this least least thing I do.
Now one word more and then I am gone indeed,
Warn'd by the bright procession of the stars.
My cousin will not love you as I love,
Floris; she will not hit thy sum of worth,
Thou jacinth; nor have skill of all thy virtues,
Floris, thou late-found All-heal;

(iv)

A. What is your name, boy?

B. George, if you please Sir.

A. Why it doesn't please me at all. I think George is a fustian name.

C. Fustian, what a word! why labourers' jackets are made of fustian. [*Aside*]

A. You see it isn't how it pleases me, but how it pleased your godfathers and godmothers—how many years ago?

B. What, Sir?

A. Why, how old are you?

B. Fourteen.

A. Fourteen? A pretty age.

C. How can one age be prettier than another? You might as well say half past nine was a very handsome time of day. [*Aside*]

(v)

With what bold grace
This sweet Deserter lists herself anew
Enroll'd and sexèd with our ruder files
And marching to false colours! those few strokes
That forge her title of inheritance
To Manhood, on the upper lip,—they look'd
Most like the silver plighted tuft about
The mouthèd centre of a violet.

Io

Forward she leans, with hollowing back, stock-still,
Her white weed-bathèd knees are shut together,
Her silky coat is sheeny, like a hill
Gem-fleeced at morn, so brilliant is the weather.
Her nostril glistens; and her wet black eye
Her lids half-meshing shelter from the sky.

Her finger-long new horns are capp'd with black;
In hollows of her form the shadow clings;
Her milk-white throat and folded dew-lap slack
Are still; her neck is creased in close-ply rings;
Her hue's a various brown with creamy lakes,
Like a cupp'd chestnut damask'd with dark breaks.

Backward are laid her pretty black-fleeced ears;
The feathery knot of locks upon her head
Plays to the breeze; where now are fled her fears,
Her jailor with his vigil-organ dead?
Morn does not now new-basilisk his stare,
Nor night is blown with flame-rings everywhere.

The rainbow

See on one hand
He drops his bright roots in the water'd sward,
And rosing part, on part dispenses green;
But with his other foot three miles beyond
He rises from the flocks of villages
That bead the plain; did ever Havering church-tower
Breathe in such ether? or the Quickly elms
{ With such a violet slight their distanced green?
{ Slight with such violet their bright-mask'd green?

or

Mask'd with such violet disallow their green?

'—Yes for a time'

A.—Yes for a time they held as well
Together, as the criss-cross'd shelly cup
Sucks close the acorn; as the hand and glove;
As water moulded to the duct it runs in;
As keel locks close to kelson—

B. Let me now
Jolt and unset your morticed metaphors.
The hand draws off the glove; the acorn-cup
Drops the fruit out; the duct runs dry or breaks;
The stranded keel and kelson warp apart;
And your two etc.

Gabriel

(i)

Scene. A cave in a quarry. Evening. Gabriel comes to ask the advice of the hermit, who has however died. He is half-mad. He runs out and finds some night-shade berries which he eats. These make him delirious. A shepherd and his wife take refuge in the cave from the violence of the rain; she crouching in the corner, he standing at the door. Re-enter Gabriel.

G. Can you remember why he set me this penance? What has happened with me? Have I wronged any man's wife? I can call none to mind.—Who are you?

S. What do you want with me?

G. Are you married?

S. Who are you that ask me these questions?

G. What, do you think I am the only man that has been shamed in his bed? Get into the wet. There is nightshade about. Out, out, cuckoo. Out of the nest. (Thrusting him out.)

S. Keep back. (Strikes him with his heavy stick. Gabriel falls with a cry.)

G. O Maurice, you have hurt me. You have struck me, Maurice. I have not wronged your wife, nor any mans wife.

You are handsome and strong and my friend: there is not such another in the court, but you strike too hard.

W. Nay, John, you have hurt him. He bleeds. Now see here, John; 'tis a thousand pities if you have hurt him. There's a face to be sure.

G. Gabrielle! I know you. But you are under a cloud. Ay, they say so: 'tis the talk of the whole court. Yes, I know your husband; good but weak. They say he still loves her very, very, very much. Oh the misery. It is a weakness. The last time I saw him he lay in a quarry bleeding. I am cold: cover me up.

W. It is wicked to laugh, but he does talk wild. Dear, dear, poor soul. There put your hands down.

G. See, it rains blood. The moon shall be turned into blood.—Why if all the jealous husbands run their horns at us as you did, shepherd, there'll be no gallantry left in these latter days.

S. Best leave him. We can do nought for him. He is clean mad.

W. Now John, how can be so hard-hearted. Come, I'll not stir; so you may do as you like.

G. No, never leave her. And yet I have been bitterly, horribly, horribly wronged.—Well the tale runs thus. The husband went away, his friend committed adultery with his wife, the husband comes back, does nothing, but goes as near madness as the scalp is to the scull, and the devil has a good find of souls.—Well 'tis the story of Launcelot and Guinevere again. Some call her Guinevera, some Guinevere, but the story is the same.

(ii)

—O Guinevere
I read that the recital of thy sin,
Like knocking thunder all round Britain's welkin,
Jarr'd down the balanced storm; the bleeding heavens
Left not a rood with curses unimpregnate;
There was no crease or gather in the clouds
But dropp'd its coil of woes: and Arthur's Britain,
The mint of current courtesies, the forge
Where all the virtues were illustrated
In gilt and blazon and mail'd shapes of bronze,

Abandon'd by her saints, turn'd black and blasted,
Like scalded banks topp'd once with principal flowers:
Such heathenish misadventure dogg'd one sin.

'I am like a slip of comet'

—I am like a slip of comet,
Scarce worth discovery, in some corner seen
Bridging the slender difference of two stars,
Come out of space, or suddenly engender'd
By heady elements, for no man knows:
But when she sights the sun she grows and sizes
And spins her skirts out, while her central star
Shakes its cocooning mists; and so she comes
To fields of light; millions of travelling rays
Pierce her; she hangs upon the flame-cased sun,
And sucks the light as full as Gideon's fleece:
But then her tether calls her; she falls off,
And as she dwindles shreds her smock of gold
Amidst the sistering planets, till she comes
To single Saturn, last and solitary;
And then goes out into the cavernous dark.
So I go out: my little sweet is done:
I have drawn heat from this contagious sun:
To not ungentle death now forth I run.

'No, they are come'

No, they are come; their horn is lifted up;
They stand, they shine in the sun; Fame has foregone
All quests save the recital of their greatness;
Their clarions from all corners of the field
With potent lips call down cemented towers;
Their harness beams like scythes in morning grass;
Like flame they gather on our cliffs at evening,
At morn they come upon our lands like rains;
They plough our vales; you see the unsteady flare

Flush thro' their heaving columns; when they halt,
They seem to fold the hills with golden capes;
They draw all coverts, cut the fields, and suck
The treasure from all cities. etc.

'Now I am minded'

Now I am minded to take pipe in hand
And yield a song to the decaying year;
Now while the full-leaved hursts unalter'd stand,
    And scarcely does appear
The Autumn yellow feather in the boughs;
    While there is neither sun nor rain;
And a grey heaven does the hush'd earth house,
And bluer gray the flocks of trees look in the plain.

So late, the hoar green chestnut breaks a bud,
And feeds new leaves upon the winds of Fall;
So late there is no force in sap or blood;
    The fruit against the wall
Loose on the stem has done its summering;
These should have starv'd with the green broods of spring,
    Or never been at all;
Too late or else much, much too soon,
Who first knew moonlight by the hunters' moon.

A Voice from the World

Fragments of 'An Answer to Miss Rossetti's *Convent Threshold*'

At last I hear the voice well known;
Doubtless the voice: now fall'n, now spent,
Now coming from the alien eaves,—
You would not house beneath my own;
To alien eaves you fled and went,—
Now like the bird that shapes alone
A turn of seven notes or five,

When skies are hard as any stone,
The fall is o'er, told off the leaves,
'Tis marvel she is yet alive.
Once it was scarce perceivèd Lent
For orience of the daffodil;
Once, jostling thick, the bluebell sheaves
The peacock'd copse were known to fill;
Through other bars it used to thrill,
And carried me with ravishment
Your signal, when apart we stood,
Tho' far or sick or heavy or still
Or thorn-engaged, impalèd and pent
With just such sweet-potential skill,
Late in the green weeks of April
Cuckoo calls cuckoo up the wood.
Five notes or seven, late and few.
From parts unlook'd-for, alter'd, spent,
At last I hear the voice I knew.

. . . .

I plead: familiarness endears
My evil words thorny with pain:
I plead: and you will give your tears:
I plead: and ah! how much in vain!

. . . .

I know I mar my cause with words:
So be it; I must maim and mar.
Your comfort is as sharp as swords;
And I cry out for wounded love.
And you are gone so heavenly far
You hear nor care of love and pain,
My tears are but a cloud of rain
My passion like a foolish wind
Lifts them a little way above.
But you, so spherèd, see no more—
You see but with a holier mind—
You hear and, alter'd, do not hear
Being a stoled apparel'd star.
You should have been with me as near

As halves of sweet-pea-blossom are;
But now are fled, and hard to find
As the last Pleiad, yea behind
Exilèd most remote El Khor.

. . . .

The love of women is not so strong,—
'Tis falsely given—as love in men;
A thing that weeps, enduring long:
But mine is dreadful leaping pain,
Phrenzy, but edged and clear of brain
Ruinous heart-beat, wandering, death.
I walk towards eve our walks again;
When lily-yellow is the west.
Say, o'er it hangs a water-cloud
And ravell'd into strings of rain.
At once I struggle with my breath.
'The light was so, the wind so loud
No louder, when I was with you.
Always the time remembereth
His very looks in other years,
Only with us is old and new.'
I fall, I tear and shower the weed,
I bite my hands, my looks I shroud;
My cry is like a bleat; a few
Intolerable tears I bleed.
Then is my misery full indeed:
I die, I die, I do not live.—
Alas! I rave, where calm is due;
I would remember. Love, forgive.
I cannot calm, I cannot heed.
I storm and shock you. So I fail.
And like a self-outwitted blast
Fling to the convent wicket fast.
Who would not shelter from the hail?
But is there a place for tenderness,
There was a charm would countervail
The spell of woe if any could.
Once in a drawer of Indian wood
You folded (did you not?) your dress.

The essence ne'er forgot the fold;
And I esteem'd the sandal good
And now I get some precious slips.

. . . .

. . . upon you dreamed:
I [dream'd] my counterpart. It seem'd
[A bell] at midnight woke the town
[And all] into the Duomo ran:
You met me, I had hasten'd down:
That night the judgment day began:
'Twas said of none but all men knew:
Nocturns I thought were hurried through.
Some knelt, some stood: I seem'd to feel
Who knelt were for the Lord's right hand;
They are the goats who stand, said I.
I stood; but does she stand or kneel?
I strove to look; I lost the trick
Of nerve; the clammy ball was dry.
Then came the benediction.
His lips moved fast in sense too thick!
The others heard; I could not hear
Him . . . .
Save me: and you were standing near.

An angel came: 'The judgment done,
Mercy is left enough for one:
Choose, one for hell and one for heaven!'
You cried 'But I have served thee well,
O Lord; but I have wrought and striven;
Duly, dear Lord, my prize is won.
I did repent; I am forgiven.
Give him the gift.' I cannot tell
But all the while it seem'd to me
I reason'd the futility.
Or this, or else I do not love,
I inly said; but could not move
My fast-lodged tongue. '[To her the gift]
I yield' I would have cried. At last,

Something I said; I swooned and fell.
The angel lifted us above.
The bitterness of death was past,
My love; and all was sweet and well.

. . . .

But what indeed is ask'd of me?
Not this. Some spirits, it is told,
Have will'd to be disparadised
For love and greater glory of Christ.
But I was ignorantly bold
To dream I dared so much for thee.
This was not ask'd, but what instead?
Waking I thought; and it sufficed:
My hopes and my unworthiness,
At once perceivèd, with excess
Of burden came and bow'd my head.
Yea, crush'd my heart, and made me dumb.
I thought: Before I gather strength. . . .

. . . .

Who say that angels, in your ear
Are heard, that cry 'She does repent',
Let charity thus begin at home,—
Teach me the paces that you went
I can send up an Esau's cry;
Tune it to words of good intent.
This ice, this lead, this steel, this stone,
This heart is warm to you alone;
Make it to God. I am not spent
So far but I have yet within
The penetrative element
That shall unglue the crust of sin.
Steel may be melted and rock rent.
Penance shall clothe me to the bone.
Teach me the way: I will repent.

. . . .

But grant my penitence begun:
I need not, love, I need not break
Remember'd sweetness. For my thought
No house of Rimmon may I take,
To bow but little, and worship not?
Is not some little Bela set
Before the mountain?—No, not one,
The heaven-enforcèd answer comes,
Yea, to myself I answer make:
Who can but barter slender sums
By slender losses are undone;
They breathe not who are late to run.—
O hideous vice to haggle yet
For more with Him who gives thee all,
Freely forgives the monstrous debt!
Having the infinitely great
Therewith to hanker for the small!

Knowledge is strong but love is sweet.—
I found the ways were sown with salt
Where you and I were wont to tread;
Not further'd far my travell'd feet
For all the miles that they were sped;
No flowers to find, no place to halt,
No colour in the overhead,
No running in the river-bed;
And passages where we used to meet,—
Fruit-cloistering hyacinth-warding woods,
I call'd them and I thought them then—
When you were learner and I read,
Are waste, and had no wholesome foods,
Unpalateable fruits to eat.
What have I more than other men,
For learning stored and garnerèd?
And barely to escape the curse,
I who was wise would be untaught,
And fain would follow I who led.
How shall I search, who never sought?
How turn my passion-pastured thought
To gentle manna and simple bread?

For a Picture of Saint Dorothea

I bear a basket lined with grass;
I am so light, I am so fair,
That men must wonder as I pass
And at the basket that I bear,
Where in a newly-drawn green litter
Sweet flowers I carry,—sweets for bitter.

Lilies I shew you, lilies none,
None in Caesar's gardens blow,—
And a quince in hand,—not one
Is set upon your boughs below;
Not set, because their buds not spring;
Spring not, 'cause world is wintering.

But these were found in the East and South
Where Winter is the clime forgot.—
The dewdrop on the larkspur's mouth
O should it then be quenchèd not?
In starry water-meads they drew
These drops: which be they? stars or dew?

Had she a quince in hand? Yet gaze:
Rather it is the sizing moon.
Lo, linkèd heavens with milky ways!
That was her larkspur row.—So soon?
Sphered so fast, sweet soul?—We see
Nor fruit, nor flowers, nor Dorothy.

St. Dorothea (*lines for a picture*)

The Angel

I bear a basket lined with grass.
I am só light and fair
Men must start to see me pass
And the básket that I bear,

Which in newly-drawn green litter
Carries treats of sweet for bitter.

See my lilies: lilies none,
None in Caesar's gardens blow—
Quinces, loók, whén not one
Is set in any orchard, no;
Not set because their buds not spring;
Spring not, 'cause world is wintering.

The Protonotary Theophilus

Bút they cáme fróm the south,
Where winter's out and all forgot.

The Angel

The bell-drops in my mallow's mouth
Hów are théy quenchèd not?—
These drops in starry shire they drew:
Whích are théy? stars or dew?

A Catechumen

That a quince we pore upon?
O no, it is the sizing moon.
Now her mallow-row is gone
In floats of evening sky.—So soon?
Sphered so fast, sweet soul?—We see
Nor fruit nor flowers nor Dorothy.

Theophilus

How to name it, blessed it,
Suiting its grace by *him* and *her*?
Dorothea—or was your writ
Servèd by sweet seconder?—
Your parley was not done and there!
You fell into the partless air.

You waned into the world of light,
Yet made your market here as well:
My eyes hold yet the rinds and bright
Remainder of a miracle.

O this is bringing! Tears may swarm
While such a wonder's wet and warm!

Ah myrtle-bend never sit,
Sit no more these bookish brows!
I want, I want, if I were fit,
Whát the cóld mónth allows—
Nothing green or growing but
A pale and perished palmtree-cut.

Dip in blood the palmtree-pen
And wordy warrants are flawed through;
And more shall wear this wand and then
The warpèd world it will undo.—
Próconsul,—cáll him near—
I find another Christian here.

Lines for a Picture of St. Dorothea

Dorothea and Theophilus

I bear a basket lined with grass.
I′ am so′ light′ and fair′
Men are amazed to watch me pass
With′ the básket I bear′,
Which in newly drawn green litter
Carries treats of sweet for bitter.

See my lilies: lilies none,
None in Caesar's garden blow.
Quínces, look′, when′ not one′
Is set in any orchard; no,
Not set because their buds not spring;
Spring not for world is wintering.

But′ they came′ from′ the South′,
Where winter-while is all forgot.—
The dew-bell in the mallow's mouth
Is′ it quénchèd or not′?

In starry, starry shire it grew:
Which′ is it′, star′ or dew′?—

That a quince I pore upon?
O no it is the sizing moon.
Now her mallow-row is gone
In tufts of evening sky.—So soon?
Sphered so fast, sweet soul?—We see
Fruit nor flower nor Dorothy.

How to name it, blessed it!
Suiting its grace with *him* or *her*?
Dorothea—or was your writ
Sérvèd bý méssenger′ ?
Your parley was not done and there!
You went into the partless air.

It waned into the world of light,
Yet made its market here as well:
My eyes hold yet the rinds and bright
Remainder of a miracle.
O this is bringing! Tears may swarm
Indeed while such a wonder's warm.

Ah dip in blood the palmtree pen
And wordy warrants are flawed through.
More will wear this wand and then
The warpèd world we shall undo.
Proconsul!—Is Sapricius near?—
I find another Christian here.

'Proved Etherege'

Proved Etherege prudish, selfish, hypocrite, heartless,
No scholar, a would-be critic, a *dillentante*,
  Cream-laid, a surface, who could quote, to startle us,
  The Anatomy, Politian, a little Dante,—
And so forth. Then for his looks—like pinkish paper:
  Features? A watermark; other claims as scanty.
  In such wise did the gentle . . . vapour.

Richard

(i)

He was a shepherd of the Arcadian mood,
That not Arcadia knew nor Haemony.
Affinèd to the earnest solitude,
The winds and listening downs he seem'd to be.
He went with listless strides, disorderedly.
And answer'd the dry tinkles of his sheep
With piping unexpected melody.
With absent looks inspired as drinking deep
True nectar filter'd thro' the thymy leaves of sleep.

He rested on the forehead of the down
Shaping his outlines on a field of cloud.
His sheep seem'd to step from it, past the crown
Of the hill grazing:

(ii)

As void as clouds that house and harbour none,
Whose gaps and hollows are not browzed upon,
As void as those the gentle downs appear
On such a season of the day and year.
There was no bleat of ewe, no chime of wether,
Only the bellèd foxgloves lisp'd together.
Yet there came one who sent his flock before him,
Alone upon the hill-top, heaven o'er him,
And where the brow in first descending bow'd
He sat and wrought his outline on a cloud.
His sheep seem'd to come from it as they stept,
One and then one, along their walks, and kept
Their changing feet in flicker all the time
And to their feet the narrow bells gave rhyme.
Affinèd well to that sweet solitude,
He was a shepherd of the Arcadian mood
That not Arcadia knew nor Haemony.
His tale and telling has been given to me.

. . . .

(iii)

But what drew shepherd Richard from his downs,
And bred acquaintance of unusèd towns?
What put taught graces on his country lip,
And brought the sense of gentle fellowship,
That many centres found in many hearts?
What taught the humanities and the round of arts?
And for the tinklings on the falls and swells
Gave the much music of our Oxford bells?

. . . .

(iv)

'Sylvester, come, Sylvester; you may trust
Your footing now to the much dreaded dust,
Crisp'd up and starchy from a short half-hour
Of standing to the blossom-hitting shower
That still makes counter-roundels in the pond.
A rainbow also shapes itself beyond
The shining slates and houses. Come and see.
You may quote Wordsworth, if you like, to me.'
Sylvester came: they went by Cumnor hill,
Met a new shower, and saw the rainbow fill
From one frail horn that crumbled to the plain
His steady wheel quite to the full again.
They watched the brush of the swift stringy drops,
Help'd by the darkness of a block of copse
Close-rooted in the downward-hollowing fields;
Then sought such leafy shelter as it yields,
And each drew bluebells up, and for relief
Took primroses, their pull'd and plotted leaf
Being not forgotten, for primroses note
The blue with brighter places not remote.

(v)

There was a meadow level almost: you traced
The river wound about it as a waist.
Beyond, the banks were steep; a brush of trees
Rounded it, thinning skywards by degrees,
With parallel shafts,—as upward-parted ashes,—

Their highest sprays were drawn as fine as lashes,
With centres duly touch'd and nestlike spots,—
And oaks,—but these were leaved in sharper knots.
Great butter-burr-leaves floor'd the slope corpse ground
Beyond the river, all the meadow's round,
And each a dinted circle. The grass was red
And long, the trees were colour'd, but the o'er-head,
Milky and dark, with an attuning stress
Controll'd them to a grey-green temperateness,
Making the shadow sweeter. A spiritual grace,
Which Wordsworth would have dwelt on, about the place
Led Richard with a sweet undoing pain
To trace some traceless loss of thought again.
Here at the very furthest reach away
(The furthest reach this side, on that the bay
Most dented) lay Sylvester, reading Keats'
Epistles, while the running pastoral bleats
Of sheep from the high fields and other wild
Sounds reach'd him. Richard came. Sylvester smiled
And said 'I like this: it is almost isled,
The river spans it with so deep a hip.
I hope that all the places on our trip
Will please us so.'

. . . .

'All as that moth'

All as that moth call'd Underwing, alighted,
Pacing and turning, so by slips discloses
Her sober simple coverlid underplighted
To colour as smooth and fresh as cheeks of roses,
{ Her showy leaves staid watchet counterfoiling
{ Her showy leaves with gentle watchet foiling
Even so my thought the rose and grey disposes

The Queen's Crowning

1. They were wedded at midnight
By shine of candles three,
And they were bedded till daylight
Before he went to sea.

2. 'When are you home, my love,' she said,
'When are you home from sea?'
'You may look for me home, my love,' he said,
'In two years or in three.'

3. 'Heaven make the time be short,' she said,
'Although it were years three.
Heaven make it sweet to you,' she said,
'And make it short to me.

4. And what is your true name?' she said,
'Your name and your degree?
How shall I call my love,' she said,
'When he is over the sea?'

5. 'O I am the king's son,' he said,
'Lord William they call me.
I give you my love and I give you my land,
When I come home from sea.'

6. He yearn'd, he yearn'd to have his love,
For two years and for three.
Then he set sail in a golden ship
With a golden company.

7. Or ever he set his foot to the land
He saw his brothers three.
'O have you here a foreign lady
Come with you from over the sea?'

8. 'O I have here no foreign lady
Come with me from over the sea.
'Then will you wed with an English lady,
As wedded you must be?'

9. Says 'Get you, get you a lady to wed
That has both gold and fee.
Ere you set sail the king was dead.
The crown has come to thee.'

10. 'And if I chose a love to wed
That was of low degree?
That crown should be unto her head
And what were that to thee?'

11. One has gone to the king's steward,
Shewn him both gold and fee:
Said 'Who then is this lowly woman,
And truly tell to me.'

12. The king's friend told the thing that was hid
Because of gold and fee.
Said, it was not meet the king should wed
With one of low degree.

13. They have held his eyes with blindfold bands
Because he should not see.
They have bound his feet, they have bound his hands:
It was but one to three.

14. They have taken out their long brands,
They made him kneel on knee.
'It is for the shame of the lowly woman
That this has come to thee.'

15. They have happ'd him with the sand and stone
That was beside the sea.
In his heart said everyone
The crown shall be for me.

16. Lowly Alice sat in her bower
With a two years child at her knee.
'I think it is seven days,' she said,
'Thy father thou shalt see.'

17. Lowly Alice look'd abroad
Over field and tree,
And she was ware of a servingman
Came running over the lea.

18. 'O what will you now, good servingman,
O what will you now with me?'
Says 'Are you not Lord William's love
That is of low degree?'

19. 'I am Lord William's love,' she said,
'And Alice they call me.'
'Lord William comes hunting tomorrow morning,
And he will come to thee.

20. But how will you Lord William know
Beside his brothers three?'
'Because he is my love,' she said,
'And is so fair to see.'

21. 'Yet how will you Lord William know
Besides his brothers three?
His three brothers are each as tall
And each as fair as he.

22. If it be a white rose in his hand,
A lily if it should be,
In this wise you may know your lord
Beside his brothers three:

23. If he wear the crown upon his head
Among his brothers three,
If he wear a crown upon his head
And bring a crown for thee.'

24. She heard the hunt the morrow morning
And she came out to see.
And there she never saw the king,
But saw his brothers three.

25. She stood before them in the glen,
She kneeled upon her knee.
'O where is Lord William, my lords,' she said,
'I pray you tell to me.'

26. Two made answer in one breath
And each said 'I am he.'
'Fie, you are not Lord William,' she said;
'O fie that this should be.'

27. Then up and spake the third brother,
Said 'Listen now to me.
Lord William is king of all this land
And thou of low degree.'

28. 'Fie,' she said unto them all,
'No truth between you three.
If he were king of all this land
He would have come for me.'

29. As she lay weeping at the night
She heard but knockings three.
'It is as cold as death without:
Open the door to me.'

30. Said 'Who is this that stands without?'
Said 'Open, open to me.'
When she had made the door wide
Her true-love she might see.

31. 'O why art thou so wan,' she said,
'And why so short with me?
And art thou come from English land,
Or come from over the sea?'

32. 'I am not come from English land,
Nor yet from over the sea.
If I were come from Paradise,
It were more like to be.'

33. 'Is it a lily in your hand,
    Is it a rose I see?
Did you pull it in the king's garden
    When you came forth for me?'

34. 'I did not pull it in king's garden
    When I came forth for thee.
If it were a flower of Paradise,
    It were more like to be.'

35. 'Is that the king's crown on your head,
    And have you a crown for me?'
'If it were a crown of Paradise,
    It were more like to be.'

36. The more she ask'd, the more he spoke,
    The fairer waxèd he.
The more he told, the less she spoke,
    The wanner wanèd she.

37. 'Wilt thou follow me, my true love,
    If I give thee kisses three?
Wilt thou follow me, my true love?
    I have a crown for thee.'

38. 'O I will follow thee, my true love,
    Give me thy kisses three.
Sweeter thy kisses, my own love,
    Than all the crowns to me.'

39. He gave her kisses cold as ice;
    Down upon ground fell she.
She has gone with him to Paradise.
    There shall her crowning be.

For Stephen and Barberie

—She by a sycamore,
Whose all-belated leaves yield up themselves
To the often takings of desirous winds,
Sits without consolation, marking not
The time save when her tears which still [descend]
Her barrèd fingers clasp'd upon her eyes,
Shape on the under side and size and drop.
Meanwhile a litter of the jaggèd leaves
Lies in her lap, which she anon sweeps off.
'This weary Martinmas, would it were summer'
I heard her say, poor poor afflictèd soul,—
'Would it were summer-time.' Anon she sang
The country song of *Willow*. '*The poor soul*—
(Like me)—*sat sighing by a sycamore-tree*.'
Perhaps it was for this she chose the place.

'Boughs being pruned'

'Boughs being pruned, birds preenèd, show more fair;
To grace them spires are shaped with corner squinches;
Enrichèd posts are chamfer'd; everywhere
He heightens worth who guardedly diminishes;
Diamonds are better cut; who pare, repair;
Is statuary rated by its inches?
Thus we shall profit, while gold coinage still
Is worth and current with a lessen'd mill.'

'When eyes that cast'

When eyes that cast about the heights of heaven
To canvass the retirement of the lark
(Because the music from his bill forth-driven
So takes the sister sense) can find no mark,
But many a silver visionary spark

Springs in the floating air and the skies swim,—
Then often the ears in a new fashion hark,
Beside them, about the hedges, hearing him:
At last the bird is found a flickering shape and slim.

At once the senses give the music back,
{ The proper sweet re-attributing above.
{ That sweetness re-attributing above.—

The Summer Malison

Maidens shall weep at merry morn,
And hedges break, and lose the kine,
And field-flowers make the fields forlorn,
And noonday have a shallow shine,
And barley turn to weed and wild,
And seven ears crown the lodgèd corn,
And mother have no milk for child,
  And father be overworn.

And John shall lie, where winds are dead,
And hate the ill-visaged cursing tars,
And James shall hate his faded red,
Grown wicked in the wicked wars.
No rains shall fresh the flats of sea,
Nor close the clayfield's sharded sores,
And every heart think loathingly
  Its dearest changed to bores.

St. Thecla

That his fast-flowing hours with sandy silt
Should choke sweet virtue's glory is Time's great guilt.
Who thinks of Thecla? Yet her name was known,
Time was, next whitest after Mary's own.
To that first golden age of Gospel times
And bright Iconium eastwards reach my rhymes.

Near by is Paul's free Tarsus, fabled where
Spent Pegasus down the stark-precipitous air
Flung rider and wings away; though these were none,
And Paul is Tarsus' true Bellerophon.
They are neighbours; but (what nearness could not do)
Christ's only charity charmed and chained these two.
  She, high at the housetop sitting, as they say,
Young Thecla, scanned the dazzling streets one day;
Twice lovely, tinted eastern, turnèd Greek—
Crisp lips, straight nose, and tender-slanted cheek.
Her weeds all mark her maiden, though to wed,
And bridegroom waits and ready are bower and bed.
Withal her mien is modest, ways are wise,
And grave past girlhood earnest in her eyes.
  Firm accents strike her fine and scrollèd ear,
A man's voice and a new voice speaking near.
The words came from a court across the way.
She looked, she listened: Paul taught long that day.
He spoke of God the Father and His Son,
Of world made, marred, and mended, lost and won;
Of virtue and vice; but most (it seemed his sense)
He praised the lovely lot of continence:
All over, some such words as these, though dark,
The world was saved by virgins, made the mark.
  He taught another time there and a third.
The earnest-hearted maiden sat and heard,
And called to come at mealtime she would not:
They rose at last and forced her from the spot.

Easter Communion

Pure fasted faces draw unto this feast:
God comes all sweetness to your Lenten lips.
You striped in secret with breath-taking whips,
Those crookèd rough-scored chequers may be pieced
To crosses meant for Jesu's; you whom the East
With draught of thin and pursuant cold so nips
Breathe Easter now; you sergèd fellowships,
You vigil-keepers with low flames decreased,

God shall o'er-brim the measures you have spent
With oil of gladness, for sackcloth and frieze
And the ever-fretting shirt of punishment
Give myrrhy-threaded golden folds of ease.
Your scarce-sheathed bones are weary of being bent:
Lo, God shall strengthen all the feeble knees.

'O Death, Death'

O Death, Death, He is come.
O grounds of Hell make room.
Who came from further than the stars
Now comes as low beneath.
Thy ribbèd ports, O Death
Make wide; and Thou, O Lord of Sin,
Lay open thine estates.
Lift up your heads, O Gates;
Be ye lift up, ye everlasting doors
The King of Glory will come in.

'Love me as I love thee'

Love me as I love thee. O double sweet!
But if thou hate me who love thee, albeit
Even thus I have the better of thee:
Thou canst not hate so much as I do love thee.

To Oxford

(*a*)

New-dated from the terms that reappear,
More sweet-familiar grows my love to thee,
And still thou bind'st me to fresh fealty
With long-superfluous ties, for nothing here

Nor elsewhere can thy sweetness unendear.
This is my park, my pleasaunce; this to me
As public is my greater privacy,
All mine, yet common to my every peer.

Those charms accepted of my inmost thought,
The towers musical, quiet-wallèd grove,
The window-circles, these may all be sought
By other eyes, and other suitors move,
And all like me may boast, impeachèd not,
Their special-general title to thy love.

(*continued*)

(*b*)

Thus, I come underneath this chapel-side,
So that the mason's levels, courses, all
The vigorous horizontals, each way fall
In bows above my head, as falsified
By visual compulsion, till I hide
The steep-up roof at last behind the small
Eclipsing parapet; yet above the wall
The sumptuous ridge-crest leave to poise and ride.

None besides me this bye-ways beauty try.
Of if they try it, I am happier then:
The shapen flags and drillèd holes of sky,
Just seen, may be [to] many unknown men
The one peculiar of their pleasured eye,
And I have only set the same to pen.

(*continued*)

(*c*)

As Devonshire letters, earlier in the year
Than we in the East dare look for buds, disclose
Smells that are sweeter-memoried than the rose,
And pressèd violets in the folds appear,

So is it with my friends, I note, to hear
News from Belleisle, even such a sweetness blows
(I know it, knowing not) across from those
Meadows to them inexplicably dear.

'As when a soul laments, which hath been blest'—
I'll cite no further what the initiate know.
I never saw those fields whereon their best
And undivulgèd love does overflow.

'Where art thou friend'

Where art thou friend, whom I shall never see,
Conceiving whom I must conceive amiss?
Or sunder'd from my sight in the age that is
Or far-off promise of a time to be;
Thou who canst best accept the certainty
That thou hadst borne proportion in my bliss,
That likest in me either that or this,—
Oh! even for the weakness of the plea
That I have taken to plead with,—if the sound
Of God's dear pleadings have as yet not moved thee,—
And for those virtues I in thee have found,
Who say that had I known I had approved thee,—
For these, make all the virtues to abound,—
No, but for Christ who hath foreknown and loved thee.

'Confirmed beauty'

Confirmed beauty will not bear a stress;—
Bright hues long look'd at thin, dissolve and fly:
Who lies on grass and pores upon the sky
Shall see the azure turn expressionless
And Tantalean slaty ashiness
Like Pharaoh's ears of windy harvest dry,
Dry up the blue and be not slaked thereby.
Ah! surely all who have written will profess

The sweetest sonnet five or six times read
Is tasteless nothing: and in my degree
I prove it. What then when these lines are dead
And coldly do belie the thought of thee?
I'll lay them by, and freshly turn instead
To thy not-staled uncharted memory.

The Beginning of the End

(i)

My love is lessened and must soon be past.
I never promised such persistency
In its condition. No, the tropic tree
Has not a charter that its sap shall last
Into all seasons, though no winter cast
The happy leafing. It is so with me:
My love is less, my love is less for thee.
I cease the mourning and the abject fast
And rise and go about my works again
And, save by darting accidents, forget.
But ah! if you could understand how then
That *less* is heavens higher even yet
Than treble-fervent *more* of other men,
Even your unpassion'd eyelids might be wet.

(ii)

I must feed Fancy. Show me any one
That reads or holds the astrologic lore,
And I'll pretend the credit given of yore;
And let him prove my passion was begun
In the worst hour that's measured by the sun,
With such malign conjunctions as before
No influential heaven ever wore;
That no recorded devilish thing was done
With such a seconding, nor Saturn took
Such opposition to the Lady-star
In the most murderous passage of his book;

And I'll love my distinction: Near or far
He says his science helps him not to look
At hopes so evil-heaven'd as mine are.

(iii)

You see that I have come to passion's end;
This means you need not fear the storms, the cries,
That gave you vantage when you would despise:
My bankrupt heart has no more tears to spend.
Else I am well assured I should offend
With fiercer weepings of these desperate eyes
For poor love's failure than his hopeless rise.
But now I am so tired I soon shall send

Barely a sigh to thought of hopes forgone.
Is this made plain? What have I come across
That here will serve me for comparison?
The sceptic disappointment and the loss
A boy feels when the poet he pores upon
Grows less and less sweet to him, and knows no cause.

The Alchemist in the City

My window shews the travelling clouds,
Leaves spent, new seasons, alter'd sky,
The making and the melting crowds:
The whole world passes; I stand by.

They do not waste their meted hours,
But men and masters plan and build:
I see the crowning of their towers,
And happy promises fulfill'd.

And I—perhaps if my intent
Could count on prediluvian age,
The labours I should then have spent
Might so attain their heritage,

But now before the pot can glow
With not to be discover'd gold,
At length the bellows shall not blow,
The furnace shall at last be cold.

Yet it is now too late to heal
The incapable and cumbrous shame
Which makes me when with men I deal
More powerless than the blind or lame.

No, I should love the city less
Even than this my thankless lore;
But I desire the wilderness
Or weeded landslips of the shore.

I walk my breezy belvedere
To watch the low or levant sun,
I see the city pigeons veer,
I mark the tower swallows run

Between the tower-top and the ground
Below me in the bearing air;
Then find in the horizon-round
One spot and hunger to be there.

And then I hate the most that lore
That holds no promise of success;
Then sweetest seems the houseless shore,
Then free and kind the wilderness,

Or ancient mounds that cover bones,
Or rocks where rockdoves do repair
And trees of terebinth and stones
And silence and a gulf of air.

There on a long and squarèd height
After the sunset I would lie,
And pierce the yellow waxen light
With free long looking, ere I die.

'Myself unholy'

Myself unholy, from myself unholy
To the sweet living of my friends I look—
Eye-greeting doves bright-counter to the rook,
Fresh brooks to salt sand-teasing waters shoaly:—
And they are purer, but alas! not solely
The unquestion'd readings of a blotless book.
And so my trust confusèd, struck, and shook
Yields to the sultry siege of melancholy.
He has a sin of mine, he its near brother,
Knowing them well I can but see the fall.
This fault in one I found, that in another:
And so, though each have one while I have all,
No *better* serves me now, save *best*; no other,
Save Christ: to Christ I look, on Christ I call.

'See how Spring opens'

See how Spring opens with disabling cold,
And hunting winds and the long-lying snow.
Is it a wonder if the buds are slow?
Or where is strength to make the leaf unfold?
Chilling remembrance of my days of old
Afflicts no less, what yet I hope may blow,
That seed which the good sower once did sow,
So loading with obstruction that threshold

Which should ere now have led my feet to the field.
It is the waste done in unreticent youth
Which makes so small the promise of that yield
That I may win with late-learnt skill uncouth
From furrows of the poor and stinting weald.
Therefore how bitter, and learnt how late, the truth!

Continuation of R. Garnet's *Nix*

She mark'd where I and Fabian met;
She loves his face, she knows the spot;
And there she waits with locks unwet
For Fabian that suspects her not.

I see her riving fingers tear
A branch of walnut-leaves, and that
More sweetly shades her stolen hair
Than fan or hood or strawy plait.

He sees her, O but he must miss
A something in her face of guile,
ˣAnd relish not her loveless kiss
And wonder at her shallow smile.

ˣ[*or* And half mislike her loveless kiss.]

Ah no! and she who sits beside
Bids him this way his gazes fix.
ˣThen she seems sweet who seems his bride,
She sour who seems the slighted Nix.

ˣ[*or* Then sweetest seems the seeming bride
When maddest looks the slighted Nix.]

I know of the bored and bitten rocks
Not so far outward in the sea:
There lives the witch shall win my locks
And my blue eyes again for me.

Alas! but I am all at fault,
Nor locks nor eyes shall win again.
I dare not taste the thickening salt,
I cannot meet the swallowing main.

Or if I go, she stays meanwhile,
Who means to wed or means to kill,
And speeds uncheck'd her murderous guile
Or wholly winds him to her will.

'O what a silence'

O what a silence is this wilderness!
Might we not think the sweet(?) and daring rises
Of the flown skylark, and his traverse flight
At highest when he seems to brush the clouds,
†Had been more fertile and had sown with notes

The unenduring fallows of the heaven?
Or take it thus—that the concording stars
Had let such music down, without impediment
Falling along the breakless pool of air,
*As struck with rings of sound the close-shut palms
Of the wood-sorrel and all things sensitive?

---

†[*or* Had been effectual to have sown with notes]

*[As might have struck and shook the close-shut palms]

A. As the wood-sorrel and all things sensitive 12
That thrive in the loamy greenness of this place?
B. What spirit is that makes stillness obsolete
With ear-caressing speech? Where is the tongue
Which drives this stony air to utterance?—
Who is it? how come to this forgotten land?

'Mothers are doubtless'

Mothers are doubtless happier for their babes
And risen sons: yet are the childless free
From tears shed over children's graves.
So those who [hold to] Thee
Take their peculiar thorns and natural pain
Among the lilies and Thy good domain.

Daphne

Who loves me here and has my love,
I think he will not tire of me,
But sing contented as the dove
That comes again to the woodland tree.

He shall have summer sweets and dress
His pleasure to the changing clime,
And I can teach him happiness
That shall not fail in winter-time.

[*or* He shall have summer goods and trim
His pleasure to the changing clime,
And I shall know of sweets for him
That are not less in winter-time.]

His cap shall be shining fur,
And stain'd, and knots of golden thread,
He shall be warm with miniver
Lined all with silk of juicy red.

In spring our river-banks are topt
With yellow flags will suit his brow,
In summer are our orchards knopt
With green-white apples on the bough.

But if I cannot tempt his thought
With wealth that mocks his high degree,
The shepherds, whom I value not,
Have told me I am fair to see.

Castara Victrix

(i) Scene: a bare hollow between hills. Enter Castara and her Esquire

C. What was it we should strike the road again?
E. There was a wood of dwarf and sourèd oaks
Crept all along a hill upon our left,

A wonder in the country, and a landmark
They said we could not miss. A pushing brook
Ran through it, following which we should have sight
Of mile-long reaches of our road below us.
My thought was, there to rest against the trees
And watch until our horses and the men
Circled the safe flanks of the bulky hills.
C. And how long was the way?
E. This shorter way?
Two miles indeed.
C. We have come four, do you think?
Somewhere we slipt astray, you cannot doubt.
E. True, madam, I am sorry now to see
I better'd all our path with sanguine eyes.

. . . .

(ii) At the picnic or whatever we call it. Daphnis, Castara

D. —Can I do any harm?
C. If you are silent, that I know of, none.
D. Ill meant, yet true. I best should flatter then,
In copying well what you have well begun.
C. In copying? how?
D. Must I give tongue again?
In copying your sweet silence.
C. Am I so
Guilty of silence?
D. Quite, as ladies go.
Yet what you are, the world would say, remain:
It never yet so sweetly was put on
By any lauded statue, nor again
By speech so sweetly broken up and gone.
C. What if I hated flattery?
D. Say you do:
The hatred comes with a good grace from you:
Flattery's all out of place where praise is true.

. . . .

(iii) Valerian, Daphnis

V. Come, Daphnis.
D. Good Valerian, I will come. (*exit V.*
Why should I go because Castara goes?
I do not, but to please Valerian.
But why then should Castara weigh with me?
Why, there's an interest and sweet soul in beauty
Which makes us eye-attentive to the eye
That has it; and she is fairer than Colomb,
Selvaggia, Orinda, and Adela, and the rest.
Fairer? These are the flaring shows unlovely
That make my eyes sore and cross-colour things
With fickle spots of sadness; accessories
{Familiar and so hated by the sick;
{Hated and too familiar to— ——;
These are my very text of discontent;
These names, these faces? They are customary
And kindred to my lamentable days,
Of which I say there is no joy in them.
To these Castara is rain or breeze or spring,
— —— ——— – dew, is dawn, is day,
Sheet lightning to the stifling lid of night
Bright-lifting with a little-lasting smile
And breath on it. That is, her face is this.
And if it is why there is cause enough
To say I go because Castara goes.
Yet I'd not say it is her face alone
That this is true of: 'tis Castara's self;
But this distemper'd court will change it all:—
Which says at least then go while all is fresh,—
Much cause to go because Castara goes.

'My prayers must meet a brazen heaven'

My prayers must meet a brazen heaven
And fail and scatter all away.
Unclean and seeming unforgiven
My prayers I scarcely call to pray.

I cannot buoy my heart above;
Above I cannot entrance win.
I reckon precedents of love,
But feel the long success of sin.

My heaven is brass and iron my earth:
Yea, iron is mingled with my clay,
So harden'd is it in this dearth
Which praying fails to do away.
Nor tears, nor tears this clay uncouth
Could mould, if any tears there were.
A warfare of my lips in truth,
Battling with God, is now my prayer.

Shakspere

In the lodges of the perishable souls
He has his portion. God, who stretch'd apart
Doomsday and death—whose dateless thought must chart
All time at once and span the distanced goals,
Sees what his place is; but for us the rolls
Are shut against the canvassing of art.
Something we guess or know: some spirits start
Upwards at once and win their aureoles.

. . . .

'Trees by their yield'

Trees by their yield
Are known; but I—
My sap is sealed,
My root is dry.
If life within
I none can shew
(Except for sin),

Nor fruit above,—
It must be so—
I do not love.

Will no one show
I argued ill?
Because, although
Self-sentenced, still
I keep my trust.
If He would prove
And search me through
Would He not find
(What yet there must
Be hid behind

. . . .

'Let me be to Thee'

Let me be to Thee as the circling bird,
Or bat with tender and air-crisping wings
That shapes in half-light his departing rings,
From both of whom a changeless note is heard.
I have found my music in a common word,
Trying each pleasurable throat that sings
And every praisèd sequence of sweet strings,
And know infallibly which I preferred.

The authentic cadence was discovered late
Which ends those only strains that I approve,
And other science all gone out of date
And minor sweetness scarce made mention of:
I have found the dominant of my range and state—
Love, O my God, to call Thee Love and Love.

The Half-way House

Love I was shewn upon the mountain-side
And bid to catch Him ere the drop of day.
See, Love, I creep and Thou on wings dost ride;
Love, it is evening now and Thou away;
Love, it grows darker here and Thou art above;
Love, come down to me if Thy name be Love.

My national old Egyptian reed gave way;
I took of vine a cross-barred rod or rood.
Then next I hungered: Love when here, they say,
Or once or never took love's proper food;
But I must yield the chase, or rest and eat.—
Peace and food cheered me where four rough ways meet.

Hear yet my paradox: Love, when all is given,
To see Thee I must [see] Thee, to love, love;
I must o'ertake Thee at once and under heaven
If I shall overtake Thee at last above.
You have your wish; enter these walls, one said:
He is with you in the breaking of the bread.

A Complaint

I thought that you would have written: my birthday came and went,
And with the last post over, I knew no letter was sent.
And now if at last you write it never can be the same:
What *would* be a birthday letter that after the birthday came?

I know what you will tell me, Neglectful you were not:
But is not that my grievance—you promised and you forgot?
It's the day that makes the charm; no after-words can succeed
Though they took till the seventeenth of next October to read.

Think this, my birthday falls in a saddening time of year;
Only the dahlias blow, and all is Autumn here.
Hampstead was never bright, and whatever Miss Cully's charms,
It's hardly a proper treat for a birthday to rest in her arms.

Our sex should be born in April perhaps or the lily time,
But the lily is past, as I say, and the rose is not in its prime:
What I *did* ask then was a circle of rose-red sealing wax
And a few leaves not lily-white but charactered over with blacks.

But late is better than never. You see you have managed so,
You have made me quote almost the dismalest proverb I know;
For a letter comes at last (shall I say before Christmas is come?),
And I must take your amends, cry 'Pardon', and then be dumb.

'Moonless darkness'

Moonless darkness stands between.
Past, the Past, no more be seen!
But the Bethlehem-star may lead me
To the sight of Him Who freed me
From the self that I have been.
Make me pure, Lord: Thou art holy;
Make me meek, Lord: Thou wert lowly;
Now beginning, and alway:
Now begin, on Christmas day.

'The earth and heaven'

The earth and heaven, so little known,
Are measured outwards from my breast.
I am the midst of every zone
And justify the East and West;

The unchanging register of change
My all-accepting fixèd eye,
While all things else may stir and range,
All else may whirl or dive or fly.

The swallow, favourite of the gale,
Will on the moulding strike and cling,
Unvalve or shut his vanèd tail
And sheathe at once his leger wing.

He drops upon the wind again;
His little pennon is unfurled.
In motion is no weight or pain,
Nor permanence in the solid world.

There is a vapour stands in the wind;
It shapes itself in taper skeins:
You look again and cannot find,
Save in the body of the rains.

And these are spent and ended quite;
The sky is blue, and the winds pull
Their clouds with breathing edges white
Beyond the world; the streams are full

And millbrook-slips with pretty pace
Gallop along the meadow grass.—
O lovely ease in change of place!
I have desired, desired to pass

The Nightingale

'From nine o'clock till morning light
The copse was never more than grey.
The darkness did not close that night
  But day passed into day.
And soon I saw it shewing new
Beyond the hurst with such a hue
As silky garden-poppies do.

A crimson East, that bids for rain.
So from the dawn was ill begun
The day that brought my lasting pain
  And put away my sun.

But watching while the colour grew
I only feared the wet for you
Bound for the Harbour and your crew.

I did not mean to sleep, but found
I had slept a little and was chill.
And I could hear the tiniest sound,
  The morning was so still—
The bats' wings lisping as they flew
And water draining through and through
The wood: but not a dove would coo.

You know you said the nightingale
In all our western shires was rare,
That more he shuns our special dale
  Or never lodges there:
And I had thought so hitherto—
Up till that morning's fall of dew,
And now I wish that it were true.

For he began at once and shook
My head to hear. He might have strung
A row of ripples in the brook,
  So forcibly he sung,
The mist upon the leaves have strewed,
And danced the balls of dew that stood
In acres all above the wood.

I thought the air must cut and strain
The windpipe when he sucked his breath
And when he turned it back again
  The music must be death.
With not a thing to make me fear,
A singing bird in morning clear
To me was terrible to hear.

Yet as he changed his mighty stops
Betweens I heard the water still
All down the stair-way of the copse
  And churning in the mill.
But that sweet sound which I preferred,
Your passing steps, I never heard
For warbling of the warbling bird.'

Thus Frances sighed at home, while Luke
Made headway in the frothy deep.
She listened how the sea-gust shook
  And then lay back to sleep.
While he was washing from on deck
She pillowing low her lily neck
Timed her sad visions with his wreck.

The Habit of Perfection

Elected Silence, sing to me
And beat upon my whorlèd ear,
Pipe me to pastures still and be
The music that I care to hear.

Shape nothing, lips; be lovely-dumb:
It is the shut, the curfew sent
From there where all surrenders come
Which only makes you eloquent.

Be shellèd, eyes, with double dark
And find the uncreated light:
This ruck and reel which you remark
Coils, keeps, and teases simple sight.

Palate, the hutch of tasty lust,
Desire not to be rinsed with wine:
The can must be so sweet, the crust
So fresh that come in fasts divine!

Nostrils, your careless breath that spend
Upon the stir and keep of pride,
What relish shall the censers send
Along the sanctuary side!

O feel-of-primrose hands, O feet
That want the yield of plushy sward,
But you shall walk the golden street
And you unhouse and house the Lord.

And, Poverty, be thou the bride
And now the marriage feast begun,
And lily-coloured clothes provide
Your spouse not laboured-at nor spun.

Nondum

'Verily Thou art a God that hidest Thyself.'
ISAIAH xlv. 15.

God, though to Thee our psalm we raise
No answering voice comes from the skies;
To Thee the trembling sinner prays
But no forgiving voice replies;
Our prayer seems lost in desert ways,
Our hymn in the vast silence dies.

We see the glories of the earth
But not the hand that wrought them all:
Night to a myriad worlds gives birth,
Yet like a lighted empty hall
Where stands no host at door or hearth
Vacant creation's lamps appal.

We guess; we clothe Thee, unseen King,
With attributes we deem are meet;
Each in his own imagining
Sets up a shadow in Thy seat;
Yet know not how our gifts to bring,
Where seek Thee with unsandalled feet.

And still th'unbroken silence broods
While ages and while aeons run,
As erst upon chaotic floods
The Spirit hovered ere the sun
Had called the seasons' changeful moods
And life's first germs from death had won.

And still th'abysses infinite
Surround the peak from which we gaze.

Deep calls to deep, and blackest night
Giddies the soul with blinding daze
That dares to cast its searching sight
On being's dread and vacant maze.

And Thou art silent, whilst Thy world
Contends about its many creeds
And hosts confront with flags unfurled
And zeal is flushed and pity bleeds
And truth is heard, with tears impearled,
A moaning voice among the reeds.

My hand upon my lips I lay;
The breast's desponding sob I quell;
I move along life's tomb-decked way
And listen to the passing bell
Summoning men from speechless day
To death's more silent, darker spell.

Oh! till Thou givest that sense beyond,
To shew Thee that Thou art, and near,
Let patience with her chastening wand
Dispel the doubt and dry the tear;
And lead me child-like by the hand
If still in darkness not in fear.

Speak! whisper to my watching heart
One word—as when a mother speaks
Soft, when she sees her infant start,
Till dimpled joy steals o'er its cheeks.
Then, to behold Thee as Thou art,
I'll wait till morn eternal breaks.

Easter

Break the box and shed the nard;
Stop not now to count the cost;
Hither bring pearl, opal, sard;
Reck not what the poor have lost;

Upon Christ throw all away:
Know ye, this is Easter Day.

Build His Church and deck His shrine,
Empty though it be on earth;
Ye have kept your choicest wine—
Let it flow for heavenly mirth;
Pluck the harp and breathe the horn:
Know ye not 'tis Easter morn?

Gather gladness from the skies;
Take a lesson from the ground;
Flowers do ope their heavenward eyes
And a Spring-time joy have found;
Earth throws Winter's robes away,
Decks herself for Easter Day.

Beauty now for ashes wear,
Perfumes for the garb of woe,
Chaplets for dishevelled hair,
Dances for sad footsteps slow;
Open wide your hearts that they
Let in joy this Easter Day.

Seek God's house in happy throng;
Crowded let His table be;
Mingle praises, prayer, and song,
Singing to the Trinity.
Henceforth let your souls alway
Make each morn an Easter Day.

Summa

The best ideal is the true
  And other truth is none.
All glory be ascribèd to
  The holy Three in One.

Man is most low, God is most high.
  As sure as heaven it is
There must be something to supply
  All insufficiencies.
For souls that might have blessed the time
  And breathed delightful breath
In sordidness of care and crime
  The city tires to death.
And faces fit for leisure gaze
  And daylight and sweet air,
Missing prosperity and praise,
  Are never known for fair.

Jesu Dulcis Memoria

Jesus to cast one thought upon
Makes gladness after He is gone,
But more than honey and honeycomb
Is to come near and take Him home.

No music so can touch the ear,
No news is heard of such sweet cheer,
Thought half so dear there is not one
As Jesus God the Father's Son.

Jesu, their hope who go astray,
So kind to those who ask the way,
So good to those who look for Thee,
To those who find what must Thou be?

To speak of that no tongue will do
Nor letters suit to spell it true:
But they can guess who have tasted of
What Jesus is and what is love.

Jesu, a springing well Thou art,
Daylight to head and treat to heart,
And matched with Thee there's nothing glad
That men have wished for or have had.

Wish us Good morning when we wake
And light us, Lord, with Thy day-break.
Beat from our brains the thicky night
And fill the world up with delight.

Who taste of Thee will hunger more,
Who drink be thirsty as before:
What else to ask they never know
But Jesus' self, they love Him so.

— — — — — — —

And a sweet singing in the ear
And in the mouth a honey zest
And drinks of heaven in the breast.

Thou art the hope, Jesu my sweet,
The soul has in its sighing-fit;
The loving tears on Thee are spent,
The inner cry for Thee is meant.

Be our delight, O Jesu, now
As by and by our prize art Thou,
And grant our glorying may be
World without end alone in Thee.

'Not kind! to freeze me'

Not kind! to freeze me with forecast,
Dear grace and girder of mine and me.
You to be gone and I lag last—
Nor I nor heaven would have it be.

Horace: *Persicos odi, puer, apparatus*

(ODES I. xxxviii)

Ah child, no Persian-perfect art!
Crowns composite and braided bast
They tease me. Never know the part
        Where roses linger last.
Bring natural myrtle, and have done:
Myrtle will suit your place and mine:
And set the glasses from the sun
        Beneath the tackled vine.

Horace: *Odi profanum volgus et arceo*

(ODES III. i)

Tread back—and back, the lewd and lay!—
Grace love your lips!—what never ear
Heard yet, the Muses' man, today
I make the boys and maidens hear.

Kings herd it on their subject droves
But Jove's the herd that keeps the kings—
Jove of the Giants: simple Jove's
Mere eyebrow rocks this round of things.

Say man than man may rank his rows
Wider, more wholesale; one with claim
Of blood to our green hustings goes;
One with more conscience, cleaner fame;

One better backed comes crowding by:—
That level power whose word is Must
Dances the balls for low or high:
Her urn takes all, her deal is just.

Sinner who saw the blade that hung
Vertical home, could Sicily fare

Be managed tasty to that tongue?
Or bird with pipe, viol with air

Bring sleep round then? sleep not afraid
Of country bidder's calls or low
Entries or banks all over shade
Or Tempe with the west to blow.

Who stops his asking mood at par
The burly sea may quite forget
Nor fear the violent calendar
At Haedus-rise, Arcturus-set,

For hail upon the vine nor break
His heart at farming, what between
The dog-star with the fields abake
And spiting snows to choke the green.

Fish feel their waters drawing to
With our abutments: there we see
The lades discharged and laded new,
And Italy flies from Italy.

But fears, fore-motions of the mind
Climb quits: one boards the master there
On brazèd barge and hard behind
Sits to the beast that seats him—Care.

O if there's that which Phrygian stone
And crimson wear of starry shot
Not sleek away; Falernian-grown
And oils of Shushan comfort not,

Why . . . . . .
. . . .
Why should I change a Sabine dale
For wealth as wide as weariness?

The Elopement

All slumbered whom our rud red tiles
Do cover from the starry spread,
When I with never-needed wiles
  Crept trembling out of bed.
Then at the door what work there was, good lack,
To keep the loaded bolt from plunging back.

When this was done and I could look
I saw the stars like flash of fire.
My heart irregularly shook,
  I cried with my desire.
I put the door to with the bolts unpinned,
Upon my forehead hit the burly wind.

No tumbler woke and shook the cot,
The rookery never stirred a wing,
At roost and rest they shifted not,
  Blessed be everything.
And all within the house were sound as posts,
Or listening thought of linen-winded ghosts.

The stars are packed so thick to-night
They seem to press and droop and stare,
And gather in like hurdles bright
  The liberties of air.
I spy the nearest daisies through the dark,
The air smells strong of sweetbriar in the park.

I knew the brook that parts in two
The cart road with a shallowy bed
Of small and sugar flints, I knew
  The footway, Stephen said,
And where cold daffodils in April are
Think you want daffodils and follow as far

As where the little hurling sound
To the point of silence in the air
Dies off in hyacinthed ground,

And I should find him there.
O heart, have done, you beat you beat so high,
You spoil the plot I find my true love by.

Oratio Patris Condren: O Jesu vivens in Maria

Jesu that dost in Mary dwell,
Be in thy servants' hearts as well,
In the spirit of thy holiness,
In the fulness of thy force and stress,
In the very ways that thy life goes
And virtues that thy pattern shows,
In the sharing of thy mysteries;
And every power in us that is
Against thy power put under feet
In the Holy Ghost the Paraclete
  To the glory of the Father. Amen.

Ad Mariam

When a sister, born for each strong month-brother,
  Spring's one daughter, the sweet child May,
Lies in the breast of the young year-mother
  With light on her face like the waves at play,
Man from the lips of him speaketh and saith,
At the touch of her wandering wondering breath
Warm on his brow: lo! where is another
  Fairer than this one to brighten our day?

We have suffered the sons of Winter in sorrow
  And been in their ruinous reigns oppressed,
And fain in the springtime surcease would borrow
  From all the pain of the past's unrest;
And May has come, hair-bound in flowers,
With eyes that smile thro' the tears of the hours,
With joy for to-day and hope for to-morrow
  And the promise of Summer within her breast!

And we that joy in this month joy-laden,
  The gladdest thing that our eyes have seen,
Oh thou, proud mother and much proud maiden—
  Maid yet mother as May hath been—
To thee we tender the beauties all
Of the month by men called virginal
And, where thou dwellest in deep-groved Aidenn,
  Salute thee, mother, the maid-month's Queen!

For thou, as she, wert the one fair daughter
  That came when a line of kings did cease,
Princes strong for the sword and slaughter,
  That, warring, wasted the land's increase,
And like the storm-months smote the earth
Till a maid in David's house had birth,
That was unto Judah as May, and brought her
  A son for King, whose name was peace.

Wherefore we love thee, wherefore we sing to thee,
  We, all we, thro' the length of our days,
The praise of the lips and the hearts of us bring to thee,
  Thee, oh maiden, most worthy of praise;
For lips and hearts they belong to thee
Who to us are as dew unto grass and tree,
For the fallen rise and the stricken spring to thee,
  Thee, May-hope of our darkened ways!

O Deus, ego amo te

O God, I love thee, I love thee—
Not out of hope of heaven for me
Nor fearing not to love and be
  In the everlasting burning.
Thou, thou, my Jesus, after me
  Didst reach thine arms out dying,
For my sake sufferedst nails and lance,
Mocked and marrèd countenance,
  Sorrows passing number,
  Sweat and care and cumber,

Yea and death, and this for me,
  And thou couldst see me sinning:
Then I, why should not I love thee,
Jesu so much in love with me?
Not for heaven's sake; not to be
Out of hell by loving thee;
Not for any gains I see;
But just the way that thou didst me
I do love and I will love thee:
What must I love thee, Lord, for then?—
For being my king and God. Amen.

Rosa Mystica

1.

The rose in a mystery, where is it found?
Is it anything true? Does it grow upon ground?—
It was made of earth's mould but it went from men's eyes
And its place is a secret and shut in the skies.
Refrain—
In the gardens of God, in the daylight divine
Find me a place by thee, mother of mine.

2.

But where was it formerly? which is the spot
That was blest in it once, though now it is not?—
It is Galilee's growth: it grew at God's will
And broke into bloom upon Nazareth hill.
In the gardens of God, in the daylight divine
I shall look on thy loveliness, mother of mine.

3.

What was its season then? how long ago?
When was the summer that saw the bud blow?—
Two thousands of years are near upon past
Since its birth and its bloom and its breathing its last.
In the gardens of God, in the daylight divine
I shall keep time with thee, mother of mine.

4.

Tell me the name now, tell me its name.
The heart guesses easily: is it the same?—
Mary the Virgin, well the heart knows,
She is the mystery, she is that rose.
In the gardens of God, in the daylight divine
I shall come home to thee, mother of mine.

5.

Is Mary the rose then? Mary the tree?
But the blossom, the blossom there, who can it be?—
Who can her rose be? It could be but one:
Christ Jesus our Lord, her God and her son.
In the gardens of God, in the daylight divine
Shew me thy son, mother, mother of mine.

6.

What was the colour of that blossom bright?—
White to begin with, immaculate white.
But what a wild flush on the flakes of it stood
When the rose ran in crimsonings down the cross-wood!
In the gardens of God, in the daylight divine
I shall worship His wounds with thee, mother of mine.

7.

How many leaves had it?—Five they were then,
Five like the senses and members of men;
Five is their number by nature, but now
They multiply, multiply who can tell how.
In the gardens of God, in the daylight divine
Make me a leaf in thee, mother of mine.

8.

Does it smell sweet too in that holy place?—
Sweet unto God, and the sweetness is grace:
O breath of it bathes great heaven above
In grace that is charity, grace that is love.
To thy breast, to thy rest, to thy glory divine
Draw me by charity, mother of mine.

On St. Winefred

besides her miraculous cures
filling a bath and turning a mill

As wishing all about us sweet,
She brims her bath in cold or heat;
She lends, in aid of work and will,
Her hand from heaven to turn a mill—
Sweet soul! not scorning honest sweat
And favouring virgin freshness yet.

S. Thomae Aquinatis Rhythmus ad SS. Sacramentum

'Adoro te supplex, latens deitas'

Godhead, I adore thee fast in hiding; thou
God in these bare shapes, poor shadows, darkling now:
See, Lord, at thy service low lies here a heart
Lost, all lost in wonder at the God thou art.

Seeing, touching, tasting are in thee deceived;
How says trusty hearing? that shall be believed:
What God's Son has told me, take for truth I do;
Truth himself speaks truly or there's nothing true.

On the cross thy godhead made no sign to men;
Here thy very manhood steals from human ken:
Both are my confession, both are my belief,
And I pray the prayer of the dying thief.

I am not like Thomas, wounds I cannot see,
But can plainly call thee Lord and God as he:
This faith each day deeper be my holding of,
Daily make me harder hope and dearer love.

O thou our reminder of Christ crucified,
Living Bread the life of us for whom he died,
Lend this life to me then: feed and feast my mind,
There be thou the sweetness man was meant to find.

Like what tender tales tell of the Pelican;
Bathe me, Jesu Lord, in what thy bosom ran—
Blood that but one drop of has the worth to win
All the world forgiveness of its world of sin.

Jesu whom I look at veilèd here below,
I beseech thee send me what I thirst for so,
Some day to gaze on thee face to face in light
And be blest for ever with thy glory's sight.

Author's Preface

The poems in this book are written some in Running Rhythm, the common rhythm in English use, some in Sprung Rhythm, and some in a mixture of the two. And those in the common rhythm are some counterpointed, some not.

Common English rhythm, called Running Rhythm above, is measured by feet of either two or three syllables and (putting aside the imperfect feet at the beginning and end of lines and also some unusual measures in which feet seem to be paired together and double or composite feet to arise) never more nor less.

Every foot has one principal stress or accent, and this or the syllable it falls on may be called the Stress of the foot and the other part, the one or two unaccented syllables, the Slack. Feet (and the rhythms made out of them) in which the Stress comes first are called Falling Feet and Falling Rhythms, feet and rhythm in which the Slack comes first are called Rising Feet and Rhythms, and if the Stress is between two Slacks there will be Rocking Feet and Rhythms. These distinctions are real and true to nature; but for purposes of scanning it is a great convenience to follow the example of music and take the stress always first, as the accent or the chief accent always comes first in a musical bar. If this is done there will be in common English verse only two possible feet—the so-called accentual Trochee and Dactyl, and correspondingly only two possible uniform rhythms, the so-called Trochaic and Dactylic. But they may be mixed and then what the Greeks called a Logaoedic Rhythm arises. These are the facts and according to these the scanning of ordinary regularly-written English verse is very simple indeed and to bring in other principles is here unnecessary.

But because verse written strictly in these feet and by these principles will become same and tame the poets have brought in licences and departures from rule to give variety, and especially when the natural rhythm is rising, as in the common ten-syllable or five-foot verse, rhymed or blank. These irregularities are chiefly Reversed Feet and Reversed or Counterpoint Rhythm, which two things are two steps or degrees of licence in the same kind. By a reversed foot I mean the putting the stress where, to judge by the rest of the measure, the slack should be and the slack where the stress, and this is done freely at the beginning of a line and, in the course of a line, after a pause; only scarcely ever in the second foot or place and never in the last, unless when the poet designs some extraordinary effect; for these places are characteristic and sensitive and cannot well be touched. But the reversal of the first foot and of some middle foot after a strong pause is a thing so natural that our poets have generally done it, from Chaucer down, without remark and it commonly passes unnoticed and cannot be said to amount to a formal change of rhythm, but rather is that irregularity which all natural growth and motion shews. If however the reversal is repeated in two feet running, especially so as to include the sensitive second foot, it must be due either to great want of ear or else is a calculated effect, the superinducing or *mounting* of a new rhythm upon the old; and since the new or mounted rhythm is actually heard and at the same time the mind naturally supplies the natural or standard foregoing rhythm, for we do not forget what the rhythm is that by rights we should be hearing, two rhythms are in some manner running at once and we have something answerable to counterpoint in music, which is two or more strains of tune going on together, and this is Counterpoint Rhythm. Of this kind of verse Milton is the great master and the choruses of *Samson Agonistes* are written throughout in it—but with the disadvantage that he does not let the reader clearly know what the ground-rhythm is meant to be and so they have struck most readers as merely irregular. And in fact if you counterpoint throughout, since one only of the counter rhythms is actually heard, the other is really destroyed or cannot come to exist and what is written is one rhythm only and probably Sprung Rhythm, of which I now speak.

Sprung Rhythm, as used in this book, is measured by feet of from one to four syllables, regularly, and for particular effects any number of weak or slack syllables may be used. It has one stress, which falls on the only syllable, if there is only one, or, if there are more, then scanning as above, on the first, and so gives rise to four sorts of feet, a monosyllable and the so-called accentual Trochee, Dactyl, and the First Paeon. And there will be four corresponding natural rhythms; but nominally the feet are mixed and any one may follow any other. And hence Sprung Rhythm differs from Running Rhythm in having or being only one nominal rhythm, a mixed or 'logaoedic' one, instead of three, but on the other hand in having twice the flexibility of foot, so that any two stresses may either follow one another running or be divided by one, two, or three slack syllables. But strict Sprung Rhythm cannot be counterpointed. In Sprung Rhythm, as in logaoedic rhythm generally, the feet are assumed to be equally long or strong and their seeming inequality is made up by pause or stressing.

Remark also that it is natural in Sprung Rhythm for the lines to be *rove over*, that is for the scanning of each line immediately to take up that of the one before, so that if the first has one or more syllables at its end the other must have so many the less at its beginning; and in fact the scanning runs on without break from the beginning, say, of a stanza to the end and all the stanza is one long strain, though written in lines asunder.

Two licences are natural to Sprung Rhythm. The one is rests, as in music; but of this an example is scarcely to be found in this book, unless in the *Echos*, second line. The other is *hangers* or *outrides*, that is one, two, or three slack syllables added to a foot and not counting in the nominal scanning. They are so called because they seem to hang below the line or ride forward or backward from it in another dimension than the line itself, according to a principle needless to explain here. These outriding half feet or hangers are marked by a loop underneath them, and plenty of them will be found.

The other marks are easily understood, namely accents, where the reader might be in doubt which syllable should have the stress; slurs, that is loops *over* syllables, to tie them together into the time of one; little loops at the end of a line to shew that the rhyme goes on to the first letter of the next line; what in music are called pauses 𝄐, to shew that the syllable should be dwelt on; and twirls ∾, to mark reversed or counterpointed rhythm.

Note on the nature and history of Sprung Rhythm—Sprung Rhythm is the most natural of things. For (1) it is the rhythm of common speech and of written prose, when rhythm is perceived in them. (2) It is the rhythm of all but the most monotonously regular music, so that in the words of choruses and refrains and in songs written closely to music it arises. (3) It is found in nursery rhymes, weather saws, and so on; because, however these may have been once made in running rhythm, the terminations having dropped off by the change of language, the stresses come together and so the rhythm is sprung. (4) It arises in common verse when reversed or counterpointed, for the same reason.

But nevertheless in spite of all this and though Greek and Latin lyric verse, which is well known, and the old English verse seen in *Pierce Ploughman* are in sprung rhythm, it has in fact ceased to be used since the Elizabethan age, Greene being the last writer who can be said to have recognized it. For perhaps there was not, down to our days, a single, even short, poem in English in which sprung rhythm is employed—not for single effects or in fixed places—but as the governing principle of the scansion. I say this because the contrary has been asserted: if it is otherwise the poem should be cited.

Some of the sonnets in this book are in five-foot, some in six-foot or Alexandrine lines.

Nos. 1 and 25 are Curtal-Sonnets, that is they are constructed in proportions resembling those of the sonnet proper, namely 6 + 4 instead of 8 + 6, with however a half line tailpiece (so that the equation is rather $\frac{12}{2} + \frac{9}{2} = \frac{21}{2} = 10\frac{1}{2}$).

(98)

The Wreck of the Deutschland

Dec. 6, 7 1875

to the happy memory of five Franciscan nuns,
exiles by the Falck Laws, drowned between
midnight and morning of December 7.

Part the first

Thou mastering me
God! giver of breath and bread;
World's strand, sway of the sea;
Lord of living and dead;
Thou hast bound bones and veins in me, fastened me flesh,
And after it álmost únmade, what with dread,
Thy doing: and dost thou touch me afresh?
Over again I feel thy finger and find theé.

2

I did say yes
O at lightning and lashed rod;
Thou heardst me truer than tongue confess
Thy terror, O Christ, O God;
Thou knowest the walls, altar and hour and night:
The swoon of a heart that the sweep and the hurl of thee trod
Hard down with a horror of height:
And the midriff astrain with leaning of, laced with fire of stress.

3

The frown of his face
Before me, the hurtle of hell
Behind, where, where was a, where was a place?
I whirled out wings that spell
And fled with a fling of the heart to the heart of the Host.
My heart, but you were dovewinged, I can tell,
Carrier-witted, I am bold to boast,
To flash from the flame to the flame then, tower from the grace to the grace.

4

I am sóft síft
In an hourglass—at the wall
Fast, but mined with a motion, a drift,
And it crowds and it combs to the fall;
I steady as a water in a well, to a poise, to a pane,
But roped with, always, all the way down from the tall
Fells or flanks of the voel, a vein
Of the gospel proffer, a pressure, a principle, Christ's gift.

5

I kiss my hand
To the stars, lovely-asunder
Starlight, wafting him out of it; and
Glow, glory in thunder;
Kiss my hand to the dappled-with-damson west:
Since, though he is under the world's splendour and wonder,
His mystery must be instressed, stressed;
For I greet him the days I meet him, and bless when I
understand.

6

Not out of his bliss
Springs the stress felt
Nor first from heaven (and few know this)
Swings the stroke dealt—
Stroke and a stress that stars and storms deliver,
That guilt is hushed by, hearts are flushed by and melt—
But it rides time like riding a river
(And here the faithful waver, the faithless fable and miss.)

7

It dates from day
Of his going in Galilee;
Warm-laid grave of a womb-life grey;
Manger, maiden's knee;
The dense and the driven Passion, and frightful sweat;
Thence the discharge of it, there its swelling to be,
Though felt before, though in high flood yet—
What none would have known of it, only the heart, being hard at bay,

8

Is out with it! Oh,
We lash with the best or worst
Word last! How a lush-kept plush-capped sloe
Will, mouthed to flesh-burst,
Gush!—flush the man, the being with it, sour or sweet,
Brim, in a flash, full!—Hither then, last or first,
To hero of Calvary, Christ,'s feet—
Never ask if meaning it, wanting it, warned of it—men go.

9

Be adored among men,
God, three-numberèd form;
Wring thy rebel, dogged in den,
Man's malice, with wrecking and storm.
Beyond saying sweet, past telling of tongue,
Thou art lightning and love, I found it, a winter and warm;
Father and fondler of heart thou hast wrung;
Hast thy dark descending and most art merciful then.

10

With an anvil-ding
And with fire in him forge thy will
Or rather, rather then, stealing as Spring
Through him, melt him but master him still:
Whether át ónce, as once at a crash Paul,
Or as Austin, a lingering-out sweet skill,
Make mercy in all of us, out of us all
Mastery, but be adored, but be adored King.

Part the second

11

'Some find me a sword; some
The flange and the rail; flame,
Fang, or flood' goes Death on drum,
And storms bugle his fame.
But wé dréam we are rooted in earth—Dust!
Flesh falls within sight of us, we, though our flower the same,

Wave with the meadow, forget that there must
The sour scythe cringe, and the blear share come.

12

On Saturday sailed from Bremen,
American-outward-bound,
Take settler and seamen, tell men with women,
Two hundred souls in the round—
O Father, not under thy feathers nor ever as guessing
The goal was a shoal, of a fourth the doom to be drowned;
Yet díd the dark side of the bay of thy blessing
Not vault them, the million of rounds of thy mercy not reeve even
them in?

13

Into the snows she sweeps,
Hurling the haven behind,
The Deutschland, on Sunday; and so the sky keeps,
For the infinite air is unkind,
And the sea flint-flake, black-backed in the regular blow,
Sitting Eastnortheast, in cursed quarter, the wind;
Wiry and white-fiery and whírlwind-swivellèd snow
Spins to the widow-making unchilding unfathering deeps.

14

She drove in the dark to leeward,
She struck—not a reef or a rock
But the combs of a smother of sand: night drew her
Dead to the Kentish Knock;
And she beat the bank down with her bows and the ride of her
keel;
The breakers rolled on her beam with ruinous shock;
And canvass and compass, the whorl and the wheel
Idle for ever to waft her or wind her with, these she endured.

15

Hope had grown grey hairs,
Hope had mourning on,
Trenched with tears, carved with cares,

Hope was twelve hours gone;
And frightful a nightfall folded rueful a day
Nor rescue, only rocket and lightship, shone,
And lives at last were washing away:
To the shrouds they took,—they shook in the hurling and horrible
airs.

16

One stirred from the rigging to save
The wild woman-kind below,
With a rope's end round the man, handy and brave—
He was pitched to his death at a blow,
For all his dreadnought breast and braids of thew:
They could tell him for hours, dandled the to and fro
Through the cobbled foam-fleece. What could he do
With the burl of the fountains of air, buck and the flood of the
wave?

17

They fought with God's cold—
And they could not and fell to the deck
(Crushed them) or water (and drowned them) or rolled
With the sea-romp over the wreck.
Night roared, with the heart-break hearing a heart-broke
rabble,
The woman's wailing, the crying of child without check—
Till a lioness arose breasting the babble,
A prophetess towered in the tumult, a virginal tongue told.

18

Ah, touched in your bower of bone
Are you! turned for an exquisite smart,
Have you! make words break from me here all alone,
Do you!—mother of being in me, heart.
O unteachably after evil, but uttering truth,
Why, tears! is it? tears; such a melting, a madrigal start!
Never-eldering revel and river of youth,
What can it be, this glee? the good you have there of your own?

19

Sister, a sister calling
A master, her master and mine!—
And the inboard seas run swirling and hawling;
The rash smart sloggering brine
Blinds her; but shé that weather sees óne thing, one;
Has óne fetch ín her: she rears herself to divine
Ears, and the call of the tall nun
To the men in the tops and the tackle rode over the storm's brawling.

20

She was first of a five and came
Of a coifèd sisterhood.
(O Deutschland, double a desperate name!
O world wide of its good!
But Gertrude, lily, and Luther, are two of a town,
Christ's lily and beast of the waste wood:
From life's dawn it is drawn down,
Abel is Cain's brother and breasts they have sucked the same.)

21

Loathed for a love men knew in them,
Banned by the land of their birth,
Rhine refused them, Thames would ruin them;
Surf, snow, river and earth
Gnashed: but thou art above, thou Orion of light;
Thy unchancelling poising palms were weighing the worth,
Thou martyr-master: in thý sight
Storm flakes were scroll-leaved flowers, lily showers—sweet heaven was astrew in them.

22

Five! the finding and sake
And cipher of suffering Christ.
Mark, the mark is of man's make
And the word of it Sacrificed.
But he scores it in scarlet himself on his own bespoken,
Before-time-taken, dearest prizèd and priced—

Stigma, signal, cinquefoil token
For lettering of the lamb's fleece, ruddying of the rose-flake.

23

Joy fall to thee, father Francis,
Drawn to the Life that died;
With the gnarls of the nails in thee, niche of the lance, his
Lovescape crucified
And seal of his seraph-arrival! and these thy daughters
And five-livèd and leavèd favour and pride,
Are sisterly sealed in wild waters,
To bathe in his fall-gold mercies, to breathe in his all-fire glances.

24

Away in the loveable west,
On a pastoral forehead of Wales,
I was under a roof here, I was at rest,
And they the prey of the gales;
She to the black-about air, to the breaker, the thickly
Falling flakes, to the throng that catches and quails
Was calling 'O Christ, Christ, come quickly':
The cross to her she calls Christ to her, christens her wild-worst
Best.

25

The majesty! what did she mean?
Breathe, arch and original Breath.
Is it lóve in her of the béing as her lóver had béen?
Breathe, body of lovely Death.
They were else-minded then, altogether, the men
Wóke thee with a *We are périshing* in the wéather of
Gennésaréth.
Or ís it that she cried for the crown then,
The keener to come at the comfort for feeling the combating
keen?

26

For how to the heart's cheering
The down-dugged ground-hugged grey

Hovers off, the jay-blue heavens appearing
Of pied and peeled May!
Blue-beating and hoary-glow height; or night, still higher,
With belled fire and the moth-soft Milky Way,
What by your measure is the heaven of desire,
The treasure never eyesight got, nor was ever guessed what for the
hearing?

27

Nó, but it was nót these.
The jading and jar of the cart,
Time's tásking, it is fathers that asking for ease
Of the sodden-with-its-sorrowing heart,
Not danger, electrical horror; then further it finds
The appealing of the Passion is tenderer in prayer apart:
Other, I gather, in measure her mind's
Burden, in wind's burly and beat of endragonèd seas.

28

But how shall I . . . make me room there:
Reach me a . . . Fancy, come faster—
Strike you the sight of it? look at it loom there,
Thing that she . . . There then! the Master,
Ipse, the only one, Christ, King, Head:
He was to cure the extremity where he had cast her;
Do, deal, lord it with living and dead;
Let him ride, her pride, in his triumph, despatch and have done
with his doom there.

29

Ah! there was a heart right!
There was single eye!
Read the unshapeable shock night
And knew the who and the why;
Wording it how but by him that present and past,
Heaven and earth are word of, worded by?—
The Simon Peter of a soul! to the blast
Tárpëïan-fast, but a blown beacon of light.

30

Jesu, heart's light,
Jesu, maid's son,
What was the feast followed the night
Thou hadst glory of this nun?—
Féast of the óne wóman withóut stáin.
For so conceivèd, so to conceive thee is done;
But here was heart-throe, birth of a brain,
Word, that heard and kept thee and uttered thee óutríght.

31

Well, shé has thée for the pain, for the
Patience; but pity of the rest of them!
Heart, go and bleed at a bitterer vein for the
Comfortless unconfessed of them—
No not uncomforted: lovely-felicitous Providence
Fínger of a ténder of, O of a féathery délicacy, the bréast of the
Maiden could obey so, be a bell to, ring óf it, and
Startle the poor sheep back! is the shipwrack then a harvest, does
tempest carry the grain for thee?

32

I admire thee, master of the tides,
Of the Yore-flood, of the year's fall;
The recurb and the recovery of the gulf 's sides,
The girth of it and the wharf of it and the wall;
Stanching, quenching ocean of a motionable mind;
Ground of being, and granite of it: pást áll
Grásp Gód, thróned behínd
Death with a sovereignty that heeds but hides, bodes but abides;

33

With a mercy that outrides
The all of water, an ark
For the listener; for the lingerer with a love glides
Lower than death and the dark;
A vein for the visiting of the past-prayer, pent in prison,
The-last-breath penitent spirits—the uttermost mark
Our passion-plungèd giant risen,

The Christ of the Father compassionate, fetched in the storm of his
strides.

34

Now burn, new born to the world,
Double-naturèd name,
The heaven-flung, heart-fleshed, maiden-furled
Miracle-in-Mary-of-flame,
Mid-numberèd he in three of the thunder-throne!
Not a dooms-day dazzle in his coming nor dark as he
came;
Kind, but royally reclaiming his own;
A released shówer, let flásh to the shíre, not a líghtning of fíre
hard-húrled.

35

Dame, at our door
Drówned, and among oúr shóals,
Remember us in the roads, the heaven-haven of the
reward:
Our Kíng back, Oh, upon Énglish sóuls!
Let him easter in us, be a dayspring to the dimness of us, be a
crimson-cresseted east,
More brightening her, rare-dear Britain, as his reign rolls,
Pride, rose, prince, hero of us, high-priest,
Our héarts' charity's héarth's fíre, our thóughts' chivalry's thróng's
Lórd.

The Silver Jubilee

to James First Bishop of Shrewsbury on the
25th Year of his Episcopate July 28 1876

Though no high-hung bells or din
Of braggart bugles cry it in—
What is sound? Nature's round
Makes the Silver Jubilee.

Five and twenty years have run
Since sacred fountains to the sun
   Sprang, that but now were shut,
Showering Silver Jubilee.

Feasts, when we shall fall asleep,
Shrewsbury may see others keep;
   None but you this her true,
This her Silver Jubilee.

Not today we need lament
Your wealth of life is some way spent:
   Toil has shed round your head
Silver but for Jubilee.

Then for her whose velvet vales
Should have pealed with welcome, Wales,
   Let the chime of a rhyme
Utter Silver Jubilee.

Moonrise June 19 1876

I awoke in the midsummer not-to-call night, | in the white and the walk of the morning:
The móon, dwíndled and thínned to the frínge | of a fíngernail héld to the cándle,
Or páring of páradisáïcal frúit, | lóvely in wáning but lústreless,
Stepped from the stool, drew back from the barrow, | of dark Maenefa the mountain;
A cusp still clasped him, a fluke yet fanged him, | entangled him, not quit utterly.
This was the prized, the desirable sight, | unsought, presented so easily,
Parted me leaf and leaf, divided me, | eyelid and eyelid of slumber.

The Woodlark

Teevo cheevo cheevio chee:
O where, what can thát be?
Weedio-weedio: there again!
So tiny a trickle of sóng-strain
And all round not to be found
For brier, bough, furrow, or gréen ground
Before or behind or far or at hand
Either left either right
Anywhere in the súnlight.
Well, after all! Ah but hark—
'I am the little wóodlark.

Today the sky is two and two
With white strokes and strains of the blue

Round a ring, around a ring
And while I sail (must listen) I sing

The skylark is my cousin and he
Is known to men more than me

. . . when the cry within
Says Go on then I go on
Till the longing is less and the good gone

But down drop, if it says Stop,
To the all-a-leaf of the tréetop
And after that off the bough

I ám so véry, O só very glád
That I dó thínk there is not to be had

The blue wheat-acre is underneath
And the corn is corded and shoulders its sheaf,
The ear in milk, lush the sash,
And crusk-silk poppies aflash,
The blood-gush blade-gash

Flame-rash rudred
Bud shelling or broad-shed
Tatter-tangled and dingle-a-danglèd
Dandy-hung dainty head.

And down . . . the furrow dry
Sunspurge and oxeye
And lace-leaved lovely
Foam-tuft fumitory

Through the velvety wind V-winged
To the nest's nook I balance and buoy
With a sweet joy of a sweet joy,
Sweet, of a sweet, of a sweet joy
Of a sweet—a sweet—sweet—joy.'

Penmaen Pool:

for the Visitors' Book at the Inn

Who long for rest, who look for pleasure
Away from counter, court, or school
O where live well your lease of leisure
But here at, here at Penmaen Pool?

You'll dare the Alp? you'll dart the skiff?—
Each sport has here its tackle and tool:
Come, plant the staff by Cadair cliff;
Come, swing the sculls on Penmaen Pool.

What's yonder?—Grizzled Dyphwys dim:
The triple-hummocked Giant's Stool,
Hoar messmate, hobs and nobs with him
To halve the bowl of Penmaen Pool.

And all the landscape under survey,
At tranquil turns, by nature's rule,
Rides repeated topsyturvy
In frank, in fairy Penmaen Pool.

And Charles's Wain, the wondrous seven,
And sheep-flock clouds like worlds of wool,
For all they shine so, high in heaven,
Shew brighter shaken in Penmaen Pool.

The Mawddach, how she trips! though throttled
If floodtide teeming thrills her full,
And mazy sands all water-wattled
Waylay her at ebb, past Penmaen Pool.

But what's to see in stormy weather,
When grey showers gather and gusts are cool?—
Why, raindrop-roundels looped together
That lace the face of Penmaen Pool.

Then even in weariest wintry hour
Of New Year's Month or surly Yule
Furred snows, charged tuft above tuft, tower
From darksome darksome Penmaen Pool.

And ever, if bound here hardest home,
You've parlour-pastime left and (who'll
Not honour it?) ale like goldy foam
That frocks an oar in Penmaen Pool.

Then come who pine for peace or pleasure
Away from counter, court, or school,
Spend here your measure of time and treasure
And taste the treats of Penmaen Pool.

(*Margaret Clitheroe*)

I

God's counsel cólumnar-severe
But chaptered in the chief of bliss
Had always doomed her down to this—
Pressed to death. He plants the year;
The weighty weeks without hands grow,

Heaved drum on drum; but hands alsó
Must deal with Margaret Clitheroe.

2

The very victim would prepare.
Like water soon to be sucked in
Will crisp itself or settle and spin
So she: one sees that here and there
She mends the way she means to go.
The last thing Margaret's fingers sew
Is a shroud for Margaret Clitheroe.

3

The Christ-ed beauty of her mind
Her mould of features mated well.
She was admired. The spirit of hell
Bring to her virtue clinching-blind
No wonder therefore was not slow
To the bargain of its hate to throw
The body of Margaret Clitheroe.

Fawning fawning crocodiles
Days and days came round about
With tears to put her candle out;
They wound their winch of wicked smiles
To take her; while their tongues would go
God lighten your dark heart—but no,
Christ lived in Margaret Clitheroe.

She caught the crying of those Three,
The Immortals of the eternal ring.
The Utterer, Utterèd, Uttering,
And witness in her place would she.
She not considered whether or no
She pleased the Queen and Council. So
To the death with Margaret Clitheroe!

She was a woman upright, outright;
Her will was bent at God. For that
Word went she should be crushed out flat

Within her womb the child was quick.
Small matter of that then! Let him smother
And wreck in ruins of his mother

Great Thecla, the plumed passionflower,
Next Mary mother of maid and nun,
— — — — — — —

And every saint of bloody hour
And breath immortal thronged that show;
Heaven turned its starlight eyes below
To the murder of Margaret Clitheroe.

She held her hands to, like in prayer;
They had them out and laid them wide
(Just like Jesus crucified);
They brought their hundredweights to bear.
Jews killed Jesus long ago
God's son; these (they did not know)
God's daughter Margaret Clitheroe.

When she felt the kill-weights crush
She told His name times-over three;
I suffer this she said *for Thee.*
After that in perfect hush
For a quarter of an hour or so
She was with the choke of woe.—
It is over, Margaret Clitheroe.

'Hope holds to Christ'

Hope holds to Christ the mind's own mirror out
To take His lovely likeness more and more.
It will not well, so she would bring about
A growing burnish brighter than before
And turns to wash it from her welling eyes
And breathes the blots off all with sighs on sighs.

Her glass is blest but she as good as blind
Holds till hand aches and wonders what is there;

Her glass drinks light, she darkles down behind,
All of her glorious gainings unaware.
I told you that she turned her mirror dim
Betweenwhiles, but she sees herself not Him.

God's Grandeur

The world is charged with the grandeur of God.
  It will flame out, like shining from shook foil;
  It gathers to a greatness, like the ooze of oil
Crushed. Why do men then now not reck his rod?
Generations have trod, have trod, have trod;
  And all is seared with trade; bleared, smeared with toil;
  And wears man's smudge and shares man's smell: the soil
Is bare now, nor can foot feel, being shod.

And, for all this, nature is never spent;
  There lives the dearest freshness deep down things;
And though the last lights off the black West went
  Oh, morning, at the brown brink eastwards, springs—
Because the Holy Ghost over the bent
  World broods with warm breast and with ah! bright wings.

The Starlight Night

Look at the stars! look, look up at the skies!
  O look at all the fire-folk sitting in the air!
  The bright boroughs, the circle-citadels there!
Down in dim woods the diamond delves! the elves'-eyes!
The grey lawns cold where gold, where quickgold lies!
  Wind-beat whitebeam! airy abeles set on a flare!
  Flake-doves sent floating forth at a farmyard scare!—
Ah well! it is all a purchase, all is a prize.

Buy then! bid then!—What?—Prayer, patience, alms, vows.
Look, look: a May-mess, like on orchard boughs!
  Look! March-bloom, like on mealed-with-yellow sallows!

These are indeed the barn; withindoors house
The shocks. This piece-bright paling shuts the spouse
Christ home, Christ and his mother and all his hallows.

'As kingfishers catch fire'

As kingfishers catch fire, dragonflies draw flame;
As tumbled over rim in roundy wells
Stones ring; like each tucked string tells, each hung bell's
Bow swung finds tongue to fling out broad its name;
Each mortal thing does one thing and the same:
Deals out that being indoors each one dwells;
Selves—goes its self; *myself* it speaks and spells,
Crying *What I do is me: for that I came.*

I say more: the just man justices;
Keeps grace: that keeps all his goings graces;
Acts in God's eye what in God's eye he is—
Christ. For Christ plays in ten thousand places,
Lovely in limbs, and lovely in eyes not his
To the Father through the features of men's faces.

Spring

Nothing is so beautiful as Spring—
When weeds, in wheels, shoot long and lovely and lush;
Thrush's eggs look little low heavens, and thrush
Through the echoing timber does so rinse and wring
The ear, it strikes like lightnings to hear him sing;
The glassy peartree leaves and blooms, they brush
The descending blue; that blue is all in a rush
With richness; the racing lambs too have fair their fling.

What is all this juice and all this joy?
A strain of the earth's sweet being in the beginning
In Eden garden.—Have, get before it cloy,

Before it cloud, Christ, lord, and sour with sinning,
Innocent mind and Mayday in girl and boy,
Most, O maid's child, thy choice and worthy the winning.

The Sea and the Skylark

On ear and ear two noises too old to end
Trench—right, the tide that ramps against the shore;
With a flood or a fall, low lull-off or all roar,
Frequenting there while moon shall wear and wend.

Left hand, off land, I hear the lark ascend,
His rash-fresh re-winded new-skeinèd score
In crisps of curl off wild winch whirl, and pour
And pelt music, till none's to spill nor spend.

How these two shame this shallow and frail town!
How ring right out our sordid turbid time,
Being pure! We, life's pride and cared-for crown,

Have lost that cheer and charm of earth's past prime:
Our make and making break, are breaking, down
To man's last dust, drain fast towards man's first slime.

In the Valley of the Elwy

I remember a house where all were good
To me, God knows, deserving no such thing:
Comforting smell breathed at very entering,
Fetched fresh, as I suppose, off some sweet wood.
That cordial air made those kind people a hood
All over, as a bevy of eggs the mothering wing
Will, or mild nights the new morsels of Spring:
Why, it séemed of coúrse; séemed of ríght it shóuld.

Lovely the woods, waters, meadows, combes, vales,
All the air things wear that build this world of Wales;
Only the inmate does not correspond:

God, lover of souls, swaying considerate scales,
Complete thy creature dear O where it fails,
Being mighty a master, being a father and fond.

The Windhover:

to Christ our Lord

I caught this morning morning's minion, king-
dom of daylight's dauphin, dapple-dáwn-drawn Falcon, in his riding
Of the rólling level úndernéath him steady áir, and stríding
High there, how he rung upon the rein of a wimpling wing
In his ecstacy! then off, off forth on swing,
As a skate's heel sweeps smooth on a bow-bend: the hurl and gliding
Rebuffed the big wind. My heart in hiding
Stirred for a bird,—the achieve of, the mastery of the thing!

Brute beauty and valour and act, oh, air, pride, plume, here
Buckle! AND the fire that breaks from thee then, a billion
Times told lovelier, more dangerous, O my chevalier!

No wónder of it: shéer plód makes plóugh down síllion
Shine, and blue-bleak embers, ah my dear,
Fall, gáll themsélves, and gásh góld-vermílion.

Pied Beauty

Glory be to God for dappled things—
For skies of couple-colour as a brinded cow;
For rose-moles all in stipple upon trout that swim;
Fresh-firecoal chestnut-falls; finches' wings;
Landscape plotted and pieced—fold, fallow, and plough;
And áll trades, their gear and tackle and trim.

All things counter, original, spáre, strange;
  Whatever is fickle, frecklèd (who knows how?)
    With swíft, slów; sweet, sóur; adázzle, dím;
He fathers-forth whose beauty is pást change:
                                        Práise hím.

The Caged Skylark

As a dare-gale skylark scanted in a dull cage,
  Man's mounting spirit in his bone-house, mean house, dwells—
  That bird beyond the remembering hís free fells;
This in drudgery, day-labouring-out life's age.

Though aloft on turf or perch or poor low stage
  Both sing sometímes the sweetest, sweetest spells,
  Yet both droop deadly sómetimes in their cells
Or wring their barriers in bursts of fear or rage.

Not that the sweet-fowl, song-fowl, needs no rest—
Why, hear him, hear him babble and drop down to his nest,
  But his own nest, wild nest, no prison.

Man's spirit will be flesh-bound, when found at best,
But úncúmberèd: meadow-dówn is nót distréssed
  For a ráinbow fóoting it nor hé for his bónes rísen.

'To him who ever thought'

To him who ever thought with love of me
Or ever did for my sake some good deed
I will appear, looking such charity
And kind compassion, at his life's last need
That he will out of hand and heartily
Repent he sinned and all his sins be freed.

Hurrahing in Harvest

Summer ends now; now, barbarous in beauty, the stooks rise
Around; up above, what wind-walks! what lovely behaviour
Of silk-sack clouds! has wilder, wilful-wavier
Meal-drift moulded ever and melted across skies?

I wálk, I líft up, Í lift úp heart, éyes,
Down all that glory in the heavens to glean our Saviour;
And, éyes, héart, what looks, what lips yet gáve you a
Rapturous love's greeting of realer, of rounder replies?

And the azurous hung hills are his world-wielding shoulder
Majestic—as a stallion stalwart, very-violet-sweet!—
These things, these things were here and but the beholder
Wánting; whích two whén they ónce méet,
The heart rears wings bold and bolder
And hurls for him, O half hurls earth for him off under his feet.

The Lantern out of Doors

Sometimes a lantern moves along the night.
  That interests our eyes. And who goes there?
  I think; where from and bound, I wonder, where,
With, all down darkness wide, his wading light?

Men go by me, whom either beauty bright
  In mould or mind or what not else makes rare:
  They rain against our much-thick and marsh air
Rich beams, till death or distance buys them quite.

Death or distance soon consumes them: wind,
  What most I may eye after, be in at the end
I cannot, and out of sight is out of mind.

Christ minds: Christ's interest, what to avow or amend
  There, éyes them, heart wánts, care háunts, foot fóllows kínd,
Their ránsom, théir rescue, ánd first, fást, last fríend.

The Loss of the Eurydice

foundered March 24 1878

The Eurydice—it concerned thee, O Lord:
Three hundred souls, O alas! on board,
  Some asleep unawakened, all un-
Warned, eleven fathoms fallen

Where she foundered! One stroke
Felled and furled them, the hearts of oak!
  And flockbells off the aerial
Downs' forefalls beat to the burial.

For did she pride her, freighted fully, on
Bounden bales or a hoard of bullion?—
  Precious passing measure,
Lads and men her lade and treasure.

She had come from a cruise, training seamen—
Men, boldboys soon to be men:
  Must it, worst weather,
Blast bole and bloom together?

No Atlantic squall overwrought her
Or rearing billow of the Biscay water:
  Home was hard at hand
And the blow bore from land.

And you were a liar, O blue March day.
Bright sun lanced fire in the heavenly bay;
  But what black Boreas wrecked her? he
Came equipped, deadly-electric,

A beetling baldbright cloud thorough England
Riding: there did storms not mingle? and
  Hailropes hustle and grind their
Heavengravel? wolfsnow, worlds of it, wind there?

Now Carisbrook keep goes under in gloom;
Now it overvaults Appledurcombe;
    Now near by Ventnor town
It hurls, hurls off Boniface Down.

Too proud, too proud, what a press she bore!
Royal, and all her royals wore.
    Sharp with her, shorten sail!
Too late; lost; gone with the gale.

This was that fell capsize.
As half she had righted and hoped to rise
    Death teeming in by her portholes
Raced down decks, round messes of mortals.

Then a lurch forward, frigate and men;
'All hands for themselves' the cry ran then;
    But she who had housed them thither
Was around them, bound them or wound them with her.

Marcus Hare, high her captain,
Kept to her—care-drowned and wrapped in
    Cheer's death, would follow
His charge through the champ-white water-in-a-wallow,

All under Channel to bury in a beach her
Cheeks: Right, rude of feature,
    He thought he heard say
'Her commander! and thou too, and thou this way.'

It is even seen, time's something server,
In mankind's medley a duty-swerver,
    At downright 'No or Yes?'
Doffs all, drives full for righteousness.

Sydney Fletcher, Bristol-bred,
(Low lie his mates now on watery bed)
    Takes to the seas and snows
As sheer down the ship goes.

Now her afterdraught gullies him too down;
Now he wrings for breath with the deathgush brown;
    Till a lifebelt and God's will
Lend him a lift from the sea-swill.

Now he shoots short up to the round air;
Now he gasps, now he gazes everywhere;
    But his eye no cliff, no coast or
Mark makes in the rivelling snowstorm.

Him, after an hour of wintry waves,
A schooner sights, with another, and saves,
    And he boards her in Oh! such joy
He has lost count what came next, poor boy.—

They say who saw one sea-corpse cold
He was all of lovely manly mould,
    Every inch a tar,
Of the best we boast our sailors are.

Look, foot to forelock, how all things suit! he
Is strung by duty, is strained to beauty,
    And brown-as-dawning-skinned
With brine and shine and whirling wind.

O his nimble finger, his gnarled grip!
Leagues, leagues of seamanship
    Slumber in these forsaken
Bones, this sinew, and will not waken.

He was but one like thousands more.
Day and night I deplore
    My people and born own nation,
Fast foundering own generation.

I might let bygones be—our curse
Of ruinous shrine no hand or, worse,
    Robbery's hand is busy to
Dress, hoar-hallowèd shrines unvisited;

Only the breathing temple and fleet
Life, this wildworth blown so sweet,
These daredeaths, ay this crew, in
Unchrist, all rolled in ruin—

Deeply surely I need to deplore it,
Wondering why my master bore it,
The riving off that race
So at home, time was, to his truth and grace

That a starlight-wender of ours would say
The marvellous Milk was Walsingham Way
And one—but let be, let be:
More, more than was will yet be.—

O well wept, mother have lost son;
Wept, wife; wept, sweetheart would be one:
Though grief yield them no good
Yet shed what tears sad truelove should.

But to Christ lord of thunder
Crouch; lay knee by earth low under:
'Holiest, loveliest, bravest,
Save my hero, O Hero savest.

And the prayer thou hearst me making
Have, at the awful overtaking,
Heard; have heard and granted
Grace that day grace was wanted.'

Not that hell knows redeeming,
But for souls sunk in seeming
Fresh, till doomfire burn all,
Prayer shall fetch pity eternal.

The May Magnificat

May is Mary's month, and I
Muse at that and wonder why:
    Her feasts follow reason,
    Dated due to season—

Candlemas, Lady Day;
But the Lady Month, May,
    Why fasten that upon her,
    With a feasting in her honour?

Is it only its being brighter
Than the most are must delight her?
    Is it opportunest
    And flowers finds soonest?

Ask of her, the mighty mother:
Her reply puts this other
    Question: What is Spring?—
    Growth in everything—

Flesh and fleece, fur and feather,
Grass and greenworld all together;
    Star-eyed strawberry-breasted
    Throstle above her nested

Cluster of bugle blue eggs thin
Forms and warms the life within;
    And bird and blossom swell
    In sod or sheath or shell.

All things rising, all things sizing
Mary sees, sympathising
    With that world of good,
    Nature's motherhood.

Their magnifying of each its kind
With delight calls to mind
    How she did in her stored
    Magnify the Lord.

Well but there was more than this:
Spring's universal bliss
    Much, had much to say
    To offering Mary May.

When drop-of-blood-and-foam-dapple
Bloom lights the orchard-apple
    And thicket and thorp are merry
    With silver-surfèd cherry

And azuring-over greybell makes
Wood banks and brakes wash wet like lakes
    And magic cuckoocall
    Caps, clears, and clinches all—

This ecstacy all through mothering earth
Tells Mary her mirth till Christ's birth
    To remember and exultation
    In God who was her salvation.

'Denis'

Denis,
Whose motionable, alert, most vaulting wit
Caps occasion with an intellectual fit.
Yet Arthur is a Bowman: his three-heeled timber'll hit
The bald and bold blinking gold when all's done
Right rooting in the bare butt's wincing navel in the sight of the sun.

'The furl of fresh-leaved dogrose'

The furl of fresh-leaved dogrose down
His cheeks the forth-and-flaunting sun
Had swarthed about with lion-brown
  Before the Spring was done.

His locks like all a ravel-rope's-end,
With hempen strands in spray—
Fallow, foam-fallow, hanks—fall'n off their ranks,
Swung down at a disarray.

Or like a juicy and jostling shock
Of bluebells sheaved in May
Or wind-long fleeces on the flock
A day off shearing day.

Then over his turnèd temples—here—
Was a rose, or, failing that,
Rough-Robin or five-lipped campion clear
For a beauty-bow to his hat,
And the sunlight sidled, like dewdrops, like dandled diamonds
Through the sieve of the straw of the plait.

'He mightbe slow'

He mightbe slow and something feckless first,
Not feck at first, and here no harm,
But earnest, always earnest, *there* the charm

'What being in rank-old nature'

What being in rank-old nature should earlier have that breath been
That here personal tells off these heart-song powerful peals?—
A bush-browed beetle-browed billow is it?
With a south-westerly wind blustering, with a tide rolls reels
Of crumbling, fore-foundering, thundering all-surfy seas in; seen
Underneath, their glassy barrel, of a fairy green.

Or a jaunting vaunting vaulting assaulting trumpet telling.

Duns Scotus's Oxford

Towery city and branchy between towers;
Cuckoo-echoing, bell-swarmèd, lark-charmèd, rook-racked,
river-rounded;
The dapple-eared lily below thee; that country and town did
Once encounter in, here coped and poisèd powers;

Thou hast a base and brickish skirt there, sours
That neighbour-nature thy grey beauty is grounded
Best in; graceless growth, thou hast confounded
Rural rural keeping—folk, flocks, and flowers.

Yet ah! this air I gather and I release
He lived on; these weeds and waters, these walls are what
He haunted who of all men most sways my spirits to peace;

Of realty the rarest-veinèd unraveller; a not
Rivalled insight, be rival Italy or Greece;
Who fired Fránce for Máry withóut spót.

Binsey Poplars

felled 1879

My aspens dear, whose airy cages quelled,
Quelled or quenched in leaves the leaping sun,
Áll félled, félled, are áll félled;
Of a fresh and following folded rank
Not spared, not one
That dandled a sandalled
Shadow that swam or sank
On meadow and river and wind-wandering weed-winding bank.

O if we but knew what we do
When we delve or hew—
Hack and rack the growing green!
Since Country is so tender

To tóuch, her béing só slénder,
That, like this sleek and seeing ball
But a prick will make no eye at all,
Where we, even where we mean
To mend her we end her,
When we hew or delve:
After-comers cannot guess the beauty been.
Ten or twelve, only ten or twelve
Strokes of havoc unselve
The sweet especial scene,
Rural scene, a rural scene,
Sweet especial rural scene.

Henry Purcell

The poet wishes well to the divine genius of Purcell and praises him that, whereas other musicians have given utterance to the moods of man's mind, he has, beyond that, uttered in notes the very make and species of man as created both in him and in all men generally

Have fáir fállen, O fáir, fáir have fállen, so déar
To me, so arch-especial a spirit as heaves in Henry Purcell,
An age is now since passed, since parted; with the reversal
Of the outward sentence low lays him, listed to a heresy, here.

Not mood in him nor meaning, proud fire or sacred fear,
Of love, or pity, or all that sweet notes not his might nursle:
It is the forgèd feature finds me; it is the rehearsal
Of own, of abrupt self there so thrusts on, so throngs the ear.

Let him oh! with his air of angels then lift me, lay me! only I'll
Have an eye to the sakes of him, quaint moonmarks, to his pelted plumage under
Wings: so some great stormfowl, whenever he has walked his while

The thunder-purple seabeach, plumèd purple-of-thunder,
If a wuthering of his palmy snow-pinions scatter a colossal smile
Off him, but meaning motion fans fresh our wits with wonder.

'Repeat that, repeat'

Repeat that, repeat,
Cuckoo, bird, and open ear wells, heart-springs, delightfully sweet,
With a ballad, with a ballad, a rebound
Off trundled timber and scoops of the hillside ground, hollow
    hollow hollow ground:
The whole landscape flushes on a sudden at a sound

The Candle Indoors

Some candle clear burns somewhere I come by.
I muse at how its being puts blissful back
With yellowy moisture mild night's blear-all black
Or to-fro tender trambeams truckle at the eye.

By that window what task what fingers ply,
I plod wondering, a-wanting, just for lack
Of answer the eagerer a-wanting Jessy or Jack
There/God to aggrándise, God to glorify.—

Come you indoors, come home; your fading fire
Mend first and vital candle in close heart's vault;
You there are master, do your own desire;

What hinders? Are you beam-blind, yet to a fault
In a neighbour deft-handed? Are you that liar
And, cast by conscience out, spendsavour salt?

The Handsome Heart:

at a gracious answer

'But tell me, child, your choice, | your fancy; what to buy
You?'—'Father, what you buy me | I shall like the best'.
With the sweetest earnest air | his purport, once expressed,
Ever he swung to, push | what plea I might and ply

Him. Áh, whát the heart is! | Like carriers let fly—
Doff darkness: homing nature, | nature knows the rest—
Heart to its own fine function, | wild and self-instressed,
Falls as light as, life-long, | schooled to what and why.

Héart mánnerly | is more than handsome face,
Beauty's bearing or | muse of mounting vein;
And whát when, as ín this cáse, | bathed in high hallowing grace?—

Of heaven then now what boon | to buy you, boy, or gain
Not granted? None but this, | all your road your race
To match and more than match | its sweet forestalling strain.

'How all is one way wrought'

How all is one way wrought!
How all things suit and sit!
Then ah! the tune that thought
Trod to that fancied it.

Nor angel insight can
Learn how the heart is hence:
Since all the make of man
Is law's indifference.

Who built these walls made known
The music of his mind,
Yet here he has but shewn
His ruder-rounded rind.

Not free in this because
His powers seemed free to play:
He swept what scope he was
To sweep and must obey.

Though down his being's bent
Like air he changed in choice,
That was an instrument
Which overvaulted voice.

Therefóre this masterhood,
This piece of perfect song,
This fault-not-found-with good,
Is neither right nor wrong.

No more than red and blue,
No more than Re and Mi,
Or sweet the golden glue
That's built for by the bee.

What makes the man and what
The man within that makes:
Ask whom he serves or not
Serves and what side he takes.

For good grows wild and wide,
Has shades, is nowhere none;
But right must seek a side
And choose for chieftain one.

Cheery Beggar

Beyond Magdalen and by the Bridge, on a place called there the
    Plain,
  In Summer, in a burst of summertime
  Following falls and falls of rain,
When the air was sweet-and-sour of the flown fineflour of
Those goldnails and their gaylinks that hang along a lime;

  The motion of that man's heart is fine
  Whom want could not make pine, pine
That struggling should not sear him, a gift should cheer him
Like that poor pocket of pence, poor pence of mine.

The Bugler's First Communion

A bugler boy from barrack (it is over the hill
There)—boy bugler, born, he tells me, of Irish
Mother to an English sire (he
Shares their best gifts surely, fall how things will),

This very very day came down to us after a boon he on
My late being there begged of me, overflowing
Boon in my bestowing,
Came, I say, this day to it—to a First Communion.

Here he knelt then in regimental red.
Forth Christ from cupboard fetched, how fain I of feet
To his youngster take his treat!
Low-latched in leaf-light housel his too huge godhead.

There! and your sweetest sendings, ah divine,
By it, heavens, befall him! as a heart Christ's darling, dauntless;
Tongue true, vaunt- and tauntless;
Breathing bloom of a chastity in mansex fine.

Frowning and forefending angel-warder
Squander the hell-rook ranks sally to molest him;
March, kind comrade, abreast him;
Dress his days to a dexterous and starlight order.

How it does my heart good, visiting at that bleak hill,
When limber liquid youth, that to all I teach
Yields ténder as a púshed péach,
Hies headstrong to its wellbeing of a self-wise self-will!

Then though Í should tréad túfts of consolation
Dáys áfter, só I in a sort deserve to
And do serve God to serve to
Just such slips of soldiery Christ's royal ration.

Nothing else is like it, no, not all so strains
Us—freshyouth fretted in a bloomfall all portending

That sweet's sweeter ending;
Realm both Christ is heir to and there reigns.

O now well work that sealing sacred ointment!
O for now charms, arms, what bans off bad
And locks love ever in a lad!
Let mé though sée no more of him, and not disappointment

Those sweet hopes quell whose least me quickenings lift,
In scarlet or somewhere of some day seeing
That brow and bead of being,
An our day's God's own Galahad. Thóugh this child's drift

Seems bý a divíne doom chánnelled, nor do I cry
Disaster there; but may he not rankle and roam
In backwheels, though bound home?—
That left to the Lord of the Eucharist, I here lie by;

Recorded only, I have put my lips on pleas
Would brandle adamantine heaven with ride and jar, did
Prayer go disregarded:
Forward-like, but however, and like favourable heaven heard these.

Andromeda

Now Time's Andromeda on this rock rude,
With not her either beauty's equal or
Her injury's, looks off by both horns of shore,
Her flower, her piece of being, doomed dragon food.

Time past she has been attempted and pursued
By many blows and banes; but now hears roar
A wilder beast from West than all were, more
Rife in her wrongs, more lawless, and more lewd.

Her Perseus linger and leave her tó her extremes?—
Pillowy air he treads a time and hangs
His thoughts on her, forsaken that she seems,

All while her patience, morselled into pangs,
Mounts; then to alight disarming, no one dreams,
With Gorgon's gear and barebill/thongs and fangs.

Morning, Midday, and Evening Sacrifice

The dappled die-away
Cheek and the wimpled lip,
The gold-wisp, the airy-grey
Eye, all in fellowship—
This, all this beauty blooming,
This, all this freshness fuming,
Give God while worth consuming.

Both thought and thew now bolder
And told by Nature: Tower;
Head, heart, hand, heel, and shoulder
That beat and breathe in power—
This pride of prime's enjoyment
Take as for tool, not toy meant
And hold at Christ's employment.

The vault and scope and schooling
And mastery in the mind,
In silk-ash kept from cooling
And ripest under rind—
What death half lifts the latch of,
What hell hopes soon the snatch of,
Your offering, with despatch, of!

Peace

When will you ever, Peace, wild wooddove, shy wings shut,
Your round me roaming end, and under be my boughs?
When, when, Peace, will you, Peace?—I'll not play hypocrite

To own my heart: I yield you do come sometimes; but
That piecemeal peace is poor peace. What pure peace allows
Alarms of wars, the daunting wars, the death of it?

O surely, reaving Peace, my Lord should leave in lieu
Some good! And so he does leave Patience exquisite,
That plumes to Peace thereafter. And when Peace here does house
He comes with work to do, he does not come to coo,
He comes to brood and sit.

At the Wedding March

God with honour hang your head,
Groom, and grace you, bride, your bed
With lissome scions, sweet scions,
Out of hallowed bodies bred.

Each be other's comfort kind:
Deep, deeper than divined,
Divine charity, dear charity,
Fast you ever, fast bind.

Then let the March tread our ears:
I to him turn with tears
Who to wedlock, his wonder wedlock,
Deals triumph and immortal years.

Felix Randal

Félix Rándal the fárrier, O is he déad then? my dúty all énded,
Who have watched his mould of man, big-boned and hardy-handsome
Pining, pining, till time when reason rambled in it and some
Fatal four disorders, fleshed there, all contended?

Sickness broke him. Impatient, he cursed at first, but mended
Being anointed and all; though a heavenlier heart began some

Mónths éarlier, since Í had our swéet repriéve and ránsom
Téndered to him. Áh well, God rést him áll road éver he offénded!

This séeing the síck endéars them tó us, us tóo it endéars.
My tongue had taught thee comfort, touch had quenched thy
tears,
Thy tears that touched my heart, child, Felix, poor Felix Randal;

How far from then forethought of, all thy more boisterous years,
When thou at the random grim forge, powerful amidst peers,
Didst fettle for the great grey drayhorse his bright and battering
sandal!

Brothers

How lovely the elder brother's
Life all laced in the other's,
Love-laced!—what once I well
Witnessed; so fortune fell.
When Shrovetide, two years gone,
Our boys' plays brought on
Part was picked for John,
Young John: then fear, then joy
Ran revel in the elder boy.
Now the night come, all
Our company thronged the hall.
Henry, by the wall,
Beckoned me beside him.
I came where called and eyed him
By meanwhiles; making my play
Turn most on tender by-play.
For, wrung all on love's rack,
My lad, and lost in Jack,
Smiled, blushed, and bit his lip,
Or drove, with a diver's dip,
Clutched hands through claspèd knees;
And many a mark like these
Told tales with what heart's stress
He hung on the imp's success.

Now the óther was bráss-bóld:
He had no work to hold
His heart up at the strain;
Nay, roguish ran the vein.
Two tedious acts were past;
Jack's call and cue at last;
When Henry, heart-forsook,
Dropped eyes and dared not look.
There! the hall rung;
Dog, he did give tongue!
Oh, Harry,—in his hands he has flung
His tear-tricked cheeks of flame
For fond love and for shame.—
Ah Nature, framed in fault,
There's comfort then, there's salt!
Nature bad, base, and blind,
Dearly thou canst be kind;
There déarly thén, déarly,
Dearly thou canst be kind.

Spring and Fall:

to a Young Child

Margaret, are you grieving
Over Goldengrove unleaving?
Leaves, like the things of man, you
With your fresh thoughts care for, can you?
Ah! as the heart grows older
It will come to such sights colder
By and by, nor spare a sigh
Though worlds of wanwood leafmeal lie;
And yet you *will* weep and know why.
Now no matter, child, the name:
Sorrow's springs are the same.
Nor mouth had, no nor mind, expressed
What héart héard of, ghóst guéssed:
It is the blight man was born for,
It is Margaret you mourn for.

Inversnaid

This dárksome búrn, hórseback brówn,
His rollrock highroad roaring down,
In coop and in comb the fleece of his foam
Flutes and low to the lake falls home.

A wíndpuff-bónnet of fáwn-fróth
Turns and twindles over the broth
Of a póol so pítchblack, féll-frówning,
It rounds and rounds Despair to drowning.

Degged with dew, dappled with dew
Are the groins of the braes that the brook treads through,
Wiry heathpacks, flitches of fern,
And the beadbonny ash that sits over the burn.

What would the world be, once bereft
Of wet and of wildness? Let them be left,
O let them be left, wildness and wet;
Long live the weeds and the wilderness yet.

The Leaden Echo and the Golden Echo

(Maiden's song from *St. Winefred's Well*)

The Leaden Echo—

How to keep—is there ány any, is there none such, nowhere known some, bow or brooch or braid or brace, lace, latch or catch or key to keep
Back beauty, keep it, beauty, beauty, beauty, . . . from vanishing away?
Ó is there no frowning of these wrinkles, rankèd wrinkles deep,
Down? no waving off of these most mournful messengers, still messengers, sad and stealing messengers of grey?—
No there's none, there's none, O no there's none,
Nor can you long be, what you now are, called fair,
Do what you may do, what, do what you may,

And wisdom is early to despair:
Be beginning; since, no, nothing can be done
To keep at bay
Age and age's evils, hoar hair,
Ruck and wrinkle, drooping, dying, death's worst, winding sheets, tombs and worms and tumbling to decay;
So be beginning, be beginning to despair.
O there's none; no no no there's none:
Be beginning to despair, to despair,
Despair, despair, despair, despair.

The Golden Echo— Spare!
There is one, yes I have one (Hush there!);
Only not within seeing of the sun.
Not within the singeing of the strong sun,
Tall sun's tingeing, or treacherous the tainting of the earth's air,
Somewhere elsewhere there is ah well where! one,
One. Yes I can tell such a key, I do know such a place,
Where whatever's prizèd and passes of us, everything that's fresh and fast flying of us, seems to us sweet of us and swiftly away with, done away with, undone,
Undone, done with, soon done with, and yet dearly and dangerously sweet
Of us, the wimpledwater-dimpled, not-by-morning-matchèd face,
The flower of beauty, fleece of beauty, too too apt to, ah! to fleet,
Never fleets more, fastened with the tenderest truth
To its own best being and its loveliness of youth: it is an everlastingness of, O it is an all youth!
Cóme then, your ways and airs and looks, locks, maidengear, gallantry and gaiety and grace,
Winning ways, airs innocent, maiden manners, sweet looks, loose locks, long locks, lovelocks, gaygear, going gallant, girlgrace—
Resign them, sign them, seal them, send them, motion them with breath,
And with sighs soaring, soaring sighs, deliver
Them; beauty-in-the-ghost, deliver it, early now, long before death
Give beauty back, beauty, beauty, beauty, back to God beauty's self and beauty's giver.
See: not a hair is, not an eyelash, not the least lash lost; every hair

Is, hair of the head, numbéred.
Nay, what we had lighthanded left in surly the mere mould
Will have waked and have waxed and have walked with the wind what while we slept,
This side, that side hurling a heavy-headed hundredfold
What while we, while we slumbered.
O then, weary then whý should we tread? O why are we so haggard at the heart, so care-coiled, care-killed, so fagged, so fashed, so cogged, so cumbered,
When the thing we freely fórfeit is kept with fonder a care,
Fonder a care kept than we could have kept it, kept
Far with fonder a care (and we, we should have lost it) finer, fonder
A care kept.—Where kept? do but tell us where kept, where.—
Yonder.—What high as that! We follow, now we follow.—Yonder, yes yonder, yonder,
Yonder.

Ribblesdale

Earth, sweet Earth, sweet landscape, with leavès throng
And louchèd low grass, heaven that dost appeal
To with no tongue to plead, no heart to feel;
That canst but only be, but dost that long—

Thou canst but be, but that thou well dost; strong
Thy plea with him who dealt, nay does now deal,
Thy lovely dale down thus and thus bids reel
Thy river, and o'er gives all to rack or wrong.

And what is Earth's eye, tongue, or heart else, where
Else, but in dear and dogged man? Ah, the heir
To his own selfbent so bound, so tied to his turn,

To thriftless reave both our rich round world bare
And none reck of world after, this bids wear
Earth brows of such care, care and dear concern.

A Trio of Triolets

No. 1—*λέγεταί τι καινόν;*

'No news in the *Times* to-day,'
Each man tells his next-door neighbour.
He, to see if what they say,
'No news in the *Times* to-day'
Is correct, must plough his way
Through that: after three hours' labour,
'No news in the *Times* to-day',
Each man tells his next-door neighbour.

No. 2—Cockle's Antibilious Pills

'When you ask for Cockle's Pills,
Beware of spurious imitations.'
Yes, when you ask for every ill's
Cure, when you ask for Cockle's Pills,
Some hollow counterfeit that kills
Would fain mock that which heals the nations.
Oh, when you ask for Cockle's Pills
Beware of heartless imitations.

No. 3—'The Child is Father to the Man'
(Wordsworth)

'The child is father to the man.'
How can he be? The words are wild.
Suck any sense from that who can:
'The child is father to the man.'
No; what the poet did write ran,
'The man is father to the child.'
'The child is father to the man!'
How *can* he be? The words are wild.

The Blessed Virgin compared to the Air we Breathe

Wild air, world-mothering air,
Nestling me everywhere,
That each eyelash or hair
Girdles; goes home betwixt
The fleeciest, frailest-flixed
Snowflake; that's fairly mixed
With, riddles, and is rife
In every least thing's life;
This needful, never spent,
And nursing element;
My more than meat and drink,
My meal at every wink;
This air, which, by life's law,
My lung must draw and draw
Now but to breathe its praise,
Minds me in many ways
Of her who nót only
Gave God's infinity
Dwindled to infancy
Welcome in womb and breast,
Birth, milk, and all the rest
But mothers each new grace
That does now reach our race—
Mary Immaculate,
Merely a woman, yet
Whose presence, power is
Great as no goddess's
Was deemèd, dreamèd; who
This one work has to do—
Let all God's glory through,
God's glory which would go
Through her and from her flow
Off, and no way but so.
   I say that we are wound
With mercy round and round
As if with air: the same
Is Mary, more by name.
She, wild web, wondrous robe,

Mantles the guilty globe,
Since God has let dispense
Her prayers his providence:
Nay, more than almoner,
The sweet alms' self is her
And men are meant to share
Her life as life does air.
  If I have understood,
She holds high motherhood
Towards all our ghostly good
And plays in grace her part
About man's beating heart,
Laying, like air's fine flood,
The deathdance in his blood;
Yet no part but what will
Be Christ our Saviour still.
Of her flesh he took flesh:
He does take fresh and fresh,
Though much the mystery how,
Not flesh but spirit now
And makes, O marvellous!
New Nazareths in us,
Where she shall yet conceive
Him, morning, noon, and eve;
New Bethlems, and he born
There, evening, noon, and morn—
Bethlem or Nazareth,
Men here may draw like breath
More Christ and baffle death;
Who, born so, comes to be
New self and nobler me
In each one and each one
More makes, when all is done,
Both God's and Mary's Son.
  Again, look overhead
How air is azurèd;
O how! Nay do but stand
Where you can lift your hand
Skywards: rich, rich it laps
Round the four fingergaps.
Yet such a sapphire-shot,

Charged, steepèd sky will not
Stain light. Yea, mark you this:
It does no prejudice.
The glass-blue days are those
When every colour glows,
Each shape and shadow shows.
Blue be it: this blue heaven
The seven or seven times seven
Hued sunbeam will transmit
Perfect, not alter it.
Or if there does some soft,
On things aloof, aloft,
Bloom breathe, that one breath more
Earth is the fairer for.
Whereas did air not make
This bath of blue and slake
His fire, the sun would shake,
A blear and blinding ball
With blackness bound, and all
The thick stars round him roll
Flashing like flecks of coal,
Quartz-fret, or sparks of salt,
In grimy vasty vault.
  So God was god of old:
A mother came to mould
Those limbs like ours which are
What must make our daystar
Much dearer to mankind;
Whose glory bare would blind
Or less would win man's mind.
Through her we may see him
Made sweeter, not made dim,
And her hand leaves his light
Sifted to suit our sight.
  Be thou then, O thou dear
Mother, my atmosphere;
My happier world, wherein
To wend and meet no sin;
Above me, round me lie
Fronting my froward eye
With sweet and scarless sky;

Stir in my ears, speak there
Of God's love, O live air,
Of patience, penance, prayer:
World-mothering air, air wild,
Wound with thee, in thee isled,
Fold home, fast fold thy child.

'The times are nightfall'

The times are nightfall, look, their light grows less;
The times are winter, watch, a world undone:
They waste, they wither worse; they as they run
Or bring more or more blazon man's distress.
And I not help. Nor word now of success:
All is from wreck, here, there, to rescue one—
Work which to see scarce so much as begun
Makes welcome death, does dear forgetfulness.
Or what is else? There is your world within.
There rid the dragons, root out there the sin.
Your will is law in that small commonweal.

St. Winefred's Well

Act I. Sc. i

Enter Teryth from riding, Winefred following.

T. What is it, Gwen, my girl? | why do you hover and haunt me?
W. You came by Caerwys, sir? |
T. I came by Caerwys.
W. There
Some messenger there might have | met you from my uncle.
T. Your uncle met the messenger— | met me; and this the message:
Lord Beuno comes tonight. |

W. Tonight, sir!
T. Soon, now: therefore
Have all things ready in his room. |
W. There needs but little doing.
T. Let what there needs be done. | Stay! with him one companion,
His deacon, Dirvan. Warm | twice over must the welcome be,
But both will share one cell,— | This was good news, Gwenvrewi.
W. Áh, yes!
T. Why, get thee gone then; | tell thy mother I want her.
Exit Winefred.
No man has such a daughter. | The fathers of the world
Call no such maiden 'mine'. | The deeper grows her dearness
And more and móre times laces | round and round my heart,
The more some monstrous hand | gropes with clammy fingers there,
Támpering with those sweet bines, | draws them out, strains them, strains them;
Meantime some tongue cries 'Whát, Teryth! | what, thou poor fond father!
How when this bloom, this honeysuckle, | that rides the air so rich about thee,
Is all, all sheared away, | thus!' Then I sweat for fear.
Or else a funeral | and yet 'tis nót a funeral,
Some pageant which takes tears | and I must foot with feeling that
Alive or dead my girl | is carried in it, endlessly
Goes marching thro' my mind. | What sense is this? It has none.
This is too much the father; | nay the mother. Fanciful!
I here forbid my thoughts | to fóol themselves with fears.
Enter Gwenlo.

. . . .

ACT II.—*Scene, a wood, ending in a steep bank over a dry dean. Winefred having been murdered within, re-enter Caradoc with a bloody sword.*

C. My héart, where have we been? | What have we séen, my mind?
What stroke has Caradoc's right arm dealt? | what done? Head of a rebel
Struck óff it has; written | upon lovely limbs,
In bloody letters, lessons | of earnest, of revenge;
Mónuments of my earnest, | récords of my revenge,
On one that went against me | whereas I had warned her—
Wárned her! well she knew | I warned her of this work.
What work? what harm's done? There is | no harm done, none yet;
Perháps we struck no blow, | Gwenvrewi lives perhaps;
To mákebelieve my mood was— | móck. O I might think so
But here, here is a workman | from his day's task swéats.
Wiped I am sure this was; | it seems, not well; for still,
Still the scarlet swings | and dances on the blade.
So be it. Thou steel, thou butcher,
I cán scour thee, fresh burnish thee, | sheathe thee in thy dark lair; these drops
Never, never, never | in their blue banks again.
The wóeful, Cradock, O | the woeful word! Then what,
What have we seen? Her head, | sheared from her shoulders, fall,
And lapped in shining hair, | róll to the bank's edge; then
Down the beetling banks, | like water in waterfalls,
It stooped and flashed and fell | and ran like water away.
Her eyes, oh and her eyes!
In all her beauty, and sunlight | to it is a pit, den, darkness,
Foamfalling is not fresh to it, | rainbow by it not beaming,
In all her body, I say, | no place was like her eyes,
No piece matched those eyes | kept most part much cast down
But, being lífted, ímmortal, | of immórtal brightness.
Several times I saw them, | thrice or four times turning;

Round and round they came | and flashed towards heaven: O there,
There they did appeal. | Therefore airy vengeances
Are afoot; heaven-vault fast purpling | portends, and what first lightning
Any instant falls means me. | And I do not repent;
I do not and I will not | repent, not repent.
The blame bear who aroused me. | What Í have dóne violent
I have like a lion done, | lionlike done,
Honouring an uncontrolled | royal wrathful nature,
Mantling passion in a grandeur, | crimson grandeur.
Now be my pride then perfect, | all one piece. Henceforth
In a wide world of defiance | Caradoc lives alone,
Loyal to his own soul, laying his | own law down, no law nor
Lord now curb him for ever. | O daring! O deep insight!
What is virtue? Valour; | only the heart valiant.
And right? Only resolution; | will, his will unwavering
Who, like me, knowing his nature | to the heart home, nature's business,
Despatches with no flinching. | But will flesh, O can flesh
Second this fiery strain? | Not always; O no no!
We cannot live this life out; | sometimes we must weary
And in this darksome world | what comfort can I find?
Down this darksome world | comfort where can Í find
When 'ts light I quenched; its rose, | time's one rich rose, my hand,
By her bloom, fast by | her fresh, her fleecèd bloom,
Hideous dashed down, leaving | earth a winter withering
With no now, nó Gwenvrewi. | I must miss her most
That might have spared her were it | but for passion-sake. Yes,
To hunger and not have, yet | hope on for, to storm and strive and
Be at every assault fresh foiled, | worse flung, deeper disappointed,
The turmoil and the torment, | it has, I swear, a sweetness
Keeps a kind of joy in it, | a zest, an edge, an ecstasy,
Next after sweet success. | I am not left even this;

I all my being have hacked | in half with her neck: one part,
Reason, selfdisposal, | choice of better or worse way,
Is corpse now, cannot change; | my other self, this soul,
Life's quick, this kínd, this kéen self-feeling,
With dreadful distillation | of thoughts sour as blood,
Must all day long taste murder. | What do now then? Do? Nay,
Deed-bound I am; one deed treads all down here | cramps all doing. What do? Not yield,
Not hope, not pray; despair; | ay, that: brazen despair out,
Brave all, and take what comes— | as here this rabble is come,
Whose bloods I reck no more of, | no more rank with hers
Than sewers with sacred oils. | Mankind, that mob, comes. Come!

Enter a crowd, among them Teryth, Gwenlo, Beuno, etc.

. . . .

(C.) After Winefred's raising from the dead and the breaking out of the fountain.

Beuno. O now while skies are blue, | now while seas are salt,
While rushy rains shall fall | or brooks shall fleet from fountains,
While sick men shall cast sighs, | of sweet health all despairing,
While blind men's eyes shall thírst after | daylight, draughts of daylight,
Or deaf ears shall desire that | lípmusic that's lóst upon them,
While cripples are, while lepers, | dancers in dismal limb-dance,
Fallers in dreadful frothpits, | waterfearers wild,
Stone, palsy, cancer, cough, | lung-wasting, womb-not-bearing,
Rupture, running sores, | what more? in brief, in burden,
As long as men are mortal | and God merciful,
So long to this sweet spot, | this leafy lean-over,
This Dry Dean, now no longer dry | nor dumb, but moist and musical

With the uproll and the downcarol | of day and night delivering
Water, which keeps thy name, | (for not in róck written,
But in pale water, fráil water, | wild rash and reeling water,
That will not wear a print, | that will not stain a pen,
Thy venerable record, | virgin, is recorded)
Here to this holy well | shall pilgrimages be,
And not from purple Wáles only | nor from elmy England,
But from beyond seas, Erin, | France and Flanders, everywhere
Pilgrims, still pilgrims, móre | pilgrims, still more poor pilgrims

. . . .

What sights shall be when some | that swung, wretches, on crutches
Their crutches shall cast from them, | on heels of air departing,
Or they go rich as roseleaves | hence that loathsome cáme hither!
Not now to náme even
Those dearer, more divine | boons whose haven the heart is.

. . . .

As sure as what is most sure, | sure as that spring primroses
Shall new-dapple next year, | sure as tomorrow morning,
Amóngst come-back-agáin things, | thíngs with a revival, things with a recovery,
Thy name . . .

. . . .

'To seem the stranger'

To seem the stranger lies my lot, my life
Among strangers. Father and mother dear,
Brothers and sisters are in Christ not near
And he my peace/my parting, sword and strife.

England, whose honour O all my heart woos, wife
To my creating thought, would neither hear
Me, were I pleading, plead nor do I: I wéar-
Y of idle a being but by where wars are rife.

I am in Ireland now; now I am at a thírd
Remove. Not but in all removes I can
Kind love both give and get. Only what word

Wisest my heart breeds dark heaven's baffling ban
Bars or hell's spell thwarts. This to hoard unheard,
Hear unheeded, leaves me a lonely began.

'I wake and feel'

I wake and feel the fell of dark, not day.
What hours, O what black hours we have spent
This night! what sights you, heart, saw; ways you went!
And more must, in yet longer light's delay.

With witness I speak this. But where I say
Hours I mean years, mean life. And my lament
Is cries countless, cries like dead letters sent
To dearest him that lives alas! away.

I am gall, I am heartburn. God's most deep decree
Bitter would have me taste: my taste was me;
Bones built in me, flesh filled, blood brimmed the curse.

Selfyeast of spirit a dull dough sours. I see
The lost are like this, and their scourge to be
As I am mine, their sweating selves; but worse.

'Strike, churl'

Strike, churl; hurl, cheerless wind, then; heltering hail
May's beauty massacre and wispèd wild clouds grow
Out on the giant air; tell Summer No,
Bid joy back, have at the harvest, keep Hope pale.

'No worst'

No worst, there is none. Pitched past pitch of grief,
More pangs will, schooled at forepangs, wilder wring.
Comforter, where, where is your comforting?
Mary, mother of us, where is your relief?
My cries heave, herds-long, huddle in a main, a chief-
Woe, wórld-sorrow; on an áge-old ánvil wínce and síng—
Then lull, then leave off. Fury had shrieked 'No ling-
Ering! Let me be fell: force I must be brief.'
O the mind, mind has mountains; cliffs of fall
Frightful, sheer, no-man-fathomed. Hold them cheap
May who ne'er hung there. Nor does long our small
Durance deal with that steep or deep. Here! creep,
Wretch, under a comfort serves in a whirlwind: all
Life death does end and each day dies with sleep.

To what serves Mortal Beauty?

To what serves mortal beauty— | dangerous; does set danc-
Ing blood—the O-seal-that-so | feature, flung prouder form
Than Purcell tune lets tread to? | See: it does this: keeps warm
Men's wit to the things that are; | to what good means—where a glance
Master more may than gaze, | gaze out of countenance.
Those lovely lads once, wet-fresh | windfalls of war's storm,
How then should Gregory, a father, | have gleanèd else from swarm-
Èd Rome? But God to a nation | dealt that day's dear chance.

To man, that once would worship | block or barren stone,
Our law says/love what are | love's worthiest, were all known;
World's loveliest—men's selves. Self | flashes off frame and face.
What do then? how meet beauty? | Merely meet it; own,
Home at heart, heaven's sweet gift; | then leave, let that alone.
Yea, wish that though, wish all, | God's better beauty, grace.

(*Carrion Comfort*)

Not, I'll not, carrion comfort, Despair, not feast on thee;
Not untwist—slack they may be—these last strands of man
In me ór, most weary, cry *I can no more*. I can;
Can something, hope, wish day come, not choose not to be.

But ah, but O thou terrible, why wouldst thou rude on me
Thy wring-earth right foot rock? lay a lionlimb against me? scan
With darksome devouring eyes my bruisèd bones? and fan,
O in turns of tempest, me heaped there; me frantic to avoid thee
and flee?

Why? That my chaff might fly; my grain lie, sheer and clear.
Nay in all that toil, that coil, since (seems) I kissed the rod,
Hand rather, my heart lo! lapped strength, stole joy, would laugh,
cheer.

Cheer whóm though? The héro whose héaven-handling flúng me,
fóot tród
Me? or mé that fóught him? O whích one? is it éach one? That
níght, that yéar
Of now done darkness I wretch lay wrestling with (my God!) my
God.

(*The Soldier*)

Yes. Whý do we áll, séeing of a | soldier, bless him? bléss
Our redcoats, our tars? Both | thése being, the greater part,
But frail clay, nay but foul clay. | Hére it is: the heart,
Since, proud, it calls the calling | manly, gives a guess

That, hopes that, mákesbelieve, | the men must be no less;
It fancies, feigns, deems, déars | the artist after his art;
And fain will find as sterling | all as all is smart
And scarlet wéar the spirit of war thére express.
Mark Christ our King. He knows war, served this soldiering
through;
He of all can reave a rope best. | There he bides in bliss
Now, and seeing somewhere some man | do all that man can do,
For love he léans forth, needs | his neck must fall on, kiss,
And cry 'O Christ-done deed! | So God-made-flesh does too:
Were I come o'er again' cries | Christ 'it should be this'.

'Thee, God, I come from'

Thee, God, I come from, to thee go,
All dáy long I like fountain flow
From thy hand out, swayed about
Mote-like in thy mighty glow.

What I know of thee I bless,
As acknowledging thy stress
On my being and as seeing
Something of thy holiness.

Once I turned from thee and hid,
Bound on what thou hadst forbid;
Sow the wind I would; I sinned:
I repent of what I did.

Bad I am, but yet thy child.
Father, be thou reconciled.
Spare thou me, since I see
With thy might that thou art mild.

I have life left with me still
And thy purpose to fulfil;
Yea a debt to pay thee yet:
Help me, sir, and so I will.

But thou bidst, and just thou art,
Me shew mercy from my heart
Towards my brother, every other
Man my mate and counterpart.

. . . .

Jesus Christ sacrificed
On the cross

Moulded, he, in maiden's womb,
Lived and died and from the tomb
Rose in power and is our
Judge that comes to deal our doom.

'Patience, hard thing'

Patience, hard thing! the hard thing but to pray,
But bid for, patience is! Patience who asks
Wants war, wants wounds; weary his times, his tasks;
To do without, take tosses, and obey.

Rare patience roots in these, and, these away,
No-where. Natural heart's-ivy Patience masks
Our ruins of wrecked past purpose. There she basks
Purple eyes and seas of liquid leaves all day.

We hear our hearts grate on themselves: it kills
To bruise them dearer. Yet the rebellious wills
Of us wé do bid God bend to him even so.

And where is he who more and more distills
Delicious kindness?—He is patient. Patience fills
His crisp combs, and that comes those ways we know.

'My own heart'

My own heart let me more have pity on; let
Me live to my sad self hereafter kind,
Charitable; not live this tormented mind
With this tormented mind tormenting yet.

I cast for comfort I can no more get
By groping round my comfortless than blind
Eyes in their dark can day or thirst can find
Thirst's all-in-all in all a world of wet.

Soul, self; come, poor Jackself, I do advise
You, jaded, lét be; call off thoughts awhile
Elsewhere; leave comfort root-room; let joy size

At God knows when to God knows what; whose smile
'S not wrung, see you; unforseentimes rather—as skies
Betweenpie mountains—lights a lovely mile.

To his Watch

Mortal my mate, bearing my rock-a-heart,
Warm beat with cold beat company, shall I
Earlier or you fail at our force and lie
The ruins of, rifled, once a world of art?
The telling time our task is; time's some part,
Not all, but we were framed to fail and die—
One spell and well that one. There, ah thereby
Is sweetest comfort's carol or worst woe's smart.

Field-flown, the departed day no morning brings
Saying 'This was yours' with her, but new one, worse,
And then that last and shortest.

Spelt from Sibyl's Leaves

Earnest, earthless, equal, attuneable, | vaulty, voluminous, . . . stupendous
Evening strains to be tíme's vást, | womb-of-all, home-of-all, hearse-of-all night.
Her fond yellow hornlight wound to the west, | her wild hollow hoarlight hung to the height
Waste; her earliest stars, earlstars, | stars principal, overbend us,
Fíre-féaturing héaven. For éarth | her béing has unbóund; her dápple is at énd, as-
Tray or aswarm, all throughther, in throngs; | self ín self stéepèd and páshed—qúite
Disremembering, dismembering | all now. Heart, you round me right
With: Óur évening is óver us; óur night | whélms, whélms, ánd will énd us.
Only the beakleaved boughs dragonish | damask the tool-smooth bleak light; black,
Ever so black on it. Óur tale, O óur oracle! | Lét life, wáned, ah lét life wínd
Off hér once skéined stained véined varíety | upon, áll on twó spools; párt, pen, páck
Now her áll in twó flocks, twó folds—bláck, white; | ríght, wrong; réckon but, réck but, mínd
But thése two; wáre of a wórld where bút these | twó tell, éach off the óther; of a ráck
Where, selfwrung, selfstrung, sheathe- and shelterless, | thóughts agáinst thoughts ín groans grínd.

On the Portrait of Two Beautiful Young People

a Brother and Sister

O I admire and sorrow! The heart's eye grieves
Discovering you, dark tramplers, tyrant years.
A juice rides rich through bluebells, in vine leaves,
And beauty's dearest veriest vein is tears.

Happy the father, mother of these! Too fast:
Not that, but thus far, all with frailty, blest
In one fair fall; but, for time's aftercast,
Creatures all heft, hope, hazard, interest.

And are they thus? The fine, the fingering beams
Their young delightful hour do feature down
That fleeted else like day-dissolvèd dreams
Or ringlet-race on burling Barrow brown.

She leans on him with such contentment fond
As well the sister sits, would well the wife;
His looks, the soul's own letters, see beyond,
Gaze on, and fall directly forth on life.

But ah, bright forelock, cluster that you are
Of favoured make and mind and health and youth,
Where lies your landmark, seamark, or soul's star?
There's none but truth can stead you. Christ is truth.

There's none but good can bé good, both for you
And what sways with you, maybe this sweet maid;
None good but God—a warning wavèd to
One once that was found wanting when Good weighed.

Man lives that list, that leaning in the will
No wisdom can forecast by gauge or guess,
The selfless self of self, most strange, most still,
Fast furled and all foredrawn to No or Yes.

Your feast of; that most in you earnest eye
May but call on your banes to more carouse.
Worst will the best. What worm was here, we cry,
To have havoc-pocked so, see, the hung-heavenward boughs?

Enough: corruption was the world's first woe.
What need I strain my heart beyond my ken?
O but I bear my burning witness though
Against the wild and wanton work of men.

Harry Ploughman

Hard as hurdle arms, with a broth of goldish flue
Breathed round; the rack of ribs; the scooped flank; lank
Rope-over thigh; knee-knave; and barrelled shank—
Head and foot, shouldér and shank—
By a grey eye's heed steered well, one crew, fall to;
Stand at stress. Each limb's barrowy brawn, his thew
That onewhere curded, onewhere sucked or sank—
Soared ór sank—,
Though as a beechbole firm, finds his, as at a rollcall, rank
And features, in flesh, what deed he each must do—
His sinew-service where do.
He leans to it, Harry bends, look. Back, elbow, and liquid waist
In him, all quáil to the wallowing o' the plough. 'S cheek crímsons; curls
Wag or crossbridle, in a wind lifted, windlaced—
Wind-lilylocks-laced;
Churlsgrace too, chíld of Amansstrength, how it hángs or hurls
Them—broad in bluff hide his frowning feet lashed! raced
With, along them, cragiron under and cold furls—
With-a-fountain's shining-shot furls.

(Ashboughs)

Not of all my eyes see, wándering on the world,
Is anything a milk to the mind so, só sighs déep
Poetry to it, as a tree whose boughs break in the sky.
Say it is áshboughs: whether on a December day and furled
Fast or they in clammyish láshtender combs creep
Apart wide and new-nestle at heaven most high.
They touch heaven, tabour on it; how their talons sweep
The smouldering enormous winter welkin! May
Mells blue and snowwhite through them, a fringe and fray
Of greenery: it is old earth's groping towards the steep
Heaven whom she childs us by.

(Second version from l.7)

They touch, they tabour on it, hover on it; here, there hurled,
With talons sweep
The smouldering enormous winter welkin. Eye,
But more cheer is when May
Mells blue with snowwhite through their fringe and fray
Of greenery and old earth gropes for, grasps at steep
Heaven with it whom she childs things by.

Tom's Garland:

upon the Unemployed

Tom—garlanded with squat and surly steel
Tom; then Tom's fallowbootfellow piles pick
By him and rips out rockfire homeforth—sturdy Dick;
Tom Heart-at-ease, Tom Navvy: he is all for his meal
Sure, 's bed now. Low be it: lustily he his low lot (feel
That ne'er need hunger, Tom; Tom seldom sick,
Seldomer heartsóre; that treads through, prickproof, thick
Thousands of thorns, thoughts) swings though. Commonweal
Little Í reck ho! lacklevel in, if all had bread:
What! country is honour enough in all us—lordly head,
With heaven's lights high hung round, or, mother-ground
That mammocks, mighty foot. But nő way sped,
Nor mind nor mainstrength; gold go garlanded
With, perilous, O nó; nor yet plod safe shod sound;
Undenizened, beyond bound
Of earth's glory, earth's ease, all; no-one, nowhere,
In wide the world's weal; rare gold, bold steel, bare
In both; care, but share care—
This, by Despair, bred Hangdog dull; by Rage,
Manwolf, worse; and their packs infest the age.

Epithalamion

Hark, hearer, hear what I do; lend a thought now, make believe
We are leaf-whelmed somewhere with the hood
Of some branchy bunchy bushybowered wood,
Southern dean or Lancashire clough or Devon cleave,
That leans along the loins of hills, where a candycoloured, where a gluegold-brown
Marbled river, boisterously beautiful, between
Roots and rocks is danced and dandled, all in froth and waterblowballs, down.
We are there, when we hear a shout
That the hanging honeysuck, the dogeared hazels in the cover
Makes dither, makes hover
And the riot of a rout
Of, it must be, boys from the town
Bathing: it is summer's sovereign good.
By there comes a listless stranger: beckoned by the noise
He drops towards the river: unseen
Sees the bevy of them, how the boys
With dare and with downdolfinry and bellbright bodies huddling out,
Are earthworld, airworld, waterworld thorough hurled, all by turn and turn about.
This garland of their gambol flashes in his breast
Into such a sudden zest
Of summertime joys
That he hies to a pool neighbouring; sees it is the best
There; sweetest, freshest, shadowiest;
Fairyland; silk-beech, scrolled ash, packed sycamore, wild wychelm, hornbeam fretty overstood
By. Rafts and rafts of flake leaves light, dealt so, painted on the air,
Hang as still as hawk or hawkmoth, as the stars or as the angels there,
Like the thing that never knew the earth, never off roots
Rose. Here he feasts: lovely all is! Nó more: off with—down he dings
His bleachèd both and woolwoven wear:
Careless these in coloured wisp
All lie tumbled-to; then with loop-locks

Forward falling, forehead frowning, lips crisp
Over fingerteasing task, his twiny boots
Fast he opens, last he off wrings
Till walk the world he can with bare his feet
And come where lies a coffer, burly all of blocks
Built of chancequarrièd, selfquainèd, hoar-huskèd rocks
And the water warbles over into, filleted | with glassy grassy quicksilvery shivès and shoots
And with heavenfallen freshness down from moorland still brims,
Dark or daylight, on and on. Here he will then, here he will the fleet
Flinty kindcold element let break across his limbs
Long. Where we leave him, froliclavish, while he looks about him, laughs, swims.

Enough now; since the sacred matter that I mean
I should be wronging longer leaving it to float
Upon this only gambolling and echoing-of-earth note
What is the delightful dean?
Wedlock. What the water? Spousal love

to Everard, as I surmise,
Sparkled first in Amy's eyes
turns
Father, mother, brothers, sisters, friends
Into fairy trees, wildflowers, woodferns
Rankèd round the bower

'The sea took pity'

The sea took pity: it interposed with doom:
'I have tall daughters dear that heed my hand:
Let Winter wed one, sow them in her womb,
And she shall child them on the New-world strand.'

That Nature is a Heraclitean Fire and of the comfort of the Resurrection

Cloud-puffball, torn tufts, tossed pillows | flaunt forth, then chevy
on an air—
Built thoroughfare: heaven-roysterers, in gay-gangs | they throng;
they glitter in marches.
Down roughcast, down dazzling whitewash, | wherever an elm
arches,
Shivelights and shadowtackle in long | lashes lace, lance, and pair.
Delightfully the bright wind boisterous | ropes, wrestles, beats
earth bare
Of yestertempest's creases; in pool and rutpeel parches
Squandering ooze to squeezed | dough, crust, dust; stanches,
starches
Squadroned masks and manmarks | treadmire toil there
Footfretted in it. Million-fuelèd, | nature's bonfire burns on.
But quench her bonniest, dearest | to her, her clearest-selvèd
spark
Man, how fast his firedint, | his mark on mind, is gone!
Both are in an únfathomable, all is in an enormous dark
Drowned. O pity and indig | nation! Manshape, that shone
Sheer off, disseveral, a star, | death blots black out; nor mark
Is any of him at all so stark
But vastness blurs and time | beats level. Enough! the Resurrection,
A heart's-clarion! Away grief's gasping, | joyless days, dejection.
Across my foundering deck shone
A beacon, an eternal beam. | Flesh fade, and mortal trash
Fall to the residuary worm; | world's wildfire, leave but ash:
In a flash, at a trumpet crash,
I am all at once what Christ is, | since he was what I am, and
This Jack, joke, poor potsherd, | patch, matchwood, immortal
diamond,
Is immortal diamond.

'What shall I do for the land that bred me'

What shall I do for the land that bred me,
Her homes and fields that folded and fed me?—
Be under her banner and live for her honour:
Under her banner I'll live for her honour.
 CHORUS. Under her banner [we] live for her honour.

Not the pleasure, the pay, the plunder,
But country and flag, the flag I am under—
There is the shilling that finds me willing
To follow a banner and fight for honour.
 CH. We follow her banner, we fight for her honour.

Call me England's fame's fond lover,
Her fame to keep, her fame to recover.
Spend me or end me what God shall send me,
But under her banner I live for her honour.
 CH. Under her banner we march for her honour.

Where is the field I must play the man on?
O welcome there their steel or cannon.
Immortal beauty is death with duty,
If under her banner I fall for her honour.
 CH. Under her banner we fall for her honour.

In honour of
St. Alphonsus Rodriguez

Laybrother of the Society of Jesus upon the
first falling of his feast after his canonisation
For the College of Palma in the Island
of Majorca, where the saint lived for 40 years as
Hall porter

Glory is a flame off exploit, so we say,
And those fell strokes that once scarred flesh, scored shield,
Should tongue that time now, trumpet now that field,

Record, and on the fighter forge the day.
On Christ they do, they on the martyr may;
But where war is within, what sword we wield
Not seen, the heroic breast not outward-steeled,
Earth hears no hurtle then from fiercest fray.
Yet, he that hews out mountain, continent,
Earth, all, at last; who, with fine increment
Trickling, veins violets and tall trees makes more
Could crowd career with conquest while there went
Those years and years by of world without event
That in Majorca Alfonso watched the door.

Justus quidem tu es, Domine

si disputem tecum; verumtamen justa loquar ad te: quare via impiorum prosperatur? etc (Jerem. xii. 1.)

Thou art indeed just, Lord, if I contend
With thee; but, sir, so what I plead is just.
Why do sinners' ways prosper? and why must
Disappointment all I endeavour end?

Wert thou my enemy, O thou my friend,
How wouldst thou worse, I wonder, than thou dost
Defeat, thwart me? Oh, the sots and thralls of lust
Do in spare hours more thrive than I that spend,

Sir, life upon thy cause. See, banks and brakes
Now, leavèd how thick! lacèd they are again
With fretty chervil, look, and fresh wind shakes

Them; birds build—but not I build; no, but strain,
Time's eunuch, and not breed one work that wakes.
Mine, O thou lord of life, send my roots rain.

'The shepherd's brow'

The shepherd's brow, fronting forked lightning, owns
The horror and the havoc and the glory
Of it. Angels fall, they are towers, from heaven—a story
Of just, majestical, and giant groans.
But man—we, scaffold of score brittle bones;
Who breathe, from groundlong babyhood to hoary
Age gasp; whose breath is our *memento mori*—
What bass is *our* viol for tragic tones?
He! Hand to mouth he lives, and voids with shame;
And, blazoned in however bold the name,
Man Jack the man is, just; his mate a hussy.
And I that die these deaths, that feed this flame,
That . . . in smooth spoons spy life's masque mirrored: tame
My tempests there, my fire and fever fussy.

To R. B.

The fine delight that fathers thought; the strong
Spur, live and lancing like the blowpipe flame,
Breathes once and, quenchèd faster than it came,
Leaves yet the mind a mother of immortal song.

Nine months she then, nay years, nine years she long
Within her wears, bears, cares and combs the same:
The widow of an insight lost she lives, with aim
Now known and hand at work now never wrong.

Sweet fire the sire of muse, my soul needs this;
I want the one rapture of an inspiration.
O then if in my lagging lines you miss

The roll, the rise, the carol, the creation,
My winter world, that scarcely breathes that bliss
Now, yields you, with some sighs, our explanation.

Notes

Abbreviations used in the Notes are listed on p. x

References to the Bible are to the Authorized Version except where otherwise stated.

For explanations of such terms as standard rhythm, counterpoint, sprung rhythm, over-rove, see Author's Preface and notes, pp. 95–7, 243–4.

The metrical marks shown are all Hopkins's own, taken generally from the manuscript chosen as text (see Note on the Text, p. xxii). Hopkins's stresses are incorporated in the text while the rest of his metrical symbols are included in the notes. A list of most of these, with his explanations, follows:

~	quiver or circumflexion, making one syllable nearly two.
⌒	over three or more syllables gives them the time of one half foot.
:	great colons signify a stress on the syllables either side of the colon; a sprung opening, i.e. a great colon at the beginning of a line, indicates a stress on the initial syllable.
∾ ∽	counterpoint signs (see p. 96).
‿	between syllables slurs them into one.
‿	outride; under one or more syllables makes them extrametrical.
″	heavy stress.
\\	stresses of sense; independent of the natural stress of the verse.
⌐¬	over two neighbouring syllables means that, though one has and the other has not the metrical stress, in recitation-stress they are to be about equal.

Other symbols are explained in notes to poems in which they occur.

Hopkins also used a number of musical terms such as rallentando (slowing down), staccato (▼; short, detached sounds), sforzando (suddenly loud), and the pause (⌒; a dwelling on a syllable which need not have the metrical stress).

1 *The Escorial*. Dated 'Easter 1860'. Hopkins won the Poetry Prize at Highgate School at the age of 15 with this poem on a subject set also for the Newdigate Poetry Prize at Oxford that year. It is a vividly imaginative and well-organized account of the creation and gradual dissolution of the building, for which he drew on facts gathered largely from William H. Prescott's *History of the Reign of Philip II*,

iii (London, [1859]), which his family owned. The disapproval of the Inquisition, evident in Prescott, is clear in Hopkins's poem. The entry had to be anonymous, and Hopkins chose as identifying motto the modest line from Theocritus (Idyll 7, l. 41): 'I compete like a frog against the cicadas.' The text of the poem was written out by Hopkins's mother, but he may have inscribed the notes, which are printed at the foot of the page, himself. A line above l. 22 and stanza 9 may have been omitted to comply with the stipulated length. The form is Spenserian stanzas and Mariani draws attention to 'a pale resemblance to Keats's *The Eve of St. Agnes* in its stanza form, use of narrative, luxurious descriptions, and oblique but nevertheless strong moral undertone' (p. 4).

3 st. 8 n. *Velasquez.* The architect, as Prescott notes, was actually Juan Bautista de Toledo.

5 l. 122. *null.* MS originally read 'full'. Amendment retained since this was probably the version submitted; 'full', although idiomatic, could have been a copiest's error—there was one in the previous line. 'Null' in the sense of 'null and void' (with 'only' elided); the title 'eighth wonder of the earth' rendered 'only too empty', with overtones of 'nullified', alluding to the change in the building's religious and moral significance dealt with in the rest of the stanza.

6 *Aeschylus: Promêtheus Desmotês.* ll. 1–19 from school notebook also used at Oxford; ll. 20–36 from Hopkins's letter of 3–6 September 1862 in which he told E. H. Coleridge that he had been reading *Prometheus Bound* and considered it 'immensely superior to anything else of Aeschylus' ' he had read, 'really full of splendid poetry' (*L.* III 6). He enclosed ll. 20–36 as an example of the 'beautiful lyric passages' in the soliloquy which Prometheus delivers after the exit of the gods who have chained him to the rocks in punishment for having given fire to men and deceived the gods. Prometheus, who has the gift of prophecy which allows him to know how long his punishment is to last, calls on the elements to witness the price he has to pay for loving too well the race of man.

N. H. MacKenzie draws attention to the skill with which Hopkins's translation draws out the meaning in the metaphors and imagery (OET 219–20). Todd Bender commented that the close reading Hopkins later applied to English literature was learnt through translating and pondering upon the meaning of classical texts (pp. 56–7).

l. 3. *countless laughter.* F. A. Paley, *Tragedies of Aeschylus* (2nd edn., rev. and enlarged, London, 1861), comments on 'the quivering or rippling motion, which suggests the notion of "countless" because the surface is never for an instant still. "To count the waves" was a proverb implying impossibility' (pp. 97–8).

l. 11. *young chief of the bless'd of heaven*. In his introduction Paley says 'between the infernal powers of the old elemental mythology, including demons, heroes, and Erinyes,—gloomy, vengeful, and terrible,—and the newer and more benign deities of the Jovian dynasty, the Olympian gods generally, [Aeschylus] draws a clear distinction. The former are the genii of death and Nature's sternest laws; the latter interfere closely and sympathetically in the affairs of men, as protectors of cities and of the people in their social and political relations. It was the great object of the poet to explain away the old legends which represented these two powers in continual conflict, and to show that there was a real and material union between them . . . that the government of the world and the law of Nature could not be other than a harmonious principle' (pp. xvii–xviii). Paley draws on Hesiod Theog. 567, Opp. 52, to make the point that Prometheus' rebellious act in stealing fire had frustrated Zeus' attempt to 'restore the balance of advantages between the gods and mankind' (p. 99).

l. 18. *unending pains*. Paley remarks that this must be understood in a limited sense, for in v. 793 Prometheus foretells that he shall be liberated fourteen generations after Io.

l. 21. *scent*. 'smell unaccompanied by any vision . . . was generally regarded as the token of a divine presence' (Paley, 99).

l. 29. Prometheus' deceit made him an outcast among the gods, forbidden to enter Zeus' abode.

ll. 32–6. Prometheus 'foreknows the approach of the dreaded vulture: hence his alarm at the rustling of wings' (Paley, 100). Instead, Ocean nymphs, ministers of mercy and consolation, appear.

7 *Il Mystico*. Only extant passages printed in *L*. III 9–13 (3–6 Sept. 1862). Hopkins sent 'extracts' from it in the same letter as 'Promêtheus Desmotês' to E. H. Coleridge, saying that it was the best thing that he had done recently and was in imitation of 'Il Penseroso'. Hopkins told Coleridge that 'the description at the beginning [of the section from l. 65?] is founded on Milton's "The Cherub Contemplation" ['Il Penseroso', l. 54 ff.]' (*L*. III 13). The poem also reflects Hopkins's recent reading of Aeschylus and Shelley. It remains unfinished.

8 ll. 48–63. The rhyme scheme suggests that two lines are missing although the sense could run straight on from l. 47 to l. 48. The passage draws on the book of Ezekiel for such incidents as the prophet's vision on the banks of the river Chebar of four winged creatures who fly off into the firmament (ch. 1) and his recurrent impression of the radiant presence of God (1: 28, 2: 23, 8: 4, etc.). Ezekiel is told by God of the sins of the children of Israel and sees in ch. 8 images that tell of the way in which the elders of the tribes have

turned away from the worship of God to that of idols. The biblical story ends with God's restoration of the Israelites to his favour, but Hopkins's poem does not bring out the anger and violent jealousy of God evident in Ezekiel nor the extent to which the prophet is urged to berate the people.

9 l. 65. *lark*: skylark. See 'The Sea and Skylark'.

ll. 75–6. 'I had formerly instead of the lines resembling them which I have put in the enclosed copy, "And when the silent heights were won, Alone in air to face the sun". Now is that or is it not a plagiarism from Tennyson's *Eagle*, "Close to the sun in lonely lands," (see the poem)? I am in that state that I want an unprejudiced decision' (*L.* III 14).

10 l. 119. See Rev. 21: 19–20.

11 *A windy day in summer.* Also enclosed in Hopkins's letter of 3–6 September 1862 to E. H. Coleridge. Hopkins mentioned that he had been 'writing numbers of descriptions of sunrises, sunsets, sunlight in the trees, flowers, windy skies etc. etc.' (*L.* III 13).

A fragment of anything you like. Written below 'A windy day' in the letter mentioned above. 'Hopkins compares the pale, delicate sorrow of a woman to the late-rising and forlorn moon wandering aimlessly in broad daylight across the heavens. It is an image which calls Shelley to mind' (Mariani, 6).

A Vision of the Mermaids. The autograph is written below one of Hopkins's circular drawings. It shows groups of mermaids standing waist-deep in the sea admiring a spectacular sunset (reproduced *J.* pl. 3). See Hopkins's description of his family's seaside holiday in July 1863 (*L.* III 201): 'My brothers and cousin catch us shrimps, prawns and lobsters, and keep aquariums . . . I thought it would look strikingly graceful etc to wear sea-anemones round my forehead. (Mermaids do it, you know. Fragment from an unpublished?) . . . '. Hopkins owned Anne Pratt's *Chapters on the Common Things of the Sea Coast* (SPCK, 1853), and his appreciation of the fragile beauty of such things is evident in his almost brittle descriptions (ll. 53–74). He transcribed into his commonplace book Dr [Oliver Wend.] Holmes's poem, 'On a Broken Shell of the Chambered Nautilus', . . . 'quoted in Woods' *Illustrated Natural History*, published by Routledge'. The poem is written in heroic couplets. Mariani notes the influence on the lush imagery of Keats's *Endymion* (p. 6). Cf. Tennyson's 'Tithonus' for a similarly sensual description of dawn (ll. 19–26).

15 *Winter with the Gulf Stream.* Published in *Once a Week* (14 Feb. 1863) and revised in August 1871. Written in terza rima.

16 l. 27. *Pactolus*: the river whose golden sands are said to have come

from Midas, who bathed in it to lose his unwanted gift of turning everything he touched into gold.

Spring and Death. 1863? Cf. the poignancy in this poem that comes from appreciation of the brevity of the life of plants with Hopkins's handling of the subconscious foreknowledge of mortality in 'Spring and Fall'. See Wendell Johnson (*Hopkins Quarterly*, 10/3 (Fall 1983), 117) for a comparison with Tennyson's 'A spirit haunts the year's last hours'.

17 *Pilate.* June 1864. The sequence is uncertain, stanzas 2, 3, 5–7 are numbered; the other stanzas are printed in the order in which they occur in the manuscript with the exception of the first stanza, which is placed first following MacKenzie's OET text. GMH may have been influenced by Tennyson's 'St. Simeon Stylites', which he greatly admired (*L.* III 8), both in choosing to write the poem as a dramatic monologue and for the descriptions of Pilate's sufferings. The imagery suggests that he also had *Prometheus Bound* in mind.

l. 5. *other Pilates.* People who neglected responsibility were called 'Pilates' (MacKenzie, OET 229).

l. 7. MacKenzie points out that the line requires 'me' after 'keep'; 'stay' in the sense of legal postponement of proceedings (OET 229).

ll. 8–14. Hopkins began a revision but did not carry through the changes necessary to incorporate it:

> Betwixt the morsels of the snow,
> Under the mastering blue black heat,
> When the winds blow, when strong rains twist and flow
> Along my face and hands and feet. (OET)

19 ll. 52–9. See Matt. 27: 20–6.

l. 76. *But if this overlast the day . . .* Two pages were separated from Hopkins's diary at this point. On one occurs the first half of this stanza, printed (*J.* 49).

20 *'She schools the flighty pupils'.* June 1864. MacKenzie suggests that this is the octave from an incomplete Spenserian sonnet (OET 231), although the sense seems complete as it stands.

21 *A Soliloquy of One of the Spies left in the Wilderness.* July 1864. There are many variants. Final variants have been chosen for stanzas 4 and 9. See Num. 13–14. The speaker in this dramatic monologue is one of the spies whom Moses sent into Canaan. Afraid of the strength of the inhabitants who would have to be defeated before the Israelites could possess their land of milk and honey, the spy told lies about what the land was like. God, his people disobedient yet again, condemned the unfaithful spies to die of plague and the Israelites to wander forty years in the wilderness so that only their children would inherit

Canaan. The speaker is dying, self-deluded about what life in Egypt had been like and delirious as to where he is. The story is, on an allegorical level, a warning against preferring the *status quo* to risking dangers that must be incurred in carrying out God's design for one.

21 l. 9. *manna-bushes.* There is discussion as to what manna was, with suggestions ranging from quails and locusts to the fruit of a bush or tree (OET 232–3).

l. 14. *wide*: eliptical, wide of the mark, inaccurate.

22 ll. 43–4. See Num. 12 for Miriam's and Aaron's questioning of Moses' leadership and the punishment God meted out to them in response.

l. 45. See Exod. 8–14 for the plagues which God sent upon the Egyptians to persuade Pharaoh to release the Israelites from their enslavement.

The Lover's Stars. Between drawings dated 16 July and 18 July 1864. Hopkins called it 'a trifle in something like Coventry Patmore's style' (*L.* III 213). MacKenzie notes that Hopkins reverses the love story of *The Angel in the House* in having the voyaging naval officer more successful in winning the lady than his home-bound rival (OET 234).

23 ll. 5–8 were revised to:

The other leaves the West behind
Or it may be the prodigal South,
Passes the seas and comes to find
Acceptance round his mistress' mouth.

But since the consequent revisions required to stanzas 4 and 5 were not made, the earlier version has been retained.

The peacock's eye. The second of a number of fragments written 22–5 July 1864. It shows Hopkins vivifying a description by using verbs suggestive of dramatic action in it. He commented below, 'Overloaded apparently'. Earlier read:

The peacock's eye
Winks away it's azure sheen
Barter'd for a ring of green.
The bean-shaped pupil of moist jet
Is the silkiest violet

See *J.* 209–10 (17 May 1871) for a later description of the peacock's opened train: 'I have thought it looks like a tray or green basket or fresh-cut willow hurdle set all over with Paradise fruits cut through—first through a beard of golden fibre and then through wet flesh greener than greengages or purpler than grapes . . . and then within all a sluggish corner drop of black or purple oil.'

l. 5 *jet*: deep, glossy black.

24 *Love preparing to fly*. Immediately after 'The peacock's eye'. A description in which the vehicle is almost more vivid than the tenor, 'a wind-perplexèd rose' being easier to visualize than whether Cupid is to be seen as a rosy-winged infant or a slightly older youth. MacKenzie suggests that the title may have been an afterthought to give a mythological air to a description of a clear-wing moth taking flight (OET 236). This would provide a third distinct visual image to overlay upon the partial overlap of the more obvious ones.

l. 2. *glassy*. See *J.* 231 (11 May 1873) where 'glassy' is used to mean 'a notable glare the eye may abstract and sever from the . . . colour of light'. Clear-wing moths have shiny, transparent wings.

Barnfloor and Winepress. Printed in the *Union Review*, 3 (1865), 579. Cf. George Herbert's 'The Sacrifice'.

l. 16. *Gethsemane*: the garden in which Christ was betrayed and arrested. See Matt. 26: 36–57.

25 l. 21. *Joseph's garden*: the garden in which Christ's body was interred after the crucifixion. See Matt. 27: 57–60.

l. 24. *forty days*. Christ ascended to Heaven forty days after his resurrection.

l. 25. 'Christ was gone and in 50 days the Holy Ghost the new Paraclete came. He lost no time, but from nine o'clock in the morning of the first Whitsunday began his untiring age-long ever conquering task of convincing the world about sin and justice and judgment' (*S.* 74).

l. 28. *Libanus*: Mount Lebanon, famous for its forests and fruit.

New Readings. Bridges pointed out the similarity with George Herbert's poem, 'The Sacrifice'. See too the final stanza of 'The Bunch of Grapes', which may have influenced the choice of title.

l. 1. *the letter*. Earlier read: 'God's word'.

l. 2. See Luke 6: 44: 'For every tree is known by his own fruit. For of thorns men do not gather figs, nor of a bramble bush gather they grapes.'

ll. 6–10. See Matt. 13: 4–7.

ll. 11–12. See Luke 9: 12–17. Earlier read: 'Hard ways, rough wanderings | Made Him not fruitless; in the thorns he shed.'

ll. 14–15. See Matt. 26: 53–4: 'Jesus said, Thinkest thou that I cannot now pray to my Father, and he shall presently give me more than twelve legions of angels? But how then shall the scriptures be fulfilled, that thus it must be?'

26 *'He hath abolished the old drouth'*. July 1864. It may have been included under the title 'New Readings'. MacKenzie notes the influence in form and tone of Christina Rossetti's 'The Convent Threshold' (OET 239–40). See too her poem, 'The Offering of the New Law, the One Oblation once offered', which Hopkins's mother transcribed into his commonplace book for him. References to the Psalms are to the Prayer Book version.

ll. 1–3. See Ps. 107: 35.

l. 4. Ps. 40: 3.

ll. 6–7. Ps. 118: 17.

ll. 8, 14–15. See Matt. 13: 30: 'Let both grow together until the harvest: and in the time of harvest I will say to the reapers, Gather ye together first the tares, and bind them in bundles to burn them: but gather the wheat into my barn.'

ll. 16–17. Ps. 65: 14.

Heaven-Haven. Originally titled 'Rest', July 1864. A similar version of the first two drafted stanzas occurs on the same sheet as 'For a Picture of Saint Dorothea' but is titled 'Fair Havens—The Nunnery'. Hopkins's interest in sprung rhythm is evident in both poems. For the title, see George Herbert's poem, 'The Size' (last line): 'These seas are tears, and heav'n the haven'. Cf. Tennyson's 'Morte d'Arthur', ll. 260–4, for his description of Avilion:

Where falls not hail, or rain or any snow,
Nor ever wind blows loudly; but it lies
Deep-meadowed, happy, fair with orchard-lawns
And bowery hollows crowned with summer sea. (*J*. 356 n. 140.7)

27 *'I must hunt down the prize'*. Between 25 July and 1 August 1864, when Hopkins left for a reading holiday in Wales with Edward Bond and A. E. Hardy (see *L*. III 211–14). It uses the same form as 'Rest' (Heaven-Haven), which it follows immediately in the diary but whose aspirations it inverts.

'Why should their foolish bands'. Between 1 August and 14 August 1864. A youthful criticism of mourners not comforted by Christian doctrine.

l. 8. Uncancelled alternative: 'Far from its head an angel's hoverings'.

l. 9. MacKenzie suggests that the reference is to crosses entwined with roses placed on graves. The rose, symbolizing Paradise and regeneration, is out of keeping with the grief displayed in the rest of the funeral. Hopkins argues that if the attitudes implicit in the grief are held to be true then the hope suggested by the rose and cross is mere superstition (OET 241).

'It was a hard thing'. Mid-August 1864. Written at Maentwrog. In this highly structured poem Hopkins takes pleasure in drawing distinctions between individual vision of an independent external object and solipsism.

28 *'Glimmer'd along the square-cut steep'*. Probably written at Maentwrog on 14 Aug. 1864 or shortly afterwards.

l. 4. *lawless honey.* MacKenzie suggests a reminiscence of 1 Sam. 14: 24 ff. (OET 242).

'Miss Story's character'. Aug.–Sept. 1864. Hopkins wrote to Baillie (*L.* III 213): 'We have four Miss Storys staying in the house, girls from Reading. This is a great advantage—but not to reading.' He seems to have drafted some of the verses 'in the van between Ffestiniog and Bala' and others in the 'train from Chalk Farm to Croydon' (*J.* 317), where he stayed with his grandfather (*L.* III 222). Cf. Pope, 'Of the Characters of Women' (Mariani, 13).

l. 3. among the drafts is an address evidently written by a Miss Louisa May (also from Reading). None of this rather patronizing poem would have been visible at the time the address was written.

29 ll. 19–20. Earlier variant: ' . . . but less than female tact, | Sees the right thing to do and does not act.'

(*Epigrams*). August 1864. (i) written 'in the van between Ffestiniog and Bala'.

30 (iv) *By Mrs. Hopley.* August 1864. A first version, including ll. 1–2 of the text, was cancelled. The poem seems to have been written in reaction to articles in *The Times* (14, 15, 16, and 18 July 1864) about a suit for legal separation. A Mr Thomas Hopley had been jailed for beating a pupil to death. On his release his wife sued for separation on the grounds of cruelty to herself and their children. Mr Hopley produced letters from his wife, written to him while he was in prison, suggesting that the family were all very fond of him. The jury had difficulty in reaching a decision and eventually refused the suit because, although Mrs Hopley's charges were believed, she appeared to have condoned her husband's behaviour, negating grounds for separation. Mrs Hopley was identified by Mrs E. E. Duncan-Jones (*TLS* 10 Oct. 1968, p. 1159).

l. 1 *theory. The Times* mentions that Mr Hopley held 'absurd theories' with regard to the management of women in pregnancy and young children, amounting to maltreatment. He also had strong theories about education and intended to establish a model school (15 and 18 July).

31 *Floris in Italy.* Probably begun as a poem in June or July 1864 (see *L.* III 213). In Aug. 1864 Hopkins decided to rewrite it as a play. He

wrote to Baillie, 'What do you think? It occurred to me that the story of *Floris in Italy* is dramatic, and all of a sudden I began to turn it into a play. It is a great experiment. I shall alter the plot to suit requirements a little. I fancy there is a fascination about the dramatic form' (10 Sept. 1864, *L.* III 221). There are three poetic passages that definitely belong to the play and one, very lively, prose passage in which 'A Fool dictates a letter to Giulia' (written 9 Sept.). Various other fragments have been tentatively placed with the play. Hopkins's diaries contain a wealth of poetic experiments during this period and evidence to group any of them with this work is scant, as are clues as to what order the obvious fragments were intended to have. MacKenzie suggests that most sense is made if Floris's speech arguing against reciprocating Giulia's love appears first, followed by the prose scene between Giulia and the Fool, and then the night scene in which Giulia steals away from the sleeping Floris (OET 244–7). I like this order for literary reasons and have followed it although it reverses the sequence in which the fragments appear in the diaries. However, I do not think that 'I am like a slip of comet' fits into the flow of the night scene (iii) between ll. 48 and 49; it seems to me to belong instead to the group of experiments on describing the stars written while Hopkins was staying with his grandfather at Blunt House, Croydon. I am also not convinced that the fragment 'Yes for a time they held as well' fits into 'Floris in Italy' and have placed it later. But the prose passage (iv), although the use of 'A' for Giulia casts doubt on whether it was intended for 'Floris', does make sense of passage (v) and this suggestion of MacKenzie's I also follow. There are a number of uncancelled slightly variant lines, printed in *J.*, OET, and my Oxford Authors, but not reproduced here. Hopkins's appreciation of the liveliness of such Shakespearian heroines as Viola and Olivia and the role played by Shakespearian fools is evident in (ii).

36 *Io.* September 1864 and later. Hopkins wrote to Baillie on 10 September 1864 that besides beginning to turn 'Floris in Italy' into a play he had 'done very little' since last writing (14 Aug.) 'except three verses, a fragment, being a description of Io (tranformed into a heifer.) It sounds odd' (*L.* III 221). The story of Io occurs in Aeschylus' *Prometheus Bound.* According to Aeschylus, Zeus fell in love with Io and changed her into a white heifer to hide her from his wife, Hera. The story is also told by Ovid in *Heroides* (14. 85–108) and *Metamorphoses* (I. 588 ff.). Ovid says that Hera set Argus, a huntsman with many eyes, to guard Io and prevent Zeus from seducing her. To the same end the angry Hera sent a gadfly to torment Io and this drove her, maddened, through many lands.

l. 6. variant: 'She rests half-meshing from the too-bright sky.'

ll. 11–12. variant: 'Her hue's a honied brown and creamy lakes, | Like a cupp'd chestnut damaskèd with breaks' (see *J.* 48).

l. 14. variant: 'The knot of feathery locks'.

ll. 17–18. variants:

Day brings not back his basilisking stare,
Nor night beholds a single flame-ring flare.

and

Night is not blown with flame-rings everywhere,
Nor day new-basilisks his tireless stare.

ll. 16–18 refer to Argus, who kept two of his eyes, his 'vigil-organ', open at all times until Hermes, sent by Zeus, lulled him to sleep with stories and songs and cut off his head. Argus' many eyes have sometimes been seen as a symbol of the stars. This may explain 'flame-rings', imagery that Hopkins often applied to stars.

The rainbow. Early September 1864.

l. 2. *his.* MS reads 'its', a remnant of an earlier version when 'He' read 'It'. *sward*: a literary word for lawn.

37 *'—Yes for a time'.* 7 or 8 September 1864.

l. 5. *kelson*: 'line of timber fastening ship's floor-timbers to keel' (OED).

Gabriel. Written between 10 and 14 September 1864. Possibly intended for 'Floris in Italy' but separated out here since there is no direct link. The prose scene (i) may have prompted but not been intended to be associated with the poetic fragment (ii) which follows it.

38 (ii) *Guinevere.* Evidently influenced by Tennyson's *Idylls of the King* (1859) (OET 248). Hopkins had been an avid reader of Tennyson's work as it appeared but a letter of 10 September 1864 to Baillie shows Hopkins, who was in the process of formulating criteria for assessing poetic greatness, beginning to question Tennyson's reputation (*L.* III 215). He later suggested that Tennyson should have called his *Idylls of the King* 'Charades from the Middle Ages', 'unreal in motive and incorrect, uncanonical so to say, in detail and keepings' (*L.* II 24, 27 Feb. 1879).

39 l. 13. uncancelled variant: 'Such heathenish misadventure dogs one sin.'

'I am like a slip of comet'. Mid-September 1864. A number of important comets had been sighted in the late 1850s and 1860s. Hopkins incorporates details mentioned in contemporary reports and astronomical books in this extended metaphor. It may have

been intended to fit into a play, although Hopkins vivified many of his nature descriptions at the time by dramatizing them.

39 l. 11. *Gideon's fleece*. See Judg. 6: 36–8. The fleece that Gideon left upon the floor was soaked with dew by God as a sign that He would use Gideon to save Israel.

'No, they are come'. In Hopkins's diary this follows a description of clouds dated 14 September 1864: 'Grey clouds in knops. A curious fan of this kind of cloud radiating from a crown, and covering half the sky' (*J.* 46). Margaret Patterson suggested that Hopkins was describing cloud formations ('The Hopkins Handbook' (University of Florida dissertation, 1970), 103). MacKenzie draws attention to the overtones of the OT and classical battles. At about this time Hopkins copied into his commonplace book his father's poem, 'Clouds', in which they are used as a metaphor for memories. Part of the second verse, in which the clouds are personified though less successfully than in GMH's poem, reads:

> Around the day-king's throne the vapours stand
> And change their bright robes as he waves his wand;
> From cinnabar to crimosine
> And golden flame, and emerald green,
> While not a cloud that sails the sky
> But dons the hue in sympathy.

l. 9. Uncancelled variant: 'armed' instead of 'unsteady'.

40 l. 10. Uncancelled variants: 'Heave their unsteady columns;' *or* 'Heave through their flushing columns.'

'Now I am minded'. Immediately follows previous poem.

l. 3. *hursts*: woods.

l. 17. *hunters' moon*: the next full moon after harvest moon; approximately the third week in Oct.

A Voice from the World. June 1864–January 1865. 'But what indeed', *J.* p. 62, written between 15 May and 24 June 1865, may have been intended to fit dramatically into 'A Voice from the World'; MacKenzie suggests that it was written for insertion after line 121, and this I am following. It may mark Hopkins's deepening feeling that Rossetti's speaker's moral attitudes are unsatisfactory (see his later letter to Urquhart in which he says that he no longer wants the poem to be published. 'The objection is on the score of morality rather than of art' (*L.* III 36, Jan. 1867)). It is also in keeping with the series of expressions of self-discontent that Hopkins wrote in the summer of 1865. *L.* III 36 (Jan. 1867) suggests that Hopkins may later have completed the poem, retitled it 'Beyond the Cloister', and submitted it to *Macmillan*'s. Hopkins rendered parts of Christina Rossetti's poem 'The Convent Threshold' in Latin. MacKenzie points out that Pope's 'Eloisa to Abelard' lies behind both Christina Rossetti's and Hopkins's poems (OET 252).

41 l. 13. *bluebell sheaves.* See *J.* 22, 'sheaves of bluebells', and *J.* 209 for a more detailed description written in 1871.

43 ll. 94–5. According to Matt. 25: 31–3 at the Day of Judgement God shall judge all nations as a shepherd segregating sheep on his right hand and goats on his left. The sheep, the righteous, are to be saved while the goats will be cast into hell.

44 l. 139. *Esau's cry.* Jacob tricked Isaac into giving him the blessing intended for his elder brother Esau, which included inheriting the family's wealth. When Esau and Isaac discovered the trick, Esau cried out, 'Hast thou but one blessing, my father? bless me, even me also' (Gen. 27: 38).

45 ll. 152–4. See 2 Kgs. 5: 18. Naaman, converted after being healed of leprosy by the prophet Elisha, explained apologetically to him that he would still have to behave as if he were a believer of Rimmon when accompanying the King.

l. 155. *Bela*: Gen. 19: 19–22. A town, renamed Zoar, in which Lot, in fleeing from Sodom and Gomorrah, pleaded with God to be allowed to take refuge with his daughters. They subsequently fled into the mountains (OET 254).

l. 168. *sown with salt.* 'a conquered city was sown with salt to render it permanently barren (Judg. 9: 45)' (OET 254).

46 *For a Picture of Saint Dorothea.* November? 1864. This was the first poem Hopkins showed to Bridges (in 1866?). Hopkins later wrote an expanded dramatic version with three characters (see below).

Because Dorothea was Christian, she was tortured by the Governor of Caesarea, Sapricius. She declared that God is everywhere and that he invites us to his Paradise 'where the woods are ever adorned with fruit, and lilies ever bloom white, and roses ever flower; where the fields are green, the mountains wave with fresh grass, and the springs bubble up eternally' (S. Baring-Gould, *Lives of the Saints* (Edinburgh, 1914), February, p. 176). A lawyer called Theophilus, who was present, derisively suggested that Dorothea send him some of the heavenly apples and roses. Later, just before she was executed, Dorothea prayed that his request might be fulfilled and an angel, disguised as a beautiful youth, appeared carrying three apples and three red roses. When Theophilus received the gifts, he too became a Christian and was likewise executed. (Dorothea's feast-day is 6 February.) MS title in block capitals. In this version of the poem, as MacKenzie points out, it appears to be Dorothea herself who brings the flowers and fruit (OET 257).

46 *St. Dorothea (lines for a picture)*. Bridges has dated it 1866–8, 'Balliol College/Oxford'. Handwriting suggests late 1867–8. See notes above and below. When Hopkins sent this version to Bridges in a letter of 7 August 1868, he wrote: 'I hope you will master the peculiar beat I have introduced into St. Dorothea. The development is mine but the beat is in Shakespeare—e.g. "Whý should thís desert be?" and "Thoú for whóm Jóve would swear"—where the rest of the lines are eight-syllabled or seven-syllabled.' (*L*. I 24).

Title: Perhaps Hopkins had in mind Mrs Jameson's remark in *Sacred and Legendary Art* (2nd edn., London, 1850) that 'the principal incident of her [St. Dorothea's] legend is so picturesque and poetical that one is surprised not to meet with it oftener; in fact, I have never met with it; yet the interview between Dorothea and Theophilus, and afterwards between Theophilus and the angel, are beautiful subjects: the first scene has a tragic interest, and the latter an allegorical significance . . . ' (p. 338). Hopkins changes the traditional roses to lilies perhaps to emphasize Dorothea's purity.

48 *Lines for a Picture of St. Dorothea*. Undated. MacKenzie dates it to 1870–1 (OET 260). The poem is a later version of 'For a Picture of Saint Dorothea'.

ll. 7–12. See Philip Massinger, *The Virgin-Martyr*, Act V, Sc. i, to which Mrs Jameson alludes.

ll. 10–11. *set*: 'develop fruit' (OED).

ll. 11–12. *spring*. See *J*. 134, 'Hedges springing richly', growing rapidly, as in spring.

49 l. 20. *sizing*. It appears to increase in size as it rises above the horizon. Cf. Manley Hopkins of the sun near the horizon in his poem called 'Clouds', l. 10: 'He sinks, but gathers treble size,—'.

l. 21. *mallow-row*. See *J*. 66: 'Mallowy red of sunset and sunrise clouds'. Hopkins puns upon the fact that mallow is a plant as well as a colour.

l. 23. *Sphered*: placed 'above common reach' (OED); but with overtones of heaven and astronomy.

ll. 35–6. Cf. 'The Wreck of the Deutschland', stanza 18, for Hopkins's similar reaction to the fate of the tall nun.

l. 39. *wand*: the palm, symbol of martyrdom. Cf. 'The Wreck of the Deutschland', stanza 22, for another statement that the martyr's role is to lead men to God.

'Proved Etherege'. November? 1864.

l. 4. *The Anatomy*: Burton's *Anatomy of Melancholy*. *Politian*: Angelus Politianus, a Florentine poet and translator (OET 260).

l. 7. *gentle . . . vapour.* MacKenzie suggests this refers to Sir George Etherege, the Restoration dramatist called by Rochester 'gentle George'.

50 *Richard.* (i) First version June 1864. (ii) and (iii) December 1864; (iv) and (v) 16–24 July 1865. Hopkins applies the language and conventions of pastoral to some of his experiences and friends at university and to detailed observations of nature. Reminiscences of Matthew Arnold's 'Scholar Gypsy' are evident. Hopkins wrote to Baillie that he had begun a story to be called 'Richard' (*L.* III 213–14, 20 July–14 August 1864). Written in Spenserian stanza (OET 260).

(i) l. 4. Uncancelled variant: 'The listening downs and breezes seemed he.'

l. 8. *drinking*: later alternative to 'one drunk' (uncancelled).

l. 9. *True*: later alternative to 'In' (uncancelled).

l. 10. *forehead*: later alternative to 'frontal' (uncancelled).

(ii) l. 17. *Arcadia*: an area of the Peloponnese, which in literature has been associated with shepherds.

Haemony: Haemonia, ancient name of Thessaly (OET 260).

51 (iv) l. 9. *Cumnor hill*: west of Oxford; cf. Arnold, 'The Scholar-Gipsy': 'And watch the warm, green-muffled Cumner hills', l. 69.

52 *'All as that moth'*. December 1864.

l. 3. *underplighted*: underwoven.

l. 5. *watchet*: pale blue. *foiling*: from 'foil': 'anything that sets something off by contrast' (OED).

53 *The Queen's Crowning.* December 1864. Ballad-like stories were extremely popular in the Victorian period, as can be seen, for example, by the sheer number of them printed in *Once a Week*, the journal in which a number of Manley Hopkins's poems were published and to which the family subscribed. Humphry House compares the poem to the Scottish ballad, 'Sweet William's Ghost' (*J.* 358). MacKenzie comments on Hopkins's use of such ballad techniques as the abrupt move from incident to incident and the omission of unnecessary background information (OET 262). Much of the poem's effect derives from its simple, but telling diction.

54 l. 57. *happ'd*: from 'hap', to cover.

58 *For Stephen and Barberie.* January 1865. Cf. Tennyson's poem, 'Mariana'.

l. 5. *descend*: conjectural: the MS is badly smudged here, but de . . . is visible.

l. 7. *size*: 'to assume size, to increase in size' (OED). Hopkins uses it several times: cf. 'Lines for a Picture of St. Dorothea', l. 20, and 'The May Magnificat', l. 25, 'all things sizing'.

58 ll. 13–14. *Willow*: a traditional, Elizabethan song of unrequited love. See *Othello*, IV. iii.

'Boughs being pruned'. January 1865.

l. 2. *squinches*: 'masonry built across the top corners of a tower to support the oblique sides of a spire' (Francis Bond, *An Introduction to English Church Architecture* (London, 1913), i, p. xxvii).

l. 3. *chamfer'd*: 'an edge of wood or stone sliced off in a sloping direction' (ibid., p. xxi).

l. 8. *lessen'd mill*: with edges worn.

'When eyes that cast'. February 1865. Another example of Hopkins's exploration of the relative importance of the perceiving mind in controlling what one sees. Here, because the bird, probably a skylark, is not initially seen, the mind is tricked into mislocating the source of its song. Once the bird is seen, the mind co-ordinates the impressions of the two senses. Cf. 'The rainbow' and 'All as that moth'.

59 *The Summer Malison*. February or March 1865.

malison: curse.

l. 2. cattle breaking out of their field.

l. 6 recalls Pharaoh's dream of the seven ears of good corn that were destroyed by seven ears of poor corn, which Joseph interpreted as seven years of plenty followed by seven years of famine (Gen. 41).

lodgèd: laid flat by the weather.

l. 9. *where winds are dead*: becalmed.

l. 14. *clayfield's sharded sores*: clay, perhaps intended for making bricks, rendered useless because it is so dry it peels into fragments.

St. Thecla. The poem was probably originally written in 1864–5 (OET 265).

St Thecla is considered to be the first female martyr. Mrs Jameson notes that 'such was the veneration paid to this saint in the East, and in the early ages of Christianity, that it was considered the greatest praise that could be given a woman to compare her to St. Thecla' (*Sacred and Legendary Art* (2nd edn., London, 1850), 329).

Thecla, who lived at Iconium, was engaged to be married, but, overhearing Paul preaching, was converted and abandoned her former plans to follow him. She was subsequently sentenced as a Christian to be burned at the stake but was rescued. Later, when she was recaptured, she was sentenced to be thrown to wild beasts but was again miraculously saved. She was known as the Virgin Thecla and was famous for her purity and her ability to heal the sick. Hopkins focuses on the initial impression made on Thecla by Paul's preaching and implies in the last line both the depth of her new conviction and the brutal opposition with which it would meet from the social world to which she had till then belonged.

60 l. 8. *Pegasus*: the winged horse sent by the gods to help Bellerophon fight the Chimaera. After killing the monster, Bellerophon is said to have tried to fly to heaven to join the gods and, for this presumptuous act, Jove sent a gadfly that tormented Pegasus into unseating Bellerophon, who was lamed by the fall.

l. 9. *were none*: were mythological, not real.

l. 10. Paul was from Tarsus (Acts 22: 3).

Easter Communion. Lent 1865. First draft written 2–12 March; text from copy of 26 June. Miltonic sonnet. The poem promises heavenly and spiritual rewards celebrated at Easter to those who have fasted (l. 1), chastised themselves (ll. 3–5), dressed in poor and uncomfortable clothes (ll. 6–7, 10–11), and spent long hours in prayer (ll. 8–13) during Lent in remembrance of Christ's fasting in the wilderness. MacKenzie remarks that the poem reflects Hopkins's 'intentions more accurately than his practice' (OET 266).

ll. 5–6. Cancelled variant: 'You whom the pursuant cold so wastes and nips.'

61 l. 12. Cancelled variants include: 'Give change of fragrant-threaded gold raiment.'

'O Death, Death'. March 1865. See the Apostle's Creed: 'He descended into Hell. The third day he rose again . . . He ascended into Heaven . . . '. Cf. 'The Wreck of the Deutschland', st. 33.

ll. 8–10. See Ps. 24: 9: 'Lift up your heads, O ye gates; even lift *them* up, ye everlasting doors; and the King of glory shall come in.'

'Love me as I love thee'. March 1865. A translation of an anonymous Greek original.

To Oxford (*a*) and (*b*). Dated 'Low Sunday and Monday, 1865' (23 and 24 April). Hopkins sent Addis transcriptions, now all lost, of both these sonnets and 'Easter Communion'. Hopkins wrote of the drafts: they 'are not quite right'. He later told Dixon that he had 'been very fond' of Oxford (*L*. II 12) and commented to Baillie that 'not to love my University would be to undo the very buttons of my being' (*L*. III 244). That pleasure and love is very evident in the first of these poems, which, using terms of courtly love, pictures Oxford as the lady. Hopkins makes the point that the 'charms of Oxford' are 'private as well as public property' (Bremer, 'Sonnets of 1865', 77). The second sonnet gives a specific example of how a particular sight can have a private as well as a shared value. In the process Hopkins comments on the effect on perception of the perceiving mind, the subjective element in our experience of the physical world.

61 (*a*) l. 1. Roughly paraphrased as 'freshly with each term of the repeated cycle of the academic year'; returning to Oxford after each vacation away from it, he is struck afresh by how he loves being there.

62 l. 6. *pleasaunce*: 'archaic. pleasure-ground, esp. one attached to a mansion' (OED).

l. 10. *towers musical*: college bell towers.

l. 11. *window-circles*: rose windows.

(continued) (*b*) l. 5. *visual compulsion*: optical illusion.

To Oxford (*c*). Copied out in 26 June 1865 but its subject-matter suggests composition earlier in the year (OET 268). Hopkins noted above the poem that he had given a copy to V. S. S. Coles, and below it 'the last two lines I have forgotten and must get'. Hopkins recognizes in the poem the pleasure that Balliol men get when not in Oxford from news of their college friends.

63 l. 6. *Belleisle*: Balliol (Mrs E. E. Duncan-Jones).

l. 9. *'As when . . . blest'*: Tennyson, 'A Dream of Fair Woman', l. 281.

'Where art thou friend'. 25–7 April 1865. The friend addressed may well be a reader who has an interest in Christianity (see R. Bremer, 'Where art thou friend . . . ', *Hopkins Quarterly*, 7/1 (spring 1980), 9–14). Hopkins's premiss in the sonnet is that the function of his poetry is to bring readers closer to Christ.

l. 3. Uncancelled variant: 'Either unknown to me in the age that is'.

l. 14. Uncancelled variant: 'No, no, no, but for Christ who knew and loved thee.'

'Confirmed beauty'. April 1865. In sympathizing with Dixon's loss of pleasure in Tennyson's poetry, Hopkins speculated on more general reasons for 'the loss of taste, of relish for what once charmed us' (*L.* II 38, 22 Dec. 1880): 'I understand that state of mind well enough; it used at one time to dismay and dishearten me deeply, it made the best of things seem empty. I think that many things contribute to it and play a part. One is a real disenchantment, the correction of the earlier untrained judgment or taste by the maturer one . . . Another is the shortcoming of faculty in us, because the enchanting power in the work is finite or because the mind after a certain number of shocks or stimuli . . . is spent and flags. . . . Another is that insight is more sensitive . . . earlier in life than later and especially towards elementary impressions: I remember that crimson and pure blues seemed to

me spiritual and heavenly sights fit to draw tears once . . . Another is . . . the greater impatience with technical faults.' Although the other reasons are relevant to the thought of the sonnet, it is largely about the second of the factors leading to disillusion, the slaking of appreciation through over-exposure (Bremer, 'Sonnets of 1865', 99).

l. 5. *Tantalean.* In Greek mythology Tantalus was punished by the gods either for stealing their sacred nectar or for killing his son as a sacrifice. He was placed in a pool up to his chin but the water receded whenever he tried to quench his thirst, and ripe fruit dangling from a bough above his head evaded his reach.

l. 6. *Pharaoh's ears.* See Gen. 41: 6. See 'The Summer Malison', l. 6 n. above.

64 ll. 11–14. The implications of disenchantment with literature here reverse the trope at the end of many of Shakespeare's sonnets that literature can give enduring 'life' to the beloved.

The Beginning of the End. Subtitled 'a neglected lover's address to his mistress'. 6–8 May 1865. Cf. Meredith's *Modern Love.* Many critics have suspected that behind the dramatic situation of these sonnets lies Hopkins's feelings at the time for Digby Mackworth Dolben or Susan Bond, sister of Hopkins's friend Edward Bond (M. Patterson, 'The Hopkins' Handbook', 2 vols. (University of Florida diss., 1970), 127, and Bremer, 'Sonnets of 1865', 119). The first sonnet is followed by:

> Some men may hate their rivals and desire
> Secretive moats, knives, smothering-cloths, drugs, flame;
> But I am so consumèd with my shame
> I dare feel envy scarcely, never ire.
> O worshipful the man that she sets higher

Bridges noted that the sonnets were 'in Italian form and Shakespearian mood (refused by *Cornhill Magazine*) . . .' .

65 (iii) ll. 13–14. See note to 'Confirmed Beauty'.

The Alchemist in the City. 15 May 1865. In this dramatic monologue there are expressions very similar to those found in Hopkins's confession notes of the time of self-dissatisfaction and self-doubt. A feeling of being under pressure to succeed (ll. 33 ff.) also seems evident. Hopkins's choice of an alchemist as persona may have implications of dissatisfaction over his moral state, since alchemists' success was said to depend in part on their moral state. Cf. Browning's 'Andrea del Sarto' for another exploration of the relationship between an artist's personality and success, and Milton's sonnet 'How soon hath Time' for a feeling of insufficient achievement.

66 l. 14. *not to be discover'd gold*: gold that is made alchemically rather than discovered by prospecting.

l. 26. *levant sun*: 'rising' (OED).

l. 39. *terebinth*. Often referred to in the Bible as 'oaks', terebinths were chosen places for burial and 'Victorian travellers described [them] as standing isolated in bare ravines or on hillsides, the object of veneration' (OET 275). MacKenzie also notes that they are mentioned in Virgil's *Aeneid* (x. 136) and Theocritus (Ep. 1. 6).

67 *'Myself unholy'*. June 1865. Reminiscent in its self-discontent of Shakespeare's sonnet xxix 'When, in disgrace with Fortune and men's eyes', but instead of finding satisfaction in his lover, as Shakespeare's speaker flatteringly suggests, Hopkins turns to Christ.

l. 4. Cancelled variant: 'White clouds to furnace-eaten regions coaly:'.

l. 7. Cancelled variants: 'And so my trust confusedly is shook.' and 'confidence is struck and shook.'

ll. 9–14. Cancelled variant:

He has a fault of mine, he its near brother,
And part I like and part I hate the fall;
            is sweet to me and part is gall;
In him this fault I found, in him another:
And though they each have one and I have all,
This time it serves not. I can seek no other
Than Christ: to Christ I look, on Christ I call.

'See how Spring opens'. Dated 26 June 1865. The poem may well be about Hopkins's dissatisfaction over his moral state and his conviction that ingrained habit hampered his attempts to live a moral and spiritual life. See N. H. MacKenzie, *G. M. Hopkins: Early Poetic Manuscripts and Notebooks* (London, 1989), 173–5, for example, for Hopkins's note of his sins. There are echoes in imagery of Milton's sonnet, 'How soon hath Time'.

l. 7. See Matt. 13.

l. 14. *learnt how late, the truth*. After he had become a Catholic in 1866 Hopkins wrote: 'The silent conviction that I was to become a Catholic has been present to me for a year perhaps, as strongly, in spite of my resistance to it . . . as if I had already determined it' (*L*. III 27). His note on 12 March 1865, 'A day of the great mercy of God', may relate to his new conviction.

68 *Continuation of R. Garnet's* [*recte* Garnett's] *'Nix'*. June–July 1865. Hopkins read Richard Garnett's 'Nix' in *The Children's Garland from the Best Poets*, edited by Coventry Patmore (1862). Hopkins inaccurately quoted this version of the poem, which differed slightly from

the original version, in his Platonic dialogue, 'On the Origin of Beauty' (printed *J.* 111). Hopkins's poem questions what it is in a beloved's appearance that attracts a lover.

69 *'O what a silence'*. August 1865. The poem occurs shortly after sketches and descriptions of the sky observed while on holiday in Devon and at Hampstead.

l. 3. *skylark*. See 'The Sea and the Skylark', pp. 116 and 210.

traverse flight: 'the skylark, once he has reached his ceiling, wanders horizontally above his territory' (OET 278).

'Mothers are doubtless'. August 1865.

l. 4. Very faint; 'come to' amended to 'hold to' (OET 277).

70 *Daphne*. Dated 1 September 1865. This song and the dialogue of the next few pages are all fragments of Hopkins's unfinished play, 'Castara Victrix'.

l. 15 *knopt*: studded with knobs, here fruit; also used of flower-buds.

Castara Victrix. Begun August 1865. These speeches from Hopkins's unfinished play were written in September 1865. Hopkins listed the characters: '*Castara Victrix* or *Castara Felix*. Silvan, the king, and his two sons Arcas and Valerian. Carindel. The Fool. Carabella. Pirellia, Piers Sweetgale, Daphnis. Daphne.

The melancholy Daphne doats on him.' (*J.* 65)

Possibly influenced by Shakespeare's *As You Like It*.

72 *'My prayers must meet a brazen heaven'*. 7 September 1865. MacKenzie suggests Deut. 28: 23 and Lev. 26: 19, the effects of sin will be no rain—heavens hot brass without rain clouds, and the earth parched hard. Cf. Manley Hopkins: 'Though the earth be iron, the heaven seem brass' ('Prayer'). Hopkins used similar terms a number of times: 'sky anointed with warm brassy glow' (*J.* 212) and 'The sun just risen | Flares his wet brilliance in the dintless heaven' (*J.* 58). Many of Hopkins's confession notes at the time record failures in carrying out his daily reading of religious works and insufficient attention during prayers and religious services. Cf. 'See how Spring opens' above and such late poems as 'Carrion Comfort' and 'Thou art indeed just, Lord'.

73 *Shakspere*. 13 September 1865. There had been numerous celebrations of the tercentenary of Shakespeare's birth in 1864. This poem seems to imply that there are two independent standards: worldly achievement and moral rectitude. Hopkins would later set out their relative importance in such poems of his own as 'How all is one way wrought', and assess his friends' poems against both standards.

ll. 5–7. A statement of the difficulty of gauging worldly achievement, a problem that Hopkins had been grappling with over the previous two years.

73 l. 8. *aureoles*: 'glorifying haloes' (OED). After criticizing Tennyson in a letter to Baillie of 10 September 1864, Hopkins wrote: 'Inconsequent conclusion: Shakespear is and must be utterly the greatest of poets' (*L.* III 219).

'Trees by their yield'. 28 September 1865. Above the poem Hopkins wrote: 'A verse or more has to be prefixed'.

ll. 1–2. See Luke 6: 44: 'For every tree is known by his own fruit. For of thorns men do not gather figs, nor of a bramble bush gather they grapes.' Cf. 'New Readings', l. 2.

ll. 5–6, 8. Cf. Milton's sonnet, 'How soon hath Time'.

74 *'Let me be to Thee'*. 22 October 1865. In Hopkins's diary this follows shortly after his copy of J. H. Newman's 'Lead kindly light'. Hopkins's list of sins at the time (MacKenzie, *Hopkins: Early Poetic Manuscripts and Notebooks*, 190, 'Unwisely speaking long ab[ou]t leaving our Church . . . Repeated forecasting about Ch[urch] of Rome', for example) shows that he was thinking about converting to Catholicism. The poem seems to express his conviction of the validity of the Roman Catholic Church, drawing parallels between types of music and religious sects.

l. 9. *authentic cadence*. 'The perfect (formerly termed Authentic) Cadence, or Full Close, consists of the Major Triad on the Dominant, followed by the Triad on the Tonic' (OED, citing Banister, *Music*).

l. 14. Cf. the last of the Ignation Spiritual Exercises, which urges the exercitant to seek a great and abiding love for God (Downes, *Gerard Manley Hopkins*, 110). MacKenzie draws attention to Hopkins's letter to his father defending his decision to join the Roman Church, in which he says: 'the Catholic system . . . only wants to be known in order to be loved' (*L.* III 93, 16 Oct. 1866) (OET 281). See also notes to 'The Half-way House' below.

75 *The Half-way House*. October 1865. In Hopkins's diary this follows the previous poem. The title may come from Newman's statement in the *Apologia* that Anglicanism is the half-way house between atheism and Roman Catholicism (see Sulloway, 18). Here, however, as MacKenzie points out, the Catholic Church is the half-way house to heaven (OET 282).

l. 7. *Egyptian reed*. See Isa. 36: 6. The image suggests Hopkins's resolve to leave the Anglican Church (the national religion).

l. 8. *vine*. See John 15: 1–10.

ll. 17–18. Hopkins wrote to E. H. Coleridge (1 June 1864): 'The great aid to belief and object of belief is the doctrine of the Real Presence in the Blessed Sacrament of the Altar. Religion without that is sombre, dangerous, illogical, with that it is—not to speak of its grand consistency and certainty—*loveable*. Hold that and you will gain all Catholic truth!' (*L.* III 17). 'Catholic' is used broadly here and includes Tractarians. To his father, Hopkins wrote: 'I shall hold as a Catholic what I have long held as an Anglican, that literal truth of our Lord's words by which I learn that the least fragment of the consecrated elements in the Blessed Sacrament of the Altar is the whole Body of Christ born of the Blessed Virgin, before which the whole host of saints and angels as it lies on the altar trembles with adoration. This belief once got is the life of the soul and when I doubted it I shd. become an atheist the next day' (*L.* III 92, 16 Oct. 1866).

A Complaint. Hopkins wrote to Bridges (*L.* I 87, 14 Aug. 1879): 'I had quite forgotten the sonnet you have found but can now recall almost all of it; not so the other piece, birthday lines to my sister, I fancy.' Hopkins had forgotten Milicent's birthday (17 October) in 1863 (*L.* III 84) and it may have been on this occasion that the poem was written, although late 1865 is also a strong possibility.

76 *'Moonless darkness'*. 25 December 1865, based, as MacKenzie notes, on the first Anglican lesson for Christmas—Isa. 9: 2, 6: 'The people that walked in darkness have seen a great light . . . For unto us a child is born' (OET 283). Written in Hopkins's diary among long lists of such sins as idleness, lewdness, quarrelsomeness, indulgence.

'The earth and heaven'. 5 January 1866. The poem is still in a fairly rudimentary form, with some halting lines and unsatisfactory syntax. Its ideas centre on the relativity of each thing with regard to its surroundings. N. H. MacKenzie cites Plato (*Theaetetus* 151 ff., 161, 171, 181 ff., and *Timaeus* 40–50) and Heraclitus' concept of the continual flux of the elements (OET 283). See notes to 'That Nature is a Heraclitean Fire . . . ', p. 247.

l. 9. *'favourite . . . gale'*: cancelled and not replaced.

77 *The Nightingale*. Dated 'Jan. 18, 19, 1866'.

79 ll. 54–6. Cf. Tennyson, *In Memoriam*, VI (Mariani, 35) and Surrey, 'O happy dames that may embrace'.

The Habit of Perfection. Two autographs. (i) dated 'Jan. 18, 19, 1866', subtitled '(The Novice)'; (ii) later, perhaps contemporary with the text of 'Heaven-Haven'. Mariani draws attention to the positive results of the self-denial of each of the senses, eloquence coming from 'lovely-dumb lips', darkness leading to 'the uncreated light', etc. (p. 36).

80 *Nondum*. Dated Lent 1866. Title means 'not yet'.

ll. 1–6. See Tennyson, *In Memoriam*, LVI.

ll. 7–12. Cf. Tennyson, *In Memoriam*, CXXIV.

ll. 19–24. See Gen. 1: 1–13.

81 l. 27. *Deep calls to deep.* See Ps. 42: 7.

Easter. 1866?

l. 1. *nard*: spikenard, an expensive oil sold in alabaster boxes. See Mark 14: 3–8 and John 12: 3–8.

l. 3. *sard*: either sardius: 'a semi-precious stone mentioned by ancient writers' (OED) or chalcedony.

82 l. 21. MS reads 'disshevelled'.

Summa. 'Written when GMH was an undergraduate' (Bridges). Hopkins burnt the original when he became a Jesuit (see *L.* I 24). Summa: 'the summary of what is known of a subject' (OED). Although incomplete, the thought in the poem seems to have been developing in part along lines similar to those in a letter Hopkins wrote to E. H. Coleridge (*L.* III 19–20, 22 Jan. 1866) in which he wrote: 'You said . . . yr. repugnance was to view the issues of eternity as depending on anything so trivial and inadequate as life is . . . it is incredible and intolerable if there is nothing wh. is the reverse of trivial and will correct and avenge the triviality of this life . . . the trivialness of life is . . . done away with by the Incarnation—or, I shd, say the difficulty wh. the trivialness of life presents ought to be. It is one adorable point of the incredible condescension of the Incarnation . . . that our Lord submitted not only to the pains of life . . . but also to the mean and trivial accidents of humanity.' The other strand of thought evident in the poem concerns the relation of worldly success to spiritual wellbeing. This was one of the knottiest moral problems Hopkins faced in his life and the subject occupies numerous poems and letters (cf., for example, 'To seem the stranger', 'The times are nightfall', 'Thou art indeed just, Lord').

83 ll. 6–8. See *L.* III 19–20.

l. 13. *gaze*: sb., not verb.

Jesu Dulcis Memoria. Written in pencil and ink on two sheets, undated, no title, a number of variants. On one page Hopkins drafted in pencil a translation of the Latin hymn as it appears initially in the Roman breviary. The verses are part of a much longer hymn originally attributed to St Bernard and now thought to have been written by an English Cistercian of the twelfth century (see *The Oxford Book of Medieval Latin Verse*, ed. F. J. E. Raby (Oxford, 1959), 347–53, 493–4). Using other verses from this source there are in the breviary two more hymns, 'Jesu, Rex admirabilis' and 'Jesu, decus angelicum'. Hopkins has on the verso and other sheet translated five further stanzas, mostly from the third hymn but generally in no special order. Because Hopkins's intended sequence is not clear and the later verses cannot be appended to the first hymn, the stanzas are printed in the order of the original Latin hymn with stanzas 5 and 4 transposed and the addition of the final verse. Hopkins has not translated the first line of stanza 8. For the history of the hymn see *Dictionary of Hymnology*, ed. John Julian (London, 1892). Stanzas 1, 2, 3, 4, 10 form 'Jesu dulcis memoria' in the breviary. Stanza 5 is found in 'Jesu, Rex admirabilis'. Among Hopkins's variants are:

ll. 5–7. Song never was so sweet in ear,
Word never was such news to hear,
Thought half so sweet there is not one
There's no such touching music heard,
There's never spoke so glad a word,
So sweet a thought there is not one.

ll. 17–20. Jesu, like dainties to the heart
Daylight or running brooks Thou art,
And matched with Thee there's nothing glad
That can be wished or can be had.

84 *'Not kind! to freeze me'*. Written in pencil on one of seven sheets on which Hopkins drafted a translation of Horace's ode, 'Odi profanum volgus'. The sheet contains the beginning of a letter to Hopkins's aunt, Laura Hodges (with whom he stayed in January 1868). Like 'Odi profanum volgus', the poem was probably written early in 1868 during Hopkins's final term of teaching at the Oratory, Birmingham. It is, as MacKenzie and R. Kilpatrick have shown (*Classical and Modern Literature*, 5/1 (Fall 1984)), a spirited translation of Horace, *Odes*, Book II, xvii, ll. 1–4.

85 *Horace: 'Persicos odi'*. Autograph undated, on four pages of notepaper. One of the sheets contains part of a letter mentioning the visits of Fr. Ignatius Ryder to the Oratory, and concludes: 'I do not expect to be long here: if I get a vocation to the priesthood I should go away . . .' (see *J.* 534 and *L.* III 52–5). Probably translated at the Oratory between November 1867 and Easter 1868 (*J.* 534). I am indebted to R. G. M. Nisbet and Margaret Hubbard for the following notes based on their *Commentary on Horace: Odes*, Book I (Oxford, 1970), 421–7. The poem, placed at the end of Book I, is a characteristic request for a simple style of life without luxury and ostentation.

l. 1. *child*: wine-server. There was a tradition in Greek literature of addresses to slaves.

Persian-perfect. Persia was associated with luxury.

85 l. 2. *bast*: a membrane below the bark of lime trees, used as string to bind together elaborate garlands.

l. 5. *myrtle*: a very common plant. Flowers were often interwoven to decorate garlands of it.

l. 6. Myrtle was said to dispel the fumes of wine. Hopkins does not bring out Horace's implication that he too, like the wine-server, is still handsome enough to show off a simple garland.

l. 8. *tackled*: fastened to a pergola.

Horace: 'Odi profanum volgus'. Pencil drafts on seven sides. Stanza I follows 'Not kind! to freeze me'. Probably translated early in 1868.

l. 2. Earlier read: 'Grace guard your tongues! . . . '

l. 4. *make*: earlier read 'bid'.

ll. 9–10. Earlier read:

Say man than man may more enclose
In rankèd vineyards

86 l. 21 was rewritten 'Sleep that comes light and not afraid', but the 'linkage of this line with stanza 5 seems to us too elliptical for adoption in the text' (*Poems*, 322).

I am indebted to Gordon Williams for the following notes based on his commentary on *The Third Book of Horace's Odes* (Oxford, 1969).

ll. 1–2. Two commands were given at the beginning of solemn rites: uninitiated listeners were warned to stay away and those remaining were asked to be silent.

ll. 9–16. These lines describe differences between men during life, but l. 16 shows that death takes all.

l. 17. The sword which Dionysius suspended above Damocles' head.

l. 18. Sicilian banquets were proverbial.

ll. 21–32. Unlike the rich man with many crops or ships, the simple countryman can sleep without worry.

l. 24. *Tempe*: a valley renowned for its beautiful, shady trees and singing birds.

l. 28. Stars signalling the beginning and end of stormy winter.

l. 31. The dog-star was associated with heat-waves.

ll. 33–4. Hyperbole suggesting that the many luxurious villas built into the sea encroach upon the fish.

ll. 35–6, 37–40. Anxious, rich men try in vain to divert themselves with luxurious yachts.

l. 41. *Phrygian stone*: a prized marble.

l. 42. Expensive clothes.

l. 43. *Falernian-grown*: wine.

l. 44. *oils of Shushan*: Persian balsam.

87 *The Elopement*. The Revd D. A. Bishoff, SJ writes: 'Early in 1868, two of the fifth form of the Oratory School, Edgbaston, Birmingham, joined with one of the junior masters, J. Scott Stokes, in editing a weekly journal called *The Early Bird* or *The Tuesday Tomtit*. Each issue was limited to three handwritten copies, the first appearing on 18 February 1868. It suffered an early death. One of the issues, however, carried these verses by G. M. H., then a junior master at Dr J. H. Newman's school; they were followed by a parody, "The Robbery", written by R. Bellais and W. Sparrow. The original handwritten copies have disappeared. The only record of these verses is found in an anonymous essay, "Early Magazines", *The Oratory School Magazine*, No. 13, Nov. 1895, pp. 5–8' (*Poems*, 309).

l. 1. *rud red*: the colour of red ochre. See 'The Woodlark', l. 31 (p. 122).

l. 19. Magazine omits hyphen, 'to-night' (OET 300).

ll. 19–22. These use with little variation a quatrain that Hopkins wrote in January 1866:

The stars were packed so close that night
  They seemed to press and stare
And gather in like hurdles bright
  The liberties of air.

l. 21. *hurdle*: fence. See 'The Starlight Night', l. 13, for a similar idea.

l. 22. *liberties*: the district over which a person's or corporation's privilege extends (now archaic).

l. 30. Magazine places stop at end of line (OET 300).

88 *Oratio Patris Condren*. No date. The poem is a translation of 'a prayer by Fr. Condren of the French Congregation of the Oratory of St. Philip Neri'. The principal variant is ll. 5–6:

In those most perfect ways Thou wendest,
In the virtues of that life Thou spendest,

l. 4. *fulness* in all MSS.

l. 10. *Holy Ghost the Paraclete*. See *S*. 69–71.

Ad Mariam. No manuscripts extant. Printed in *Stonyhurst Magazine* (Feb. 1894) and in *Blandyke Papers*, 26 (May 1890). Attributed to Hopkins. MacKenzie suggests that it was written in 1873 (OET 305–6). The metre is that of Swinburne's 'When the hounds of spring' from *Atalanta in Calydon*. See Schneider, *The Dragon in the Gate*, 50–7.

89 l. 23. *Aidenn*: Eden (Hebrew).

O Deus, ego amo te. Three undated, fair copies, all slightly different. Two titled 'St. Francis Xavier's Hymn' are headed AMDG. Handwriting of two of the manuscripts suggests that they date from the early 1870s. Text from the third version, written later below the end of 'S. Thomae Aquinatis Rhythmus'. Hopkins also wrote a version in Welsh titled 'Ochenaid Sant Francis Xavier; Apostol yr Indiaid' (printed OA 125 and OET 136).

l. 7. *nails and lance*. MS repeats 'lance' in mistake.

ll. 7–8. Earlier read:

> For me didst bear the nails, the lance,
> And the shaming out of countenance,

90 *Rosa Mystica*. Probably one of the two or three presentation pieces mentioned in a letter to R. W. Dixon (5 Oct. 1878).

l. 1. MacKenzie notes: 'Because the Virgin Mary was devoid of original sin, she was traditionally referred to as the Mystical Rose—the rose as it was before the Fall, before sin brought thorns into the world (Gen. 3: 18)' (OET 308–9).

ll. 9–10. Cf. 'The Wreck of the Deutschland', st. 7.

91 ll. 37–40. Cf. 'The Wreck of the Deutschland', sts. 22 and 23.

92 *On St. Winefred*. Text from autograph, headed AMDG with LDS written below. Hopkins also wrote the poem in Latin. Hopkins described a visit to the well on 8 October 1874: 'Barraud and I walked over to Holywell and bathed at the well and returned very joyously. The sight of the water in the well as clear as glass, greenish like beryl or aquamarine, trembling at the surface with the force of the springs, and shaping out the five foils of the well quite drew and held my eyes to it . . . The strong unfailing flow of the water and the chain of cures from year to year all these centuries took hold of my mind with wonder at the bounty of God in one of His saints, the sensible thing so naturally and gracefully uttering the spiritual reason of its being (which is all in true keeping with the story of St. Winefred's death and recovery) and the spring in place leading back the thoughts by its spring in time to its spring in eternity: even now the stress and buoyancy and abundance of the water is before my eyes' (*J.* 261).

S. Thomae Aquinatis Rhythmus. Four drafts with numerous variants: (i) an early draft of the complete text; (ii) a much revised draft of stanzas 5–7 (cancelled); (iii) a fair copy of the first 3½ stanzas; (iv) text, a late draft with alterations, ending above 'O Deus, ego amo te'. On an attached page Hopkins noted: 'This is what I sent to Mr. Orby Shipley—

> Godhead, I adore thee fast in hiding; thou
> God in these bare shapes, poor shadows, darkling now: etc.'

This alters the first two lines of (iv), which read:

> Godhead here in hiding, whom I do adore
> Masked by these bare shadows, shape and nothing more,

Title from (iii).

l. 10. Hopkins wrote to E. H. Coleridge (22 Jan. 1866): 'It is one adorable point of the incredible condescension of the Incarnation (the greatness of which no saint can have ever hoped to realise) that our Lord submitted not only to the pains of life, the fasting, scourging, crucifixion etc. or the insults, as the mocking, blindfolding, spitting etc, but also to the mean and trivial accidents of humanity' (*L.* III 19).

l. 12. *the prayer of the dying thief.* See Luke 23: 42–3: 'And he [the dying thief] said unto Jesus, Lord, remember me when thou comest into thy kingdom. And Jesus said unto him, Verily I say unto thee, To day shalt thou be with me in paradise.'

l. 13. See John 20: 24–9.

93 l. 21. Uncancelled variant:

> Bring the tender tale true of the Pelican;

l. 25. 'shrouded' and 'veilèd' are bracketed as equal alternatives.

94 *Author's Preface.*

this book: MS *B* (see p. xxi).

Running Rhythm. Hopkins used also the term 'Standard Rhythm'.

Stress, Slack. In the following notes the stress = ′ and the slack = ˣ or ˣˣ etc.

Logaoedic Rhythm. Elisabeth Schneider (*The Dragon in the Gate*, 50–7) shows that Hopkins may well have been influenced by Swinburne's use of the metre in his *Atalanta in Calydon*. Line 3 from 'Ad Mariam' shows Hopkins's use:

Líes in the | bréast of the | yóung year- | móther

Counterpoint Rhythm. First heard in 'God's Grandeur':

'Generations have trod, have trod, have trod,' (l. 5) (*Poems*, 46).

95 *Milton is the great master.* For Hopkins's examples of Counterpoint Rhythm in *Paradise Lost* and *Paradise Regained*, see *L.* I 38 and *L.* II 15 (*Poems*, 47).

95 *monosyllable . . . First Paeon*. e.g. in 'The Wreck of the Deutschland' (only the stressed syllables are marked in MSS):

(*a*) Monosyllabic feet:

'The sour scythe cringe, and the blear share come,' (l. 88).

(*b*) Paeons: paeonic lines often incorporate shorter feet too.

'Startle the poor sheep back! is the shipwrack then a harvest, does tempest carry the grain for thee?' (l. 248).

In example (*a*) the caesura breaks the third foot. Note the extended fifth foot in (*b*) and cf. line 6 of the same stanza (*Poems*, 47).

96 *rove over*. 'if a strong word and its epithet or other appendage are divided so that the appendage shall end one line and the supporting word begin the next, the last becomes emphasised by position and heads a fall-away or diminuendo. These little graces help the "over-reaving" of the verse at which I so much aim, make it flow in one long strain to the end of the stanza and so forth' (*L*. I 86, 14 Aug. 1879).

Echos, second line. See p. 138.

a principle needless to explain here. See note to 'Hurrahing in Harvest', p. 214.

counterpointed rhythm. See note to 'Harry Ploughman', p. 244 and *L*. I 43: 'Please remark the difference between ∞, which means a counterpoint, and ⌢ , a circumflex, over words like he͡re, hea͡r, the͡re, bea͡r, to express that they are made to approach two syllables—he-ar etc. No, it should be ~, not ⌢.' *nursery rhymes*. See *L*. II 14 (5 Oct. 1878).

97 *this book*: MS *B* (p. xxi). *Nos* 1 *and* 25. 'Pied Beauty' and 'Peace'.

98 *The Wreck of the Deutschland*.

Metrical marks: l. 13 ho͡ur l. 112 endũred l. 272 A͡ released.

Hopkins wrote to R. W. Dixon about the poem's history, 'when in the winter of '75 the Deutschland was wrecked in the mouth of the Thames and five Franciscan nuns, exiles from Germany by the Falck Laws, aboard of her were drowned I was affected by the account and happening to say so to my rector he said that he wished someone would write a poem on the subject. On this hint I set to work and, though my hand was out at first, produced one. I had long had haunting my ear the echo of a new rhythm which now I realized on paper. To speak shortly, it consists in scanning by accents or stresses alone, without any account of the number of syllables, so that a foot may be one strong syllable or it may be many light and one strong. I do not say the idea is altogether new; there are hints of it in music, in nursery rhymes and popular jingles, in the poets themselves, and, since then, I have seen it talked about as a thing possible in critics . . . But no one has professedly used it and made it the principle throughout, that I know of. Nevertheless to me it appears, I own, to be a better and more natural principle than the ordinary system, much more flexible, and capable of much greater effects. However I had to mark the stresses in blue chalk, and this and my rhymes carried on from one line into another and certain chimes suggested by the Welsh poetry I had been reading (what they call *cynghanedd*) and a great many more oddnesses could not but dismay an editor's eye, so that when I offered it to our magazine the *Month*, though at first they accepted it, after a time they withdrew and dared not print it' (*L.* II 14–15, 5 Oct. 1878). Accounts of the wreck given in *The Times* on 11 and 18 December 1875 can be found in Note F, pp. 439–43 of *L.* III.

The poem is one of conversion, telling about Hopkins's own conversion, narrating the story of the wreck and the tall nun's reaction to it, which Hopkins, following a hint in Cardinal Manning's funeral sermon for the nuns, believed had led to conversions among the shipwrecked passengers, and finally urging the conversion to Catholicism of the nation and all readers of the poem. The first Part, in which Hopkins speaks about his own experience and sets out his understanding of the relationship between God and man, establishes how the second, narrative Part is to be read. Bridges disliked the poem. To him Hopkins made several important comments about it: 'I may add . . . that what refers to myself in the poem is all strictly and literally true and did all occur; nothing is added for poetical padding' (*L.* I 47, 21 Aug. 1877). 'The Deutschland would be more generally interesting if there were more wreck and less discourse, I know, but still it is an ode and not primarily a narrative. There is some narrative in Pindar but the principal business is lyrical' (*L.* I 49, 2–3 Apr. 1878). ' . . . it needs study and is obscure, for indeed I was not over-desirous that the meaning of all should be quite clear, at least unmistakeable' (*L.* I 50, 13 May 1878).

In one manuscript the poem is preceded by a note transcribed by Bridges: 'Be pleased, reader, since the rhythm in which the following poem is written is new, strongly to mark the beats of the measure, according to the number belonging to each of the eight lines of the stanza, as the indentation guides the eye, namely two and three and four and three and five and five and four and six;* not disguising the rhythm and rhyme, as some readers do, who treat poetry as if it were prose fantastically written to rule (which they mistakenly think the perfection of reading), but laying on the beats too much stress rather than too little; nor caring whether one, two, three, or more syllables go to a beat, that is to say, whether two or more beats follow running—as there are three running in the third line of the first stanza—or with syllables between, as commonly; nor whether the line begin with a beat or not; but letting the scansion run on from one line into the next, without break to the end of the stanza: since the dividing of the lines is more to fix the places of the necessary rhymes than for any pause in the measure. Only let this be observed in the reading, that, where more than one syllable goes to a beat, then if the beating syllable is of its nature strong, the stress laid on it must be stronger the greater the number of syllables belonging to it, the voice treading and dwelling: but if on the contrary it is by nature light, then the greater the number of syllables belonging to it the less is the stress to be laid on it, the voice passing flyingly over all the syllables of the foot and in some manner distributing among them all the stress of the one beat. Which syllables however are strong and which light is better told by the ear than by any instruction that could be in short space given: but for an example, in the stanza which is fifth from the end of the poem and in the 6th line [stanza 31] the first two beats are very strong and the more the voice dwells on them the more it fetches out the strength of the syllables they rest upon, the next two beats are very light and escaping, and the last, as well as those which follow in the next line, are of a mean strength, such as suits narrative. And so throughout let the stress be made to fetch out both the strength of the syllables and the meaning and feeling of the words.'

*In Part the second the first line of each stanza has three stresses. Hopkins also noted that 'There are no outriding feet in the *Deutschland*' (*L.* I 45).

98 ll. 1–2. Earlier read:

God mastering me;
Giver of breath and bread;

ll. 5–6. See Job 10: 9–11 and Ps. 138 (Douay; AV 139) (Philip M. Martin, *Mastery and Mercy* (Oxford, 1957), p. 30).

l. 8. See *S.* 158 on elevating grace, which Hopkins describes as 'truly God's finger touching the very vein of personality, which nothing else can reach and man can respond to by no play whatever, by bare acknowledgement only, the counter stress which God alone can feel . . . the aspiration in answer to his inspiration'.

ll. 9–16. The incident described is sometimes thought to have occurred during Hopkins's first experience of the Ignation *Spiritual Exercises* in the long retreat given shortly after he entered the novitiate (see Introduction, p. xiv), but referring it to Hopkins's conversion to Catholicism makes ll. 18–19 easier to understand. See Milward, *Commentary on G. M. Hopkins' 'The Wreck of the*

Deutschland', 23, R. Boyle (in Weyand and Schoder (eds.), *Immortal Diamond*, 335), and MacKenzie (OET 324).

l. 20. *that spell*: during that time.

l. 21. *the heart of the Host*: 'God', but perhaps also 'heart' = 'meaning'. In a letter to E. H. Coleridge (1 June 1864), Hopkins said: 'The great aid to belief and object of belief is the doctrine of the Real Presence in the Blessed Sacrament of the Altar. Religion without that is sombre, dangerous, illogical, with that it is—not to speak of its grand consistency and certainty—*loveable*. Hold that and you will gain all Catholic truth' (*L.* III 17, 92).

ll. 21–3. For the image of the homing pigeon, cf. 'The Handsome Heart', ll. 5–6.

l. 24. *tower from the grace to the grace*. The underlying idea would seem to be explained in notes entitled 'On Personality, Grace and Free Will' (*S.* 146–59). Here Hopkins suggests that each man's life may be lived on a series of different degrees of moral goodness, each state called a 'pitch'. God's grace allows man to taste the degree of goodness above the one in which he is already living. In order to rise to the higher pitch man has merely to accept the opportunity. To stay at the new pitch further grace is required.

99 ll. 25–8. These lines with their traditional symbol of mortality, the hour-glass, may suggest man, and more specifically, the poet as he would be without God's grace, gradually disintegrating physically and perhaps morally.

ll. 26–7. *at the wall | Fast*: the sand at the wall of the hour-glass, which at first appears motionless.

ll. 29–32. The second image suggests that man is maintained spiritually by grace as the water in a well is replenished constantly and unnoticeably by the streams that run down the sides of the hill ('voel'). Peter Milward notes (*Commentary*, 35) the relevance of *S.* 154: 'grace is any action, activity, on God's part by which, in creating or after creating, he carries the creature to or towards the end of its being, which is its selfsacrifice to God and its salvation . . . so far as this action or activity is God's it is divine stress, holy spirit, and, as all is done through Christ, Christ's spirit.' See John 4: 14.

l. 33. *kiss my hand*: salute/greet; an ancient gesture of 'adoration and salutation', although in the Bible associated with pagan worship.

l. 35. See *J.* 254, 'As we drove home the stars came out thick: I leant back to look at them and my heart opening more than usual praised our Lord to and in whom all that beauty comes home.'

ll. 38–40. Although the wonder and splendour of nature come from Christ, in order to feel his presence with its significance ('mystery'), a special state of mind is necessary (as in *J.* 254). In this receptive state an 'instress', impression, of Christ's presence may be felt (cf. 'Hurrahing in Harvest'). To complete the communication with Christ requires that the instress be consciously accepted ('stressed'); see note to l. 8.

99 ll. 41–8. Hopkins seems here to be talking about 'actual grace', defined in the *Catholic Encyclopedia* (1909) as 'a supernatural help of God for salutary acts granted in consideration of the merits of Christ'; that is, 'a passing influence of God' helping man towards those actions necessary for his eternal salvation, given to man through and because of Christ (vi. 690). See *S.* 154, quoted in note to ll. 29–32. But see also *S.* 98–100 on the Holy Ghost.

ll. 49–56 emphasize that it is Christ's Incarnation that made this grace possible. J. E. Keating points out that 'all grace since the fall of man is bestowed through the merits of Christ' (p. 63).

ll. 56–64. In crises men turn to God.

100 ll. 58–9. 'As to final impenitence, it is absolute; and this is easily understood, for even God cannot pardon where there is no repentance, and the moment of death is the fatal instant after which no mortal sin is remitted' (*Cath. Encyc.* (1910), vii. 415). See *S.* 247 for Hopkins's statement of this.

ll. 59–62. Man's repentance and acceptance of God can fill him with a feeling of utter revulsion at his own sinfulness or overwhelming gratitude for forgiveness. Presumably both emotions are present but one dominates (the line may originally have read 'sour and sweet').

ll. 65–72 continue the description in the opening stanza of God's two very different attributes: his stern mastery and his mercy. Men whose malice is stubborn ('*dogged in den*') require harsh experience to make them acknowledge God and ask for his mercy.

ll. 70–2. Cf. Ps. 17: 10–15 (Douay; AV 18: 9–14).

l. 77. *Paul.* His Jewish name was Saul. He persecuted Christians until God temporarily blinded him and Jesus spoke to him, converting him (see Acts 9: 1–20).

l. 78. *Austin*: St Augustine (345–430). Augustine was gradually converted to Christianity by the sermons of Ambrose, Bishop of Milan.

Part the second.

l. 82. *the flange and the rail.* Railway accidents were causing hundreds of deaths in the 1870s (MacKenzie, *Reader's Guide*, 38). See *S.* 247.

ll. 85–6. *Dust*. See Gen. 3: 19 'for dust thou art, and unto dust shalt thou return', and Isa. 40: 6–8.

101 l. 88. *sour*: extremely unpleasant.

scythe cringe. Plants cut with a scythe appear to buckle or bow as they fall. Death is called 'the grim reaper'. *cringe*: transitive, 'cause to cringe or buckle'.

blear share: blind and indiscriminate ploughshare.

l. 93. *feathers*. See Ps. 91: 4: 'He (God) shall cover thee with his feathers, and under his wings shalt thou trust.'

l. 95. *bay*: architectural: recess or compartment; see *J.* 193: 'opposite bays of the sky'.

l. 96. *vault*: cover.

rounds: perhaps in the sense of a loop of rope round a reel.

reeve: fasten.

l. 107. *combs*: crests or ridges of the sandbank.

night: both the time of day when the *Deutschland* struck the bank, and in part the reason why the ship was on its mistaken course.

l. 108. *dead*: 'precisely' and 'doomed'. l. 111. *whorl*: propeller.

102 l. 128. *burl*: fullness.

buck: perhaps the rising of the wave to a crest, also the action of the wave in dislodging anyone or anything not securely fastened to the ship. 'One brave sailor, who was safe in the rigging, went down to try to save a child or woman who was drowning on deck. He was secured by a rope to the rigging, but a wave dashed him against the bulwarks, and when daylight dawned his headless body, detained by the rope, was seen swaying to and fro with the waves' (*The Times*, 11 Dec. 1875; repr. *L.* III 443).

ll. 143–4: an ecstatic joy Hopkins associates with youth.

103 l. 146. The nun may have been saying prayers for Advent, which include words translated as 'Lord, hear my cry, O Lord, make haste to aid me . . . ', a prayer Hopkins too would have uttered in the season (Griffiths, 354).

l. 147. *hawling*: perhaps from 'hawle' = hail; to throw or send down hard, like hail in a storm; or 'haul', to pull or drag forcibly (Keating, 81).

l. 148. *rash smart sloggering*: stinging, hard.

l. 150. *fetch*: a far-reaching effort (OED).

l. 151. *the tall nun. The Times* described her as 'the chief sister, a gaunt woman 6ft. high, calling out loudly and often "O Christ, come quickly!" till the end came' (11 Dec. 1875), and 'One, noted for her extreme tallness, is the lady who, at midnight on Monday, by standing on a table in the saloon, was able to thrust her body through the skylight, and kept exclaiming, in a voice heard by those in the rigging above the roar of the storm, "My God, my God, make haste, make haste"' (13 Dec. 1875).

103 l. 153. There were five nuns. l. 156. *wide of its good*: evil.

l. 157. *Gertrude.* St Gertrude the Great (1265–1301 or 1302), who died near Eisleben, the German town where Martin Luther was born. Entering the convent at the age of 5, she became a pre-eminent example of a simple Benedictine nun. She was a mystic, gifted with frequent visions (*Cath. Encyc.* 1909).

lily, and l. 158 *Christ's lily*: the symbol of purity appropriately used of St Gertrude.

ll. 157–60 state that good and evil are closely entangled on earth. The Ignatian *Spiritual Exercises* warn at a number of points of the watchfulness necessary to distinguish good from evil disguised as good.

l. 158. *beast of the waste wood.* Ps. 79: 14 (Douay; AV 80: 13) of God's vineyard the Church, 'The boar out of the wood hath laid it waste; and a . . . wild beast hath devoured it.' Martin Luther (1483–1546) was outspokenly critical of the ways in which the wealth and power of the Papacy were maintained. The political and religious rebellions which grew out of hand from his questioning of the status quo brought bloodshed and the destruction of much Church property.

l. 160. See Gen. 4.

l. 165. *Orion of light.* See Job 9 and Amos 5. Commentators say that the creation of Orion was considered to be a special example of God's power (see e.g. *The International Critical Commentary* on Amos and Hosea (Edinburgh, 1905, 1960), 115, and on Job (1921, 1964), 86–7.

l. 166. *unchancelling*: nonce-word. Perhaps Hopkins is suggesting that God is bringing the nuns into public prominence through their deaths. ('Chancels' are door-screens through which cloistered nuns can greet visitors. The word is also used of the part of a church reserved for the clergy and choir.) A large number of people visited the convent at Stratford-le-Bow where the nuns were prepared for burial. The sisters were considered by many Catholics in England to have been martyrs.

l. 169. *Five*: a holy number because of Christ's five wounds in the crucifixion. It became a cipher for Christ.

finding: emblem. Meditating on Christ's sacrifice is an important part of reaching and maintaining Christian belief, of 'coming to or finding' God.

sake. Of his use of the word in 'Henry Purcell' Hopkins wrote to Bridges: 'I mean by it the being a thing has outside itself, as a voice by its echo, a face by its reflection, a body by its shadow, a man by his name, fame, or memory, and also that in the thing by virtue of which especially it has this being abroad, and that is something distinctive, marked, specifically or individually speaking, as for a voice and echo clearness; for a reflected image light, brightness; for a shadow-casting body bulk; for a man genius, great achievements, amiability, and so on' (*L.* I 83, 26–31 May 1879).

l. 174. *before-time-taken*: predestined. See 1 Peter 1: 18–21 and *S.* 196–7.

prizèd and priced. See Zacharias 11: 13 (Douay).

104 l. 176. The red rose is a symbol of martyrdom.

l. 177. *Francis*: Francis of Assisi. The nuns were Franciscans.

ll. 178–81. Francis was given to intense meditation. On one such occasion Christ suddenly appeared to him in a vision of a crucified seraph. Francis then found that he had on his body five marks similar to the wounds Christ had received in his crucifixion: *scape* (= outward sign) of *love* (= Christ) *crucified*, a proof (= *seal*) of the vision. *The Little Flowers of St. Francis* (tr. T. W. Arnold (Chatto and Windus, 1926)) adds that Christ told Francis that every year after his death on the anniversary of his death he would go to Purgatory in order to lead from there all Franciscan orders and others devoted to Francis 'to the end that (he) mayest be conformed to (Christ) in death, as . . . in life' (p. 186).

l. 184. See Rev. 1: 14–16.

l. 186. *forehead*. St Beuno's is situated on a hillside, surrounded by fields.

l. 192. *The cross to her*: holding the crucifix against herself.

christens her wild-worst Best. Through her faith in Christ the nun makes her ordeal the opportunity for the best experience of her life. Hopkins leaves ambiguous here the suggestion that the nun identifies herself with Christ on the cross. He rejects it in ll. 209–16.

l. 194. *arch and original Breath*. See OED, *arch-* (prefix) = 'initial', or, less reduplicatively, 'sovereign'; the Spirit of God as in Gen. 1: 2.

l. 196. *body of lovely Death*: Christ crucified.

l. 198. See Matt. 8: 23–7.

104 ll. 201–4. The drooping, grey clouds of winter are 'peeled' back to reveal the blue and white skies of spring.

105 l. 208. See 1 Cor. 2: 9.

ll. 209–16 reject first the idea that the nun was asking for ease. That desire is born of dull, repetitive tasks and sorrow long-drawn-out. Nor is it likely that the nun's identification with Christ was particularly close. That requires quiet meditation.

ll. 217–24. While the language of this stanza suggests that the nun had a vision of Christ, stanza 29 makes it clear that the nun did not see Christ as a figure but, like Hopkins in 'Hurrahing in Harvest', realized that Christ is present in nature. She perceived that the storm occurred for a divine purpose.

l. 226. *single eye*: focused on God to the exclusion of everything else; see Matt. 6: 22.

l. 230. See John 1: 1–3.

l. 231. *Simon Peter.* See Matt. 16: 16–19. Simon Peter recognized Jesus as the Son of God.

l. 232. *Tarpeïan-fast*: Rome's Capitol 'on the Tarpeian rock, her citadel | Impregnable' (*Paradise Regained* iv. 49–50). As J. E. Keating points out, Hopkins is probably thinking of the Papacy ('Rome') and the nuns' adherence, despite their persecution, to Catholicism ('the true church built on the rock', Matt. 16: 18).

blown beacon of light. See Phil. 2: 15. Perhaps too the image of fires, built on headlands as warnings to ships on stormy nights, that blaze higher the stronger the wind (MacKenzie, *Reader's Guide*, p. 52).

106 ll. 233–40. The *Deutschland* was wrecked on 7 December. 8 December is the Feast of the Immaculate Conception of the Blessed Virgin Mary.

l. 238. *so to conceive thee is done.* We think of Christ as incarnated.

ll. 239–40. By thinking of Christ, recognizing his presence, and calling his name out so that others could hear it, the nun has made Christ's presence felt again in the world, 'brought it to birth' as Mary did the Incarnated Christ. See Lesson 9 on Luke 11: 28 in the Roman Breviary: 'Blessed, too, were all who conceived that same Word spiritually, by the faith that comes from hearing, and who by their good works strove to bring it to birth and, as it were, to nourish it, in their own hearts and in the hearts of their fellow men' (Keating, 98–9).

ll. 241–8. This stanza brings a reconciliation between the picture of God as sternly masterful, even destructive, and God the merciful.

ll. 241–2. Cf. John 16: 21.

l. 244. See Hopkins's notes for a sermon on death (*S.* 247–52).

ll. 246–7. Cardinal Manning's funeral sermon for the nuns was reported to include the statement that 'there was reason to believe that the sight of the calm resignation of these holy Sisters proved a useful example to some who shared their fate. Who could tell how many acts of contrition, of faith, and of submission there were during those hours of agony? The example of those sisters was like an articulate voice preaching to others' (Keating, 100). Hopkins accords this power to the cry of the tall nun rather than to the behaviour of all the sisters.

l. 250. *Yore-flood.* Perhaps an allusion to Gen. 1: 2 or to Noah's flood (Gen. 6–8) or simply to the ocean.

year's fall: perhaps the annual rainfall.

ll. 251–2. Cf. Job. 38: 8–11.

ll. 253–4. God restrains the restlessness of men's minds and gives their lives a firm foundation. Cf. ll. 29–32.

l. 256. *bodes but abides.* Foresees but waits, leaving man with free will.

ll. 257–64. See *S.* 252.

ll. 259–60. See *S.* 190, where, transcribing passages from the *Spiritual Exercises*, Hopkins writes 'after Christ had expired on the Cross . . . his blessed soul . . . united to the Divinity descended into hell, whence releasing the souls of the just'. The Creed also mentions the descent into hell.

l. 261. *pent in prison.* See 1 Peter 3: 18–19.

ll. 262–4. These people, who had almost lost any chance of salvation, were the furthermost from salvation that Christ, sent by his merciful Father, reached and gathered in his Passion and Resurrection (see *S.* 140–1).

For a summary of various interpretations of these lines see Keating, 104–6.

107 l. 268. *Mary-of-flame.* See the Roman Breviary, feasts of the Circumcision and Purification, 'Rubum quem viderat', 'The bush which Moses had beheld unburnt we have recognized as thy praiseworthy unstained virginity; Mother of God intercede for us' (Keating, 107). Cf. Rev. 12: 1 and Hopkins's commentary on it in *S.* 170–1.

l. 272. *lightning of fire hard-hurled.* See Matt. 24: 27 and Luke 9: 54–6.

l. 277. *easter in us*: come to spiritual rebirth in us. See in the Roman Breviary the pre-Christmas antiphon 'O Oriens', 'O dayspring, splendour of eternal light and sun of justice, come and illumine those who sit in darkness and in the shadow of death' (Keating, 109).

107 *crimson-cresseted east.* The rising sun is a symbol of a new and holier day. See 'God's Grandeur', ll. 12–14. A 'cresset' was a metal or stone vessel for holding oil, coal, etc., for light. It could be used as a beacon, or placed in a church beside the cross.

l. 278. *rare*: special, 'of uncommon excellence' (OED).

The Silver Jubilee. Hopkins also contributed poems in Latin and Welsh.

l. 1. 'Roman Catholic churches at the time were forbidden to ring bells' (McChesney, 51).

l. 5. Hopkins notes in a letter (*L.* I 65, 29 Jan. 1879) that it was in fact twenty-six years, not twenty-five, since the restoration of the Catholic hierarchy in Britain.

108 *Moonrise.* Dated 'June 19, 1876'. Below the poem Hopkins experimented with adding another stress to the second half of the first line.

> in the white of the dusk, in the walk of the morning
> in the wake of the yesterday, walk of the morning
> in the yesterday light, in etc.

He added 'And so alter throughout' but no further drafts are extant.

l. 3. *paring of paradisaïcal fruit*: the dull, golden skin; see *J.* 209.

l. 4. *Maenefa*: the mountain behind St Beuno's (OET 354).

l. 5. *fluke*: the triangular-shaped piece of iron near the tip of the arms of an anchor.

fanged. Earlier read: 'fanged in him': 'of an anchor: to "bite" with its fluke' (OED), to hold.

not quit utterly. Earlier read: 'not free utterly'.

l. 6. caesural mark omitted in MS.

109 *The Woodlark.* Dated 'July 5' [1876]. The poem is in the very early stages of composition, with a great many lines missing. The version printed here follows the manuscript order and shows Hopkins in the intermediate stage between the fragmentary lines of description, like those jotted into his diaries and notebooks, and the smooth coherence of his finished poems.

Metrical marks: Hopkins has put dots below words to mark the stresses in ll. 27, 29–34.

ll. 1–11. See *J.* 138 (3 June 1866) 'The cuckoo singing one side, on the other from the ground and unseen the wood-lark, as I suppose, most sweetly with a song of which the structure is more definite than the skylark's and gives the link with that of the rest of birds.'

l. 26 cancelled and not replaced.

ll. 27–34 revised several times.

110 l. 36. *oxeye*. See *J.* 144: 'Those ox-eye-like flowers in grain fields smell deliciously', and p. 138, 'The meadows . . . containing white of oxeyes'.

l. 38. *fumitory.* See *J.* 135: 'Fumitory graceful plant'.

Penmaen Pool. Dated 'Barmouth, Merionethshire. Aug. 1876'.

l. 10. Hopkins notes that the 'Giant's Stool' is the mountain, Cadair Idris.

111 l. 17. *Charles's Wain*: the Plough.

l. 32. Two transcriptions read 'darksome danksome'.

ll. 34–5. Variant: 'Who'll | But praise it?'

(*Margaret Clitheroe*). Without date or title. Stanzas 6 and 7 lack their final four lines and stanza 8 is missing line 3. The sequence is uncertain apart from the first three stanzas, which Hopkins numbered. (1876–7?)

Margaret Clitheroe (*c.*1556–86). Married to a wealthy butcher in York, she became a Catholic convert, raised her children as Catholics, and harboured priests. She became known for her outspoken faith and was imprisoned for it several times. In 1586 the government became more determined to stamp out Catholicism in York and Margaret was arrested and questioned again. She refused to plead in order to prevent her children being forced to give evidence against her. The penalty for silence was to be 'pressed to death' (*Cath. Encyc.* 1967.) She was declared a saint in 1970. See *L.* I 92 and *S.* 48.

ll. 1–4. Two ideas seem to be clear here: that Margaret was predestined to martyrdom (see 'The Wreck of the Deutschland', ll. 173–4), and that, although she suffered, her reward was the everlasting bliss of the martyrs.

l. 2. *the chief of bliss*. Earlier read: 'out-of-sight with bliss'.

112 l. 10. *crisp*: see *J.* 144: 'Strange pretty scatter-droop of barley ears, their beards part outside like the fine crispings of smooth running water on piers etc.'

l. 18. *clinching-blind*. She was sentenced by Judge Clinch.

l. 27. Comma editorial.

l. 31. The Holy Trinity.

113 l. 42. *Thecla*. See note to the poem, 'St. Thecla'.

ll. 51–61. The punishment was intended to last three days but Margaret died within a quarter of an hour.

113 *'Hope holds to Christ'*. Text from a torn scrap of paper. Cf. 2 Cor. 3: 18; 4.

l. 1. Earlier read: 'Hope holds towards Christ her home-made mirror out'; 'her home-made' was then altered to 'a living'.

l. 7. Earlier: 'Her glass can see'. Gap between ll. 10 and 11.

114 *God's Grandeur.* Dated 23 Feb. and Mar. 1877; marked 'Standard rhythm, counterpointed'.

Metrical marks: l. 1 with the grandeur l. 3 gathers l. 5 Generations. Hopkins noted that this poem and 'Starlight Night' were 'to be read, both of them, slowly, strongly marking the rhythms and fetching out the syllables'.

ll. 1–3. 'All things therefore are charged with love, are charged with God and if we know how to touch them give off sparks and take fire, yield drops and flow, ring and tell of him' (*S.* 195).

l. 2. *shining from shook foil*. 'I mean foil in its sense of leaf or tinsel . . . Shaken goldfoil gives off broad glares like sheet lightning and also, and this is true of nothing else, owing to its zigzag dints and creasings and network of small many cornered facets, a sort of fork lightning too' (*L.* I 169). One autograph read 'lightning' instead of 'shining' but Hopkins later rejected this.

l. 3. *oil*: crushed from olives. Earlier read: 'like an oozing oil | Pressed'.

ll. 13–14. See Gen. 1: 2 and Milton, *Paradise Lost*, i. 19–22. Hopkins also observed the way in which the sea 'warped to the round of the world' (*J.* 222, 251).

The Starlight Night. Dated 'Feb. 24 1877'; marked 'Standard rhythm opened and counterpointed'.

Metrical marks: l. 2 sitting in the air l. 3 boroughs l. 6 airy abeles l. 9 patience.

l. 2. See *J.* 46: 'Sky peak'd with tiny flames'.

l. 3. Areas of the sky thickly strewn with stars.

l. 4. *dim woods*: areas of the sky where fewer stars can be seen. *delves*: plural of 'delf' (obs.) a mine. Earlier read 'diamond wells'.

l. 5. *quickgold*: analogous to 'quicksilver'. Earlier read 'gold-dew'. See *J.* 150: 'the odd white-gold look of short grass in tufts'.

l. 6. *whitebeam, abeles*: trees whose leaves have silvery undersides.

l. 7. *Flake-doves*. See *J.* 261, where starlings are described as 'black flakes hurling round'.

l. 8. Bridges suggested comparing George Herbert's 'Church Porch', stanza 29:

> What skills it, if a bag of stones or gold
> About thy neck do drown thee? raise thy head;
> Take stars for money; stars not to be told
> By any art, yet to be purchased.

l. 10. See *J.* 249, lime-trees 'starrily tasselled with blossom'.

115 l. 12. *barn.* See Matt. 13: 30.

l. 13. *shocks*: sheaves.

piece-bright paling. The image is of wooden walls with knot-holes through which star-like points of light can be seen. Cf. 'The stars were packed so close' (see notes to 'The Elopement', p. 193). Cf. too 'He hath abolished the old drouth', l. 14.

'As kingfishers catch fire'.

Metrical marks: l. 1 dragonflies; l. 8 Crying; ll. 9, 11, 12 begin with great colons; l. 10 has a great colon before 'that'; l. 11 eye he.

See *S.* 238–9: 'WHY DID GOD CREATE? . . . He meant the world to give him praise, reverence and service . . . The creation does praise God, does reflect honour on him . . . *he does not need it* . . . Nevertheless he takes it. . . . "The heavens declare the glory of God". They glorify God, *but they do not know it.* The birds sing to him, the thunder speaks of his terror, the lion is like his strength, the sea is like his greatness, the honey like his sweetness; they are something like him, they make him known, they tell of him, they give him glory, but they do not know they do . . . This then is poor praise . . . Nevertheless what they can *they always do.* But AMIDST THEM ALL IS MAN, man and the angels . . . Man was created. Like the rest then to praise, reverence, and serve God; to give him glory. He does so, even by his being . . . But man can know God, *can mean to give him glory.* This then was why he was made . . . It is not only prayer that gives God glory but work. Smiting on an anvil, sawing a beam, whitewashing a wall, driving horses, sweeping, scouring, everything gives God some glory if being in his grace you do it as your duty.'

ll. 1–4. See *S.* 195: 'All things . . . are charged with God and . . . give off sparks and take fire, yield drops and flow, ring and tell of him.'

l. 3. *tucked string*: dial. for 'plucked'; earlier read 'every string taxed'.

ll. 3–4. Earlier read: 'as every sweet string tells, each bell's | Bow answers being asked and calls its name'.

l. 9. Variant in regular rhythm: 'Then I say more: the just man justices'.

115 *justices*. Acts in a godly manner aided by God's grace; see note to l. 10.

l. 10. Alternative (regular rhythm): 'Keeps grace and that keeps all his goings graces'. See *S.* 154: 'grace is any action, activity, on God's part by which, in creating or after creating, he carries the creature to or towards the end of its being, which is its selfsacrifice to God and its salvation'. To maintain such behaviour man needs further grace (*S.* 155, 240).

l. 11. Variant in regular rhythm: 'In God's eye acts what &c.'

ll. 11–14. Both sorts of grace come to man through Christ (cf. *S.* 154). It is the Christ-like part of man that experiences the initial belief, and it is through emulating Christ's behaviour that man can achieve the second type of grace.

Spring. Dated May 1877 and marked 'Standard rhythm, opening with sprung leadings'.

Metrical marks: in one autograph ll. 1, 5, 9, and 13 begin with great colons (see p. 167). In another ll. 1–9 are linked together by a curved line and marked 'staccato' while ll. 10 and 14 are marked 'Rall.' (rallentando) and in one transcription Hopkins marked: l. 5. to hear l. 8. the racing.

l. 3. The thrush's eggs are blue.

l. 6. *glassy*. 'A notable glare the eye may abstract and sever from the . . . colour of light reflected' (*J.* 231, 11 May 1873); 'the flesh being . . . sometimes glassy with reflected light' (*J.* 154).

116 *The Sea and the Skylark*. The poem was originally titled 'Walking by the Sea'. Dated 'Rhyl May 1877' and marked 'standard rhythm, in parts sprung and in others counterpointed'.

Metrical marks: in an autograph there are numerous musical signs including staccatos over l. 4 Frequenting there, l. 5 Left hand, off land, and all of l. 7; rallentando above the beginning of l. 14; accents (>) above l. 2 right, ramps, l. 9 frail; a pause (⌒) over l. 6 more, and several different metrical symbols. Later Hopkins confined his metrical marks to: l. 1 to end l. 8 music.

Hopkins was not pleased with the earlier version. Parts of the explanation which he sent to Bridges in 1882 apply to the final, revised poem:

ll. 6–7 refer to 'a headlong and exciting (*rash-fresh*) new snatch of singing, resumption by the lark of his song, which by turns he gives over and takes up again (*re-winded*) all day long, and this goes on, the sonnet says (l. 1), through all time, without ever losing its first freshness, being a thing both new and old' (*L.* I 164).

l. 6. *new-skeinèd score*. 'the lark's song, which from his height gives the impression . . . of something falling to the earth and not vertically quite but tricklingly or wavingly, something as a skein of silk ribbed by having been tightly wound on a narrow card or a notched holder . . . the laps or folds are the notes or short measures and bars of them. The same is called a score in the musical sense of score and this score is "writ upon a liquid sky trembling to welcome it", only not horizontally. The lark in wild glee races the reel round, paying or dealing out and down the turns of the skein . . . right to the . . . ground, where it lies in a heap . . . or rather is all wound off on to another winch . . . in Fancy's eye by the moment the bird touches earth and so is ready for a fresh unwinding at the next flight' (*L.* I 164).

Hopkins noted that when he had written the poem he had been fascinated with cynghanedd, or consonant-chime (*L.* I 163).

l. 2. *trench*: make a deep impression.

l. 3. *flood*: high-tide. *fall*: low tide.

l. 9. The seaside resort of Rhyl in Wales.

l. 11. *cared-for crown*. See Gen. 1: 26–9 and Matt. 6: 29–33. Cf. 'God heeds all things and cares and provides for all things but for us men he cares most and provides best' (*S.* 90).

l. 13. *make*: species.

making: things made, such as the 'frail town'.

l. 14. *dust*. Cf. the Anglican burial service: 'Forasmuch as it hath pleased Almighty God of his great mercy to take unto himself the soul of our dear brother here departed, we therefore commit his body to the ground; earth to earth, ashes to ashes, dust to dust . . . '

first slime. See Gen. 2: 7.

In the Valley of the Elwy. Dated 'May 23 1877'; marked 'standard rhythm, sprung and counterpointed'.

Metrical marks: in the final version Hopkins's marks are: l. 1 I remember l. 3 very entering l. 7 morsels l. 9 waters, meadows l. 10 the air l. 12 swaying. In one MS 'Rall.' is marked before ll. 9 and 14, and Sf (sforzando) before l. 10. In another MS l. 8 'seemed' and l. 11 'Only' are preceded by great colons.

Hopkins wrote of the poem: 'The kind people of the sonnet were the Watsons of Shooter's Hill, nothing to do with the Elwy. The facts were as stated . . . The frame of the sonnet is a rule of three sum *wrong*, thus: As the sweet smell to those kind people so the Welsh landscape is NOT to the Welsh; and then the author and principle of all four terms is asked to bring the sum right' (*L.* I 76–7). He noted that the companion poem to the above was 'Ribblesdale'.

116 l. 2. *me.* 'Swivelling on the self, [Hopkins] realizes two dimensions of the incident, the domesticated amiability and the sense of a more severe judgement (God's) behind the surfaces of life, two dimensions, each with a corresponding language, of familiar habit or of calling to account' (Griffiths, 277).

ll. 5–6. In his Journal Hopkins noted on 22 July 1873: 'Very hot, though the wind, which was south, dappled very sweetly on one's face and when I came out I seemed to put it on like a gown as a man puts on the shadow he walks into and hoods or hats himself with the shelter of a roof, a penthouse, or a copse of trees, I mean it rippled and fluttered like light linen, one could feel the folds and braids of it . . .' (*J.* 233).

117 *The Windhover.* Dated 'St Beuno's. May 30 1877'; marked 'Falling paeonic rhym [*sic*], sprung and outriding'.

Metrical marks: l. 2 dauphin l. 3 rolling . . . him l. 4 there l. 6 heel . . . the hurl l. 8 achieve of l. 9 oh, air l. 11 lovelier . . . dangerous l. 12 of it.

Windhover. A kestrel or falcon, which hunts by hovering on the wind with quivering wings and occasional rapid bursts of larger wing-movement. It can glide sideways from one level to another and dives to snatch its prey.

ll. 4–5. Earlier read: 'Hung so and rung the rein of a wimpled wing | In an ecstacy'. Wings quivering in a hover.

l. 5. All MSS read 'ecstacy'.

ll. 5–6. One of the kestrel's most beautiful movements is a rapid side-slip, gliding in a curve from one level to another.

ll. 7–8. *My heart in hiding.* Discretion would be necessary to get close to the bird, but the phrase also suggests a stark contrast between the bird with its activity and freedom and proud courage and the still, earthbound observer, his movements arrested by his admiration for the bird's skill.

l. 8. *achieve*: achievement. Earlier read: 'Stirred for a bird,—for the mastery of the thing!'

ll. 9–11. This is ambiguous, but many critics suggest that the poet has a sudden vision combining the beauty, courage, and skill of the bird into a perception of its essential nature (inscape) and, beyond that, envisages Christ, who is a billion times lovelier and mightier.

l. 10. *buckle*: come together. See MacKenzie, *Reader's Guide*, 76–84.

l. 11. *O my chevalier.* Perhaps addressed to Christ, to whom Hopkins dedicated the poem when correcting the final version. However, the dedication may be explained by the fact that Hopkins considered this poem the best he had written.

l. 12. *sillion*: a strip of arable land usually worked by a tenant farmer. A plough, rusty at the end of winter, soon becomes shiny when used.

l. 14. Apparently cold, black embers often have a hot, glowing centre.

Figuratively in the sestet light is suggestive of Christ, whose presence can be perceived even in dull daily toil (represented by ploughing) and whose sacrifice is recalled by the self-destruction of the embers. (The observation of Christ's presence in the world is frequently a subject in the poems Hopkins wrote during 1876–8.) The final six lines stress the relationship between God and the world (see also 'As kingfishers catch fire'). Man can contribute to this relationship by keeping in mind Christ's example of obscure toil and self-sacrifice and by dedicating his own physical work (also ll. 12–13) and inner spiritual life (ll. 13–14) to the glory of God (see *S.* 238–41, quoted in notes to 'As kingfishers catch fire').

Pied Beauty. Dated 'St Beuno's, Tremeirchion. summer 1877' and marked 'Curtal-sonnet: sprung paeonic rhythm'.

Metrical marks: l. 9 sŏur. *Curtal*: see Author's Preface, p. 97. Autograph has great colons before the opening of ll. 1, 5, 7, and 'finches' (l. 4), 'trades' (l. 6), 'strange' (l. 7), 'slow' (l. 9), 'change' (l. 10), 'him' (l. 11).

l. 2. *brinded*: brindled, streaked.

l. 3. Trout lose their rose-coloured marks when they die (OET 385).

l. 4. *Fresh-firecoal.* 'Chestnuts as bright as coals or spots of vermilion' (*J.* 189).

finches' wings. These have conspicuous light-coloured bands.

118 l. 7. *counter*: unusual. *spare*: undecorated.

l. 8. *fickle*: changeable.

freckled: variegated, here slightly eccentric?

l. 10. *fathers-forth*: creates. *past change*: eternal.

The Caged Skylark. Dated 'St. Beuno's. 1877'; marked 'falling paeonic rhythm, sprung and outriding'.

Metrical marks: l. 4 drudgery l. 8 barriers l. 10 babble and l. 13 uncumberèd l. 14 footing it.

Cf. Manley Hopkins's 'To a Bird Singing in a Narrow Street', which imagines without religious implications how a caged bird may lament its loss of liberty. Hopkins copied the poem into his commonplace book.

118 l. 2. *bone-house*. Perhaps from 'bānhūs', Old English for 'body', but the rib-cage provides the closest visual analogy.

l. 3. *beyond the remembering his free fells*. Earlier read: 'beyond recollection of free fells'.

fells: moors, hilltops.

l. 5. *turf*: piece of clover frequently placed in a skylark's cage.

ll. 9–11. The free bird.

l. 10. 'The lark descends, still singing. When yet at a height, the song ceases and the bird drops abruptly, recovering itself a foot or so above the grass and skimming forward before alighting' (T. A. Coward, *The Birds of the British Isles and their Eggs* (London, 1939), 93).

ll. 12–14. The belief that after the Day of Judgement, when those who believe in God have repented of their sins and are granted eternal life, they will have perfect bodies that will hinder their spirits no more than a rainbow damages the feathery seeds of thistles or dandelions (*meadow-down*).

'To him who ever thought'. Probably 1877.

Sister Mary Jeremy noted (*TLS*, 14 Nov. 1952) that Hopkins's poem is based on a passage in the *Revelations of St. Gertrude (*1865): 'Having heard a preacher declare that no person could be saved without the love of God, and that all must at least have so much of it as would lead them to repent and to abstain from sin, the Saint began to think that many, when dying, seemed to repent more from the fear of hell than from the love of God. Our Lord replied: "When I behold anyone in his agony who has thought of Me with pleasure, or who has performed any works deserving of reward, I appear to him at the moment of death with a countenance so full of love and mercy, that he repents from his inmost heart for having ever offended Me, and he is saved by this repentance"' (*The Life and Revelations of St. Gertrude* (repr., Newman's Press, Maryland, 1949), 201). For St Gertrude, see note to 'The Wreck of the Deutschland', l. 157.

l. 6. Earlier read: 'Will grieve his ever sinning and be freed'; revised to: 'Repent he sinned and so his sins be freed'.

freed: perhaps 'to clear from blame or stain; to show or declare to be guiltless; to absolve, acquit' (obsolete), OED, as in Rom. 6: 7: 'For he that is dead is freed from sin.'

Above the poem is a single line related in thought:

Matchless mercy in disasterous, a disastrous time

119 *Hurrahing in Harvest*. Dated 'Vale of Clwyd Sept. 1 1877' and marked

'sprung and outriding rhythm; no counterpoint. Take notice that the outriding feet are not to be confused with dactyls or paeons, though sometimes the line might be scanned either way. The strong syllable in an outriding foot has always a great stress and after the outrider follows a short pause. The paeon is easier and more flowing' (see *L.* I 45, *L.* II 85–7).

Metrical marks: l. 1 now; . . . barbarous l. 8a/Rapturous . . . greeting l. 9 azurous l. 10 Majestic . . . stalwart l. 14 for him . . . for him.

Hopkins said 'the Hurrahing Sonnet was the outcome of half an hour of extreme enthusiasm as I walked home alone one day from fishing in the Elwy' (*L.* I 56 [16 July 1878]).

ll. 2–3. *wind-walks . . . | . . . silk-sack clouds*: fluffy clouds blown across the sky as if making their way along a path. Cf. 'That Nature is a Heraclitean Fire', ll. 1–2. See *J.* 204: 'Clouds however solid they may look far off are I think wholly made of film in the sheet or in the tuft. The bright woolpacks that pelt before a gale in a clear sky are in the tuft and you can see the wind unravelling and rending them finer than any sponge till within one easy reach overhead they are morselled to nothing and consumed—it depends of course on their size.'

ll. 3–4. *wilful-wavier |Meal-drift*: high, wispy clouds.

ll. 7–8. *a |Rapturous.* Cf. the use of run-on rhyme in 'The Loss of the Eurydice'.

ll. 11–14. Cf. 'The Wreck of the Deutschland', ll. 38–40.

The Lantern out of Doors. Marked 'Standard rhythm, with one sprung leading' (l. 9) 'and one line counterpointed' (l. 14). Hopkins subsequently altered l. 5 so that it now opens with a spondee. Hopkins dated it 'St. Beuno's. 1877' and noted that the poem's companion is 'The Candle Indoors'.

Metrical marks: l. 13 them, heart l. 14 rescue, and.

l. 8. *distance buys them quite.* Jesuits were regularly moved from one community to another and rarely had the same daily companions for long.

ll. 9–10. winding the eye. Hopkins explained to Bridges: 'I mean that the eye winds/only in the sense that its focus or point of sight winds and that coincides with a point of the object and winds with that. For the object, a lantern passing further and further away and bearing now east, now west of one right line, is truly and properly described as winding' (*L.* I 66–7, 15 Feb. 1879).

ll. 12–14. Cf. *S.* 89: 'God knows infinite things, all things, and heeds them all in particular. We cannot "do two things at once", that is cannot give our full heed and attention to two things at once. God heeds all things at once. He takes more interest in a merchant's business than the merchant, in a vessel's steering than the pilot, in a lover's sweetheart than the . . . lover, in a sick man's pain than the sufferer, in our salvation than we ourselves. . . . God heeds all things and cares and provides for all things but for us men he cares most and provides best.'

119 l. 14. *ransom*: Christ's sacrifice for man's salvation.

120 *The Loss of the Eurydice*. Marked 'written in sprung rhythm. The 3rd line has three beats, the rest 4. The scanning runs on without break to the end of the stanza, so that each stanza is rather one long line rhymed in passage than 4 lines with rhymes at the ends' (see *L.* I 86). Dated 'Mount St. Mary's, Derbyshire. April 1878'. Slurs linking the end of third line to the beginning of the fourth to complete the rhyme occur in stanzas 6, 17, 23.

l. 6. *furled them, the hearts of oak*. The image is of 'a stroke or blast in a forest of "hearts of oak" (. . . sound oak-timber) which at one blow both lays them low and buries them in broken earth' (*L.* I 52). *hearts of oak*: also brave, doughty, see OED, *heart* 19b.

l. 8. *forefalls*: the closest, sea-facing slopes.

ll. 9–20. The *Eurydice* was a naval training vessel returning from exercises in the West Indies. Contemporary descriptions can be found in *Immortal Diamond*, ed. Weyand, 375–92.

l. 22. *bay*: 'Of heaven' (see *L.* II 33).

l. 23. *Boreas*: the Greek god, personifying the North Wind, who destroyed the Persian fleet (MacKenzie, *Reader's Guide*, 99).

121 ll. 29–32. Carisbrook, Appledurcombe, Ventnor, and Boniface Down are all places on the Isle of Wight.

l. 33. *press*: 'as much sail as wind etc. will allow' (OED).

l. 34. *royals*: above topgallant sails (OED), used only in fine weather (MacKenzie, *Reader's Guide*, 100).

l. 47. *Cheer's death*: despair.

ll. 53–6. '"Even" those who seem unconscientious will act the right part at a great push' (*L.* I 53).

122 ll. 89–92. Many Catholic shrines in England had been destroyed by Henry VIII and their contents taken.

123 l. 94. *wildworth*. Wild flowers: a reference to the men, who are hardy, healthy, and mature (*blown*) but are lost because they are outside the protection of the Catholic Church: cf. Hopkins's note

to 'Henry Purcell' (quoted below): 'May Purcell . . . have died a good death . . . so that the heavy condemnation under which he outwardly or nominally lay for being out of the true Church may in consequence of his good intentions have been reversed' (*L.* I 170–1, 4–5 Jan. 1883). See too Hopkins's sermon on Death (*S.* 244–52).

l. 98. *my master*: Christ or God.

ll. 99–100. Henry VIII had severed the link between the national church of England and Roman Catholicism.

l. 102. The Milky Way (*marvellous Milk*) was called the 'Walsingham Way' because it guided pilgrims travelling at night towards the popular Catholic shrine to the Virgin Mary at Walsingham in Norfolk.

l. 103. *And one*: Duns Scotus, 'champion of her (Mary's) Immaculate Conception' (*L.* I 77).

l. 112. *O Hero* (that) *savest*: Christ. *Hero.* See *S.* 34.

ll. 113–20 refer to the belief that those who have not been damned to hell but only appear to be doomed can be given God's mercy till the Day of Judgement through the prayers of those still living.

124 *The May Magnificat.* Dated 'Stonyhurst. May 1878'; marked 'sprung rhythm: four stresses in each line of the first couplet, three in each of the second'. The poem was requested for hanging in front of a statue but was rejected by Hopkins's superiors, perhaps because of its sprung rhythm.

Magnificat: Mary's hymn praising God. See Luke 1: 46–55.

l. 5. *Candlemas*: (2 Feb.) the feast celebrating Mary's purification after the birth of Christ and her presentation of him in the temple.

Lady Day: (25 Mar.) the Feast of the Annunciation.

l. 21. *bugle*: a plant with blue flowers (*Ajuga reptans*).

l. 25. *sizing*: growing in size.

125 ll. 37–8. Apple blossom is white with a touch of deep pink.

l. 41. Bluebells are grey when they first flower. Their colour then gradually deepens to blue (see *J.* 208–9, 231).

ll. 43–4. See *J.* 232: 'Sometimes I hear the cuckoo with wonderful clear and plump and fluty notes: it is when the hollow of a rising ground conceives them and palms them up and throws them out, like blowing into a big humming ewer—for instance under Saddle Hill one beautiful day and another time from Hodder wood when we walked on the other side of the river.'

125 *'Denis'*. Text from a draft written before 'The furl of fresh-leaved dogrose', fragments of which surround it. On the verso is a draft of 'Binsey Poplars' dated 'March 13 1879'. Early March (?) 1879.

Metrical marks: l. 3 occasion. Great colons before 'blinking' and 'done' (l. 5).

l. 4. *three-heeled timber*: traditional, wooden archer's arrow with three stabilizing vanes.

ll. 5–6. *gold*: the centre of the target (*butt*, used loosely).

'The furl of fresh-leaved dogrose'. Early March(?) 1879.

Metrical marks: l. 17 sidled . . . dewdrops . . . diamonds.

ll. 1–4. Earlier read:

> Soft childhood's carmine dew drift down
> His cheeks the forward sun
> Has swarthed about with a lion-brown
> Before Spring season is done.

l. 1. *furl*: noun perhaps drawn from the verb in its sense of 'covering or wrapping round'.

l. 3. *swarthed*: made swarthy, darkened the complexion.

126 l. 6. MS not indented, in error.

l. 9. See *J.* 209: 'The bluebells in your hand baffle you . . . : if you draw your fingers through them they are lodged and struggle/with a shock of wet heads; the long stalks rub and click and flatten to a fan on one another . . . making a brittle rub and jostle like the noise of a hurdle strained by leaning against'.

l. 11. Earlier read: 'Or like a hurdleless fleecy flock'.

'He mightbe slow'. Written above a draft of 'Binsey Poplars' (see note to 'Denis'). Spring 1879, before 13 March. It may have been written about the Arthur who is mentioned in 'Denis'.

l. 1. *slow*. Earlier read: 'dull'.

l. 2. *feck at first*: cancelled and not replaced.

'What being in rank-old nature'. The early versions were written between summer 1878 (see N. White in *Review of English Studies*, 20/79 (Aug. 1969) 319–20) and June 1879 (OET 399).

Metrical marks: l. 1 nature l. 2 personal l. 5 crumbling . . . thundering

There are great colons before 'personal' (l. 2), 'billow' (l. 3), 'westerly' and 'blustering' (l. 4), 'Underneath' (l. 6).

ll. 1–2. Earlier read:

What things in nature should have, earlier, that breath been
Which, personal, tells off these heart's-song powerful peals?—

l. 3. Earlier read:

Some billow, a casquèd billow:

MacKenzie has suggested that the poem was 'inspired by a piece of music, perhaps Purcell or Handel played on some great organ' (*Reader's Guide*, 222).

127 *Duns Scotus's Oxford*. Dated 'Oxford, March 1879'.

Metrical marks: l. 2 cuckoo-echoing, bell-swarmèd, lark-charmèd l. 3 thee l. 4 encounter in l. 8 keeping l. 10 on . . . waters l. 11 haunted . . . men l. 12 rarest-veinèd l. 13 insight.

l. 1. From almost any direction the college towers and trees of Oxford are conspicuous.

ll. 3–4. Country and town were once equally matched and balanced powers in Oxford.

ll. 5–6 contrast the ugly new, brick-built suburbs with the grey stone of the older, college buildings. Both Ruskin and William Morris were to complain of the new ugliness.

l. 8. *keeping*: harmony.

l. 10. *he*: Duns Scotus, who is thought to have taught at Oxford around the year 1300.

l. 11. Hopkins wrote: 'At this time I had first begun to get hold of the copy of Scotus on the Sentences . . . and was flush with a new stroke of enthusiasm. It may come to nothing or it may be a mercy from God. But just then when I took in any inscape of the sky or sea I thought of Scotus' (*J.* 221, 3 Aug. 1872).

l. 12. *realty*: reality.

ll. 12–3. Hopkins remarked to Patmore that Duns Scotus 'saw too far, he knew too much; his subtlety overshot his interests . . . and the ruck of talent in the Schools finding itself, as his age passed by, less and less able to understand him, voted that there was nothing important to understand and so first misquoted and then refuted him' (*L.* III 349).

l. 14. See *S.* 45: 'It is a comfort to think that the greatest of the divines and doctors of the Church who have spoken and written in favour of this truth [the Immaculate Conception] came from England: between 500 and 600 years ago he was sent for to go to Paris to dispute in its favour. The disputation or debate was held in public and someone who was there says that this wise and happy man by his answers broke the objections brought against him as Samson broke the thongs and withies with which his enemies tried to bind him.' Scotus was born in Scotland, but at the time Hopkins was writing it was thought that he might have been born in Northumbria.

127 *Binsey Poplars.* Dated 'March 13 1879'.

Metrical marks: l. 8 river and wind-wandering.

Hopkins wrote to Canon Dixon, 'I have been up to Godstow this afternoon. I am sorry to say that the aspens that lined the river are everyone felled' (*L.* II 26).

l. 1. *aspens*: an unusually broad type of poplar with fluttering leaves.

l. 6. *dandled*: used of bouncing a child up and down. Cf. Milton, *Paradise Lost*, iv. 343.

In April 1873 Hopkins wrote 'The ashtree growing in the corner of the garden was felled. It was lopped first: I heard the sound and looking out and seeing it maimed there came at that moment a great pang and I wished to die and not to see the inscapes of the world destroyed any more' (*J.* 230).

128 *Henry Purcell.* Dated 'Oxford, April 1879' and marked 'Alexandrine: six stresses to the line'.

Metrical marks: l. 1 fair fallen . . . fallen l. 2 To me l. 4 sentence . . . listed l. 5 meaning l. 6 that l. 8 there . . . on . . . the ear l. 9 angels . . . lay me! only I'll l. 10 of him . . . moonmarks l. 11 stormfowl l. 13 palmy l. 14 him . . . motion.

l. 6. *nursle*: to nurse, foster, cherish.

l. 7. *forgèd feature*: inescapable impress of personality.

l. 8. *abrupt*: frank, unselfconscious.

ll. 9–14. Hopkins wrote to Bridges: 'The sestet of the Purcell sonnet is not so clearly worked out as I could wish. The thought is that as the seabird opening his wings with a whiff of wind in your face means the whirr of the motion, but also unaware gives you a whiff of knowledge about his plumage, the marking of which stamps his species, that he does not mean, so Purcell, seemingly intent only on the thought or feeling he is to express or call out, incidentally lets you remark the individualising marks of his own genius' (*L.* I 83, 26–31 May 1879).

l. 10. *sakes.* 'It is the *sake* of "for the sake of", *forsake, namesake, keepsake.* I mean by it the being a thing has outside itself, as a voice by its echo, a face by its reflection . . . a man by his name, fame, or memory, *and also* that in the thing by virtue of which especially it has this being abroad, and that is something distinctive, marked, specifically or individually speaking, as for a voice and echo clearness . . . for a man genius, great achievements, amiability, and so on. In this case it is, as the sonnet says, distinctive quality in genius' (*L.* I 83, 26–31 May 1879).

moonmarks. 'I mean crescent shaped markings on the quillfeathers, either in the colouring of the feather or made by the overlapping of one on another' (Hopkins to Bridges, *L.* I 83, 26–31 May 1879).

l. 13. *wuthering*: 'a Northcountry word for the noise and rush of wind: hence Emily Brontë's "Wuthering Heights"' (Hopkins to Bridges, *L.* I 83, 26–31 May 1879).

Hopkins explained to Bridges that 'The sonnet on Purcell means this: 1—4. I hope Purcell is not damned for being a Protestant, because I love his genius. 5–8. And that not so much for gifts he shares, even though it shd. be in higher measure, with other musicians as for his own individuality. 9–14. So that while he is aiming only at impressing me his hearer with the meaning in hand I am looking out meanwhile for his specific, his individual markings and mottlings, 'the sakes of him'. It is as when a bird thinking only of soaring spreads its wings: a beholder may happen then to have his attention drawn by the act to the plumage displayed.—In particular, the first lines mean: May Purcell, O may he have died a good death and that soul which I love so much and which breathes or stirs so unmistakeably in his works have parted from the body and passed away, centuries since though I frame the wish, in peace with God! so that the heavy condemnation under which he outwardly or nominally lay for being out of the true Church may in consequence of his good intentions have been reversed. "Low lays him" is merely "lays him low", that is/strikes him heavily, weighs upon him. (I daresay this will strike you as more professional than you had anticipated.) It is somewhat dismaying to find I am so unintelligible though, especially in one of my very best pieces. "Listed", by the by, is "enlisted". "Sakes" is hazardous: about that point I was more bent on saying my say than on being understood in it. The "moonmarks" belong to the image only of course, not to the application; I mean not detailedly: I was thinking of a bird's quill feathers. One thing disquiets me: I *meant* "fair fall" to mean *fair (fortune be)fall*; it has since struck me that perhaps "fair" is an adjective proper and in the predicate and can only be used in cases like "fair fall the day", that is, *may the day fall, turn out, fair.* My line will yield a sense that way indeed, but I never meant it so' (*L.* I 170–1, 4–5 Jan. 1883).

129 *'Repeat that, repeat'.* Undated fragment.

Metrical marks: great colon before 'landscape' (l. 5).

See *J.* 232; notes to 'The May Magnificat', ll. 43–4.

The Candle Indoors. Dated 'Oxford 1879' and marked 'common rhythm, counterpointed'.

129 Metrical marks: l. 5 window l. 6 wondering.

Hopkins noted that the poem's companion is 'The Lantern out of Doors'.

l. 3. *blear-all black*: darkness that blurs the outlines of all things.

l. 4. Perhaps the rays of light that appear to radiate out from the candle seem to revolve, an optical illusion caused by the movement of the eyelashes. Earlier read: 'Or truckling to-fro trambeams ~~finger~~ dally at the eye.'

l. 8. The oblique slash indicates a pause in reading aloud but not the break in meaning that a comma would imply.

In ll. 9–14 the poet addresses himself.

l. 12. *beam-blind*. See Matt. 7: 3–5. The poet reminds himself to be more attentive to his own faults and less critical of others.

l. 13. *liar*: false thing, i.e. salt that is incapable of 'salting'.

l. 14. *spendsavour salt*. See Matt. 5: 13–16, in which Christ warns his disciples not to lose their power of preserving mankind but to spread Christianity through their example and teaching.

conscience: men of good conscience.

The Handsome Heart. Dated 'Oxford 1879'. All versions except the final one, which uses a 6-stress line, are in pentameters.

Metrical marks: l. 5 carriers l. 11 bathed.

Hopkins described to Bridges the incident behind the sonnet: 'last Lent, when Fr. Parkinson was laid up in the country, two boys of our congregation gave me much help in the sacristy in Holy Week. I offered them money for their services, which the elder refused, but being pressed consented to take it laid out in a book. The younger followed suit; then when some days after I asked him what I shd. buy answered as in the sonnet. His father is Italian and therefore sells ices' (*L.* I 86, 14–21 Aug. 1879).

Bridges compiled a version from earlier MSS. This more lively version reads:

> 'But tell me, child, your choice; what shall I buy
> You?'—'Father, what you buy me I like best.'
> With the sweetest air that said, still plied and pressed,
> He swung to his first poised purport of reply.
>
> What the heart is! which, like carriers let fly—
> Doff darkness, homing nature knows the rest—
> To its own fine function, wild and self-instressed,
> Falls light as ten years long taught how to and why.

Mannerly-hearted! more than handsome face—
Beauty's bearing or muse of mounting vein,
All, in this case, bathed in high hallowing grace . . .

Of heaven what boon to buy you, boy, or gain
Not granted?—Only . . . O on that path you pace
Run all your race, O brace sterner that strain!

l. 4. *swung to*: like the needle in a compass. For more complex religious ideas lying behind the octave, see *S.* 157–8, 'Notes on Fr Francis Suarez, *De Mysteriis Vitae Christi*, the passage from "The will is surrounded by the objects of desire as the needle by the points of the compass . . . the grace of the mature mind."''

130 l. 5. *carriers*: pigeons capable of flying home instinctively.

heart. Earlier read 'soul'.

l. 6. *Doff darkness*: Open the pigeons' travelling-basket.

ll. 7–8. *Heart to its . . . | Falls*: following its own fine nature, which it reveals through its actions. Cf. *J.* 261: 'naturally and gracefully uttering the spiritual reason of its being'.

l. 7 *wild*: in the sense of 'untutored', innate, or natural inclination.

ll. 9–10. In a letter to Bridges, Hopkins ranked different kinds of beauty, the lowest being beauty of the body. 'Then comes the beauty of the mind, such as genius . . . And more beautiful than the beauty of the mind is beauty of character, the "handsome heart"' (*L.* I 95, 22–5 Oct. 1879).

l. 12. *buy*: by prayers.

ll. 13–14: to fulfil the promise he has shown of living a life of which God would approve.

In his letter of 8–16 October 1879, Hopkins told Bridges that 'the little hero of the Handsome Heart has gone to school at Boulogne to be bred for a priest and he is bent on being a Jesuit'.

'How all is one way wrought'. Undated draft with many revisions. Several verses are written on a note from W. H. Pater dated 'May 20 [1879]'. It may be the poem Hopkins said in a letter of 22 June 1879 that he was writing (*L.* I 84). The sequence of stanzas printed here follows the manuscript and may well not be the arrangement Hopkins would have chosen had he finished the poem.

Earlier read:

ll. 1–4. How all's to one thing wrought!
The members how they sit!
O what a tune the thought
Must be that fancied it.

l. 7. Since all that makes the man(cancelled)

ll. 9–12. Who shaped these walls has shewn
The music of his mind,
Made known in earth and stone,
What beauty beat behind.

ll. 14–16. His hand seemed free to play
He did but draw but what he was
To draw and must obey. } (cancelled)

l. 20. That vaulted round his voice.
(full stop from earlier version)

ll. 22–3. This sweetness, all this song,
This piece of perfect good,

ll. 23–4. Punctuation from earlier versions. See *S*. 295–6.

l. 28. That's cloistered by the bee.

l. 30. With that the man shall make:

ll. 35–6. But right must choose its side
To champion, and have done.

The opening stanza suggests that a piece of art, here a piece of architecture, must be revelatory of its creator. In the second and third stanzas the idea is examined, with the conclusion that the heart cannot be revealed by a building, which is also too clumsy ('rough hew and rugged rind' in one of the alternatives) to express the subtlety of its creator's mind. Stanzas four and five suggest that artistic individuality arises from the artist's intrinsic, created nature or from inspiration that (as in Plato's *Apology*) utilizes his talent. His product, therefore, (stanzas six and seven) may be artistically perfect but is morally neutral. The final two stanzas concentrate on the artist, stressing that he has moral obligations and that it is his deliberate moral attitude that governs what he makes of that more important product—himself.

131 *Cheery Beggar*. Written at Oxford during summer 1879.

Metrical marks: great colons before 'Magdalen' (l. 1) and the second 'pine' (l. 7); l. 1 Magdalen . . . thẽre l. 4 sweet-and-so͠ur of . . . fineflo͠ur of l. 5 links.

l. 3. In February Hopkins wrote to his mother: 'the long frost, severer, it is said, at Oxford than elsewhere, has given place to great rains and those to fine weather' (*L*. III 151).

ll. 4–5. *fineflour*: pollen. *goldnails*: stamens.

l. 5: *gaylinks*. Earlier read: 'gaylatchets'.

132 *The Bugler's First Communion*. Dated 'Oxford ~~Aug. 8~~ July 27(?) 1879'

and marked 'sprung rhythm, overrove; an outride between the 3rd and 4th foot of the 4th line in each stanza'.

Metrical marks: l. 3 he l. 4 surely l. 6 me, overflowing l. 8 to it l. 12 housel his l. 16 chastity l. 20 dexterous l. 24 wellbeing of a l. 25 though I l. 28 soldiery l. 32 hĕir to . . . thĕre l. 36 of him l. 40 Galahad l. 44 Eucharist l. 48 however, and.

Hopkins's parish duties included spending one day a week at the Cowley barracks in Oxford; see Griffiths 324–7.

ll. 5–6. Hopkins explained that the soldier 'came into Oxford to our Church in quest of (or to get) a blessing which, on a late occasion of my being up at Cowley Barracks, he had requested of me' (*L.* I 97, 22 Oct. 1879).

l. 12. *housel*: the communion wafer that, in Catholic belief, becomes the body of Christ.

ll. 17–20. *angel-warder*. See *S.* 91–3: 'in appointing us guardian angels God never meant that they should make us proof against all the ills that flesh is heir to, that would have been to put us in some sort back into the state of Paradise which we have lost; but he meant them, accompanying us through this world of evil and mischance, sometimes warding off its blows and buffets, sometimes leaving them to fall, always to be leading us to a better . . . world [i.e. Heaven]'.

l. 18. *squander*: scatter. *hell-rook ranks* (that) *sally*: temptations.

l. 24. *of a self-wise self-will*. In a forthright manner ('headstrong') does what is most true to man's nature as God intended it. Cf. 'The Handsome Heart', l. 7, 'its own fine function, wild and self-instressed'.

l. 25. *tufts of consolation*: intermittent comforting thoughts.

ll. 29–30. *strains* | *Us*: inspires us to effort.

l. 30. *freshyouth*. Earlier read 'boyhood' and 'boyboughs fretted in a flowerfall and all portending | Fruit of sweet's sweeter ending;'.

The image of a tree was one that Hopkins frequently used for a youth (see 'The Loss of the Eurydice', l. 6, and 'On the Portrait of Two Beautiful Young People', l. 32, for example). Here Hopkins describes a fruit-tree, suddenly altered/ruffled (*fretted*?) by the loss of its blossom, whose fall indicates that fruit is developing, a metaphor for the growing dedication to Christ within the youths.

133 l. 37. *least me quickenings lift* = least quickenings lift me.

l. 46. *brandle*: shake.

l. 48. *forward-like*: presumptuous. *like*: belike, probably.

Hopkins noted that the solider had been 'ordered to Mooltan in the Punjaub; was to sail Sept. 30'. On 8 October 1879 Hopkins wrote to Bridges: 'I enclose a poem, the Bugler. I am half inclined to hope the Hero of it may be killed in Afghanistan' (*L.* I 92), suggesting that he had misgivings about the lad's ability to lead a Christian life.

133 *Andromeda*. Dated 'Oxford Aug. 12 1879'.

In the Greek myth the princess, Andromeda, was chained to a rock as a sacrifice to a sea monster in exchange for its promise to stop ravaging her father's kingdom. Perseus, a hero with winged shoes that enabled him to fly and who was armed with a sword and the head of Medusa that turned to stone any who looked at it, saw Andromeda and rescued her.

It has been suggested that the poem is an allegory in which Andromeda represents the Catholic Church, which has been attacked through the centuries and seems doomed to be conquered by evil ('dragon food'). The 'wilder beast from West' may be the rise of industrialization, evolutionary theory, or Liberalism, which Newman condemned as the 'subjecting to human judgment (of) those revealed doctrines which are in their nature beyond and independent of it' (*Apologia*, Note A, see M. Moore, 'Newman and the "Second Spring" of Hopkins's Poetry', *Hopkins Quarterly*, 6/3 (1979)). Perseus represents Christ who will in time rescue the faithful. Hopkins may have had in mind the Day of Judgement or, more probably, the reconversion of England to Catholicism that he hoped for and frequently mentioned in his poems (see, for example, 'The Wreck of the Deutschland', stanza 34).

Hopkins, responding to Bridges' charges of writing obscure and overly ornate poems, sent him 'Andromeda' saying of it: 'Lastly I enclose a sonnet on which I invite minute criticism. I endeavoured in it at a more Miltonic plainness and severity than I have anywhere else. I cannot say it has turned out severe, still less plain, but it seems almost free from quaintness and in aiming at one excellence I may have hit another' (*L.* I 87, 14–21 Aug. 1879).

134 *Morning, Midday, and Evening Sacrifice*. Dated 'Oxford Aug. 1879'.

l. 1. *die-away*. Suggests subtle colouring and smooth shape.

l. 2. *wimpled*: curved, Cupid's bow of the upper lip.

l. 6. *fuming*: suggestive of the fleeting, almost transparent quality of childhood beauty. See *J.* 220: 'fuming of the atmosphere marked like the shadow of smoke'.

Hopkins explained to a congregation that 'any day, any minute we bless God for our being or for anything, for food, for sunlight, we do and are what we were meant for, made for—things that give and mean to give God glory . . . It is not only prayer that gives God glory but work. . . . everything gives God some glory if being in his grace you do it as your duty. . . . To lift up the hands in prayer gives God glory, but a man with a dungfork in his hand, a woman with a sloppail, give him glory too. He is so great that all things give him glory if you mean they should' (*S.* 240–1).

l. 17. Hopkins explained, '"*In silk-ash kept from cooling*". I meant to compare grey hairs to the flakes of silky ash which may be seen round wood embers burnt in a clear fire and covering a "core of heat", as Tennyson calls it' ('In Memoriam', cvii) (*L.* I 97–8).

l. 18. *rind*: the outer covering of the ember.

l. 21. See *L.* I 98: 'Come, your offer of all this (the matured mind), and without delay either!'

Peace. Curtal sonnet in alexandrines, dated 'Oct. 2 1879'. Hopkins wrote the poem out of the unsettling knowledge that the following day he was to move yet again, from Oxford to a new post as preacher in the industrial, northern town of Bedford Leigh. *Curtal*: see Author's Preface, p. 97, and *L.* II 85–8 (29 Oct. 1881).

l. 2. Hopkins remarked that in 'under be' he had reversed the order of the words for the sake of the rhythm (*L.* I 196).

135 l. 7. *reaving*: rob (*L.* I 196).

l. 9. *plumes to*: matures into, as a fledgeling develops adult plumage.

At the Wedding March. Marked 'sprung rhythm' with numerous great colons and dated 'Bedford, Lancashire. Oct. 21 1879'.

l. 3. *scions*: shoots of plants, especially for grafting. See the Catholic mass for a bridegroom and bride: 'Thy wife shall be fruitful as the vine that grows on the walls of thy house. The children round thy table sturdy as olive branches.'

ll. 10–12. See *S.* 35, Christ is 'the true love and the bridegroom of men's souls' whose sacrifice offers man eternal life (MacKenzie, *Reader's Guide*, 135).

Felix Randal. Dated 'Liverpool. April 28 1880', and marked 'sprung and outriding rhythm; six foot lines'.

Metrical marks: l. 1 Randal . . . farrier . . . then l. 3 pining . . . in it l. 5 him . . . Impatient l. 7 earlier l. 8 to him. Ah well l. 11 child, Felix, l. 12 of l. 13 random l. 14 drayhorse.

l. 6. See *S.* 248–9.

136 l. 7. *sweet reprieve and ransom.* Holy Communion recalling Christ's sacrifice.

l. 8. *God rest him.* God forgive him.

136 *all road ever*. . . Lancashire dialect, 'for whatever (sins) he committed'.

l. 14. *sandal*: the technical name for a particular type of horseshoe (MacKenzie, *Reader's Guide*, 139).

Brothers. Dated 'Hampstead. Aug. 1880'; marked 'sprung rhythm; three feet to the line; lines free-ended and not overrove; and reversed or counterpointed rhythm allowed in the first foot'.

See *L.* I 86 (14 Aug. 1879): 'I hope to enclose a little scene that touched me at Mount St. Mary's. It is something in Wordsworth's manner; which is, I know, inimitable and unapproachable, still I shall be glad to know if you think it a success, for pathos has a point as precise as jest has and its happiness "lies ever in the ear of him that hears, not in the mouth of him that makes".' Jack may have played the part of a herald in a single-act farce called 'A Model Kingdom', which was performed after a two-act play (l. 29). The 11-year-old might have had to play a few notes on a trumpet (ll. 33–4), which further explains Harry's apprehension, and makes the description of Jack as 'brass-bold' (l. 25) still more appropriate (Fr. Francis Keegan, SJ, 'Gerard Manley Hopkins at Mount St. Mary's College Spinkhill, 1877–1878', *Hopkins Quarterly* (spring 1979), 26).

137 *Spring and Fall.* Dated 'Lydiate, Lancashire. Sept. 7 1880' and marked 'sprung rhythm'. Hopkins wrote to Bridges that the poem was 'not founded on any real incident' (*L.* I 109). The poet suggests that children intuitively feel the sorrow of death. As adults, he says, they will understand that the source of this sorrow is their own mortality, which since the Fall all men must experience (Gen. 3: 19).

l. 2. *unleaving*: losing its leaves.

l. 8. Earlier read: 'Though forests low and leafmeal lie'. See *J.* 239: 'Wonderful downpour of leaf: when the morning sun began to melt the frost they fell at one touch and in a few minutes a whole tree was flung of them; they lay masking and papering the ground at the foot. Then the tree seems to be looking down on its cast self as blue sky on snow after a long fall, its losing, its doing.'

wanwood: perhaps from 'wann', Old English for 'dark', but I prefer the associations suggested by 'wan', pale from fatigue or sorrow.

leafmeal: perhaps a more specific version of 'piecemeal'; the tree's 'cast self' disintegrating as fallen leaves. See the final note to 'Binsey Poplars'.

l. 13. *ghost*: spirit.

138 *Inversnaid.* Dated 'Inversnaid Sept. 28 1881'. Inversnaid is a small settlement in the Scottish Highlands. Hopkins described his visit to W. M. Baillie (7 Sept. 1887): 'I hurried from Glasgow one day to Loch Lomond. The day was dark and partly hid the lake, yet it did

not altogether disfigure it but gave a pensive or solemn beauty which left a deep impression on me. I landed at Inversnaid (cf. Wordsworth and Matthew Arnold) for a few hours . . . ' (*L.* III 288).

l. 3. *coop*: perhaps a hollow; 'Rushing streams may be described as inscaped ordinarily in pillows—and upturned troughs' (*J.* 176).

comb: water pouring over a rock so that it forms ridges. See *J.*, pl. 28, 'At the baths of Rosenlaui'. The picture elucidates both 'comb' and 'flutes'.

l. 4. *flutes*: the architectural meaning applied to ridges of water, used here to suggest the appearance of grooves in the falling plane of water.

l. 6. *twindles*. Perhaps Lancashire dialect 'twins', the foam divides into two or doubles. Alternatively the verb may be a combination of 'twine' (to coil) and 'spindle' (to grow into a long, slender form).

l. 9. *degged*: Lancashire dialect for 'sprinkled', 'bedewed'.

l. 11. *heathpacks*: heather.

flitches: stiff, browned fronds like thin strips of tree trunk (MacKenzie, *Reader's Guide*, 147).

l. 12. *beadbonny ash*: mountain ash, which has lots of red berries in the autumn.

ll. 13–16. See *L.* I 73–4: 'I have . . . something, if I cd. only seize it, on the decline of wild nature, beginning somehow like this—

O where is it, the wilderness,
The wildness of the wilderness?
Where is it, the wilderness?
— — — — — —
And wander in the wilderness;
In the weedy wilderness,
Wander in the wilderness.'

The Leaden Echo and the Golden Echo. Dated 'Stonyhurst. Oct. 13 1882'. Hopkins wrote on it, 'I have marked the stronger stresses, but with the degree of stress so perpetually varying no marking is satisfactory. Do you think all had best be left to the reader?'

Metrical marks: l. 1 keep . . . lace l. 4 Down *Golden Echo*: l. 7 One l. 9 dearly l. 12 more l. 17 sighs.

As early as 5 September 1880 Hopkins wrote to Bridges: 'You shall also see *The Leaden Echo* when finished. The reason, I suppose, why you feel it carry the reader along with it is that it is dramatic and meant to be popular. It is a song for St. Winefred's maidens to sing.' He announced in early October 1882 (*L.* I 153) that he had finished the poem and was pleased with it. In November 1882 (*L.* I 161) he wrote: 'I cannot satisfy myself about the first line. You must know that words like *charm* and *enchantment* will not do: the thought is of beauty as of something that can be physically kept and lost and by physical things only, like keys; then the things must come from the *mundus muliebris*; and thirdly they must not be markedly oldfashioned. You will see that this limits the choice of words very much indeed. However I shall make some changes. *Back* is not pretty, but it gives that feeling of physical constraint which I want.'

When offering to send the poem to Dixon, Hopkins noted of it: 'I never did anything more musical' (*L.* II 149). A somewhat similar theme can be seen in 'Morning, Midday, and Evening Sacrifice' (p. 134).

The Leaden Echo.

138 ll. 3–4. *frowning . . . Down*: driving away with disapproval.

rankèd: ranks of, strongly marked.

l. 8. The wise are the first to realize that physical beauty will fade with age.

The Golden Echo.

139 l. 1. *Spare*: a mechanical echo of 'Despair' marking a change in attitude between the two sections of the poem.

l. 10. Fresh, fleeting beauty.

l. 11. *fleece of beauty.* 'The velvetiness of rose-leaves, flesh and other things' (*L.* I 215).

140 l. 21. See Matt. 10: 30, quoted by Hopkins in *S.* 252.

ll. 22–5. See *L.* I 159: '"Nay what we lighthanded" etc. means "Nay more: the seed that we so carelessly and freely flung into the dull furrow, and then forgot it, will have come to ear meantime" etc.'

l. 26. *fagged*: tired, worn out. *fashed*: (Scot.) anxious.

cogged: perhaps 'vexed', 'blocked'. *cumbered*: overladen.

ll. 27–30. See *S.* 89: God 'takes more interest . . . in a lover's sweetheart than the . . . lover, in a sick man's pain than the sufferer, in our salvation than we ourselves'. The Catholic doctrine of the Resurrection promises believers that their human bodies will be restored for eternity but perfected and consequently the surest way of preserving physical beauty is to dedicate one's earthly body and life to God.

Ribblesdale. One autograph prefaces the poem with the Latin of Rom. 8: 19–20: 'Nam expectatio creaturae . . . '. Below this version Hopkins wrote: 'It is to be read very pausingly, the voice especially dwelling where the native rhythm overlaps into another line. It is common rhythm counterpointed.' Dated 'Stonyhurst. 1882' and marked, 'Companion to no. 10' ('In the Valley of the Elwy').

Metrical marks: l. 1 landscape l. 10 the heir.

Nam expectatio . . . The Douay version paraphrases Rom. 8: 19–21: 'He (St Paul) speaks of the corporeal creation, made for the use and service of man and, by occasion of his sin, made subject to vanity, that is, to a perpetual instability, tending to corruption and other defects: so that by a figure of speech it is here said to groan and be in labour and to long for its deliverance, which is then to come, when sin shall reign no more and God shall raise the bodies and unite them to their souls, never more to separate and to be in everlasting happiness in heaven.'

l. 1. *throng*. See *L*. II 109: 'I mean "throng" for an adjective as we use it here in Lancashire' ('thick or crowded', *EDD*). Cf. 'All the herbage enthronged with every fingered or fretted leaf' (*J*. 172).

l. 2: *louchèd*. See *L*. II 109: '"louchéd" is a coinage of mine and is to mean much the same as slouched, slouching.'

ll. 6–7. *deal . . . down*: to treat badly, unfairly.

l. 11. *selfbent*: absorbed by his own self-centred desires. Contrast l. 24 of 'The Bugler's First Communion' (p. 132).

ll. 13–14. *this bids . . . concern*. This is why the earth looks so troubled.

141 *'A Trio of Triolets'*. Printed in the *Stonyhurst Magazine*, 1/9 (Mar. 1883), 162. They were signed with the pseudonym, BRAN. Hopkins liked numbers 2 and 3 (*L*. I 190, 317–18), but he considered that no. 1 'was not good, and they spoilt what point it had by changing the title'. The original title is now lost (OET 434).

No. 1 λέγεταί . . . 'Is there any news today?', Demosthenes, *First Philippic*, 10.

142 *The Blessed Virgin compared*. Dated 'Stonyhurst. May 1883'. See *L*. I 179 (11 May 1883): 'We hang up polyglot poems in honour of the Blessed Virgin this month. I am on one in English in three-foot couplets . . . It is partly a compromise with popular taste, and it is too true that the highest subjects are not those on which it is easy to reach one's highest.' He told Dixon that the poem was 'in the same metre as "Blue in the mists all day" . . . '(*L*. II 108).

l. 5. *frailest-flixed*: from 'flix', the fur of various quadrupeds. Hopkins often uses it to describe clouds (see *J*. 153, 192, for example).

ll. 22–33. Papal Bull *Gloriosae Dominae* (1748) compares Mary to 'a heavenly stream through which the flow of all graces and favours reaches the soul of every wretched mortal'.

142 l. 37. Mary is called Mother of Mercy. She is seen as Queen of Heaven, possessing the power of dispensing grace but not punishment.

143 ll. 40–1. 'God has allowed her prayers to dispense his beneficent care.'

ll. 46–8. Christ's statement to John (John 19: 26–7) is often interpreted as a proclamation that Mary is the spiritual mother of the human race.

ll. 53–4. Christian doctrine states that belief in Christ is essential for salvation. (See next note on Christ's mystical body.)

ll. 60–72. Christ's presence on earth after the Resurrection continues within his believers. Contemplation of his divine conception and birth (at Nazareth and Bethlehem respectively) creates new and reaffirms old believers in the Catholic faith. Since Christ's mystical body is his Church of believers on earth, an increase in the number of believers 'more makes' or increases Christ (God's and Mary's Son) both here and in redemption. The dedication to Christ is also made 'more' in each believer.

ll. 75–80. See *J.* 154 (30 Aug.); *S.* 29: 'St. Bernard's saying, All grace given through Mary: this a mystery. Like blue sky, which for its richness of colour does not stain the sunlight, though smoke and red clouds do, so God's graces come to us unchanged but all through her. Moreover she gladdens the Catholic's heaven and when she is brightest so is the sun her son: he that sees no blue sees no sun either, so with Protestants.'

144 l. 103. *God of old*: God of the old dispensation, just but not merciful.

ll. 104–13. Mary is an intermediary between the might of Christ risen and mankind. She is perfect, the only woman completely without sin, and more powerful than all mortals but of lower rank than Christ, with whom she intercedes on man's behalf.

145 *'The times are nightfall'*. Undated draft (1885–6?). For the thought, see *L.* I 221 (1 Sept. 1885) for example: 'in the life I lead now, which is one of a continually jaded and harassed mind, if in any leisure I try to do anything I make no way—nor with my work, alas! but so it must be.' Hopkins does not appear to have written the sonnet's final three lines. See C. Phillips, 'The Effects of Incompleteness in Three Hopkins Poems', *Renascence,* 42/1–2 (Fall 1989–Winter 1990), 22–6, on the poem's form.

l. 1. Earlier read: ' . . . nightfall, light of heaven grows less'.

l. 4. Earlier read: 'More make or plainer publish our distress' (cancelled).

l. 5. Earlier read: 'I cannot help', altered to 'Could I but help'.

l. 8. *does dear*: does make (forgetfulness) dear or precious.

ll. 9–11. See 'The Candle Indoors', ll. 9–11 (p. 129).

l. 10. *dragons*: symbolic of evil; see *S.* 198–9.

St. Winefred's Well.

Metrical marks: l. 6 ready in his l. 10 A̋h l. 11 No man l. 13 mőre times l. 15 Ta̋mpering . . . drȃws l. 16 Wha̋t l. 18 all, all l. 19 nőt l. 24 főol Act II, l. 1 hea̋rt . . . se̋en l. 3 őff l. 5 Mőnuments . . . re̋cords l. 6 whéreas l. 7 Wa̋rned l. 9 Perha̋ps l. 10 ma̋kebelieve . . . mőck l. 11 here, here . . . swe̋ats l. 15 ca̋n . . . thee ín thy dárk lair; thése drops l. 17 woe̋ful l. 19 rőll l. 23 tó l. 27 li̋fted, ̋immortal . . . ímmőrtal l. 32 nót l. 34 Í . . . dóne víolent l. 35 líke a líon dóne, líonlíke dóne l. 40 Lóyal . . . ówn . . . láying . . . ówn . . . dówn, no láw l. 41 Lȏrd . . . hím l. 42 ȏnly l. 43 Ȏnly l. 44 líke l. 45 wíll . . . can flésh l. 49 cómfort whére can I̋ l. 50 time's one rich rose, mý hand l. 52 dáshed down l. 53 nő l. 54 passion-sake. Yes l. 55 nót . . . yét hope ón l. 60 hér neck l. 63 ki̋nd . . . ke̋en l. 65 Whát do nów . . . Dó l. 66 Déed-bound . . . óne . . . tréads . . . dówn (C) l. 4 thi̋rst l. 5 li̋pmusic . . . lőst l. 14 rőck l. 15 fra̋il l. 19 Wa̋les l. 21 mőre pilgrims l. 24 ca̋me l. 25 na̋me l. 26 bóons . . . háven the héart l. 28 neẃ-dapple l. 29 Amőngst come-back-aga̋in . . . thi̋ngs with.

Note that single stress-marks in the text represent double stresses in the MS, see pp. xxii–xxiii, 167.

*St. Winefred. c.*600–60. Winefred was born into a wealthy family in Holywell, Wales. She was guided by her uncle, St Beuno, to dedicate herself to an austere and religious life. Her reputation for wisdom and purity reached the ears of Caradoc, the son of a neighbouring prince. He pressed Winefred to marry him and when she, fearing for her chastity, tried to flee from him, cut off her head. The head rolled down a steep gully and where it came to rest a spring suddenly appeared. St Beuno prayed successfully for Winefred's recovery. He also asked that Caradoc be punished and he was struck dead. St

Winefred became abbess of a convent at Holywell and later at Gwytherin (*Cath. Encycl.* 1910).

Hopkins was most enthusiastic about St Winefred's well. He wrote to Bridges of her famous spring that it 'fills me with devotion every time I see it and would fill anyone that has eyes with admiration, the flow of ἀγλαὸν ὕδωρ [beautiful water] is so lavish and so beautiful' (*L.* I 40, 3–8 Apr. 1877). In 1879 (8 Oct.) he told Bridges that he was writing a drama about the subject in alexandrines. He hoped to be able to send the murder scene and some more soon. 'I mean [it]', he added, 'to be short, say in 3 or even 2 acts; the characters few.' The greatest problems, he found, were not in writing the tragic or stirring scenes, but the 'minor parts' (*L.* I 92). The play was not finished although Hopkins worked at it periodically for seven years. Most of what is extant appears to have been written between October 1884 and April 1885.

Of the rhythm Hopkins told Dixon: 'It is in an alexandrine verse, which I sometimes expand to 7 or 8 feet, very hard to manage but very effective when well used' (*L.* II 143). To Bridges he elaborated: 'I hold that each half line is by nature a dimeter, two bars or four feet, of which commonly one foot is silent or lost at the pause. You will find it sometimes employed in full . . . You will see that as the feeling rises the rhythm becomes freer and more sprung: I think I have written nothing stronger than some of those lines' (*L.* I 212).

145 l. 2. *Caerwys.* Hopkins notes: 'In English pronounced *Caris*, like *heiress.*'

146 l. 9. *Gwenvrewi*: Winefred's original, Welsh name.

147 Act II, l. 17. *Cradock.* This spelling, which gives approximately the Welsh pronunciation and stress of *Caradoc*, appears in the Dublin notebook MS.

151 *The Sonnets of Desolation.* Most of these were found after Hopkins's death, although it is clear from his letters that he had intended to send at least some of them to Bridges. Late in May 1885 he wrote: 'I have after long silence written two sonnets, which I am touching: if ever anything was written in blood one of these was' (*L.* I 219). In September of the same year he wrote to Bridges: 'I shall shortly have some sonnets to send you, five or more. Four of these came like inspirations unbidden and against my will. And in the life I lead now, which is one of a continually jaded and harassed mind, if in any leisure I try to do anything I make no way—nor with my work, alas! but so it must be' (*L.* I 221, 1 Sept. 1885). Critics do not all agree about which poems should be covered by the title, which was not chosen by Hopkins, but generally included are: 'To seem the stranger', 'I wake and feel', 'No worst', (Carrion Comfort), 'Patience, hard

thing', and 'My own heart'. The sequence is uncertain, since most of them exist only as fair copies on a single sheet of sermon-paper, but they were all most probably written in 1885–6.

'To seem the stranger'. Single stresses in the text represent double stresses in the MS; see pp. xxii–xxiii, 167.

Metrical marks: l. 7 Ȉ wĕ̋ar l. 9 Í . . . thi̋rd l. 14 unhee͡ded.

ll. 2–3. Hopkins's family was not Catholic.

l. 4. See Matt. 10: 34–7.

l. 5. See *L.* I 231 (13 Oct. 1886) on the importance of producing successful creative works. Hopkins sees them as educative and as a patriotic duty because they increase England's fame.

ll. 6–7. (England) '*would neither hear | Me, were I pleading*', perhaps alluding to his hopes that England would become Catholic again; cf. 'The Wreck of the Deutschland', stanza 35, and 'The Loss of the Eurydice', ll. 97–104, for example.

l. 8. and ll. 11–14. Cf. Hopkins's retreat notes made at St Stanislaus College, Tullabeg, in January 1889: 'the Catholic Church in Ireland and the Irish Province in it and our College in that are greatly given over to a partly unlawful cause, promoted by partly unlawful means, and against my will my pains, laborious and distasteful, like prisoners made to serve the enemies' gunners, go to help on this cause. I do not feel then that outwardly I do much good, much that I care to do or can much wish to prosper; and this is a mournful life to lead. In thought I can of course divide the good from the evil and live for the one, not the other: this justifies me but it does not alter the facts. Yet it seems to me that I could lead this life well enough if I had bodily energy and cheerful spirits. However these God will not give me. . . . What is my wretched life? Five wasted years almost have passed in Ireland. I am ashamed of the little I have done, of my waste of time, although my helplessness and weakness is such that I could scarcely do otherwise. And yet the Wise Man warns us against excusing ourselves in that fashion. I cannot then be excused; but what is life without aim, without spur, without help? All my undertakings miscarry: I am like a straining eunuch. I wish then for death: yet if I died now I should die imperfect, no master of myself, and that is the worst failure of all' (*S* 262). See too *L.* I 231 (1 Sept. 1885), and 270 (12 Jan. 1888).

ll. 9–10. *third remove*. Perhaps the first remove was the partial estrangement with his family brought about by their holding different religious beliefs (ll. 2–4). The second remove may have been from the English people who were mostly Anglican but whom Hopkins longed to see converted to Catholicism (ll. 5–7). In Ireland, although

Hopkins found himself among Catholics, they were disloyal to England (see *S*. 262).

151 l. 14. *began*: probably noun, suggesting someone whose early promise has not been fulfilled.

'I wake and feel'. This may well have been the sonnet 'written in blood' (*L*. I 219). (MacKenzie, *Reader's Guide*, 171–2.)

Metrical mark: l. 2 hōurs we.

l. 1. *fell*: 'blow', but also 'an animal's pelt'; see *J*. 174: 'the deep fell of some other animal . . . ' See Job 7: 4.

l. 2. *black*: 'miserable' as well as 'dark'.

l. 7. *dead letters*: undelivered letters.

ll. 9–14. Earlier read:

> I am gall and heartburn. God's most deep decree
> Has me taste bitter, and my taste is me.
> My bones build, my flesh fills, blood feeds/this curse
> Of my selfstuff, by self yeast soured. I see
> The lost are like this, with their loss to be
> Their sweating selves, as I am mine, but worse.

ll. 9–10. *God's most deep decree|Bitter would have me taste*. See *L*. II 108–9, 25 June 1883: 'I see no grounded prospect of my ever doing much not only in poetry but in anything at all. At times I do feel this sadly and bitterly, but it is God's will . . . '

l. 10. Cf. *S*. 243: 'sight does not shock like hearing, sounds cannot so disgust as smell, smell is not so bitter as proper bitterness, which is in taste', from Hopkins's notes on *The Spiritual Exercises*.

ll. 12–14. *I see . . . but worse*. See *S*. 241–4, which makes it clear that the punishments endured by 'the lost' in hell are directly related to their sins: 'we are our own tormentors, for every sin we then shall have remorse and with remorse torment.'

152 *'Strike, churl'*. Written on the same page as a cancelled draft of the sestet of 'I wake and feel'. May? 1885. Hopkins wrote to his mother (17 May 1885), 'The hail today lay long like pailfuls of coarse rice' (*L*. III 171) (OET 449).

l. 4. *have at*: attack, beat; earlier 'aim at'.

'No worst'.

Metrical marks: l. 6 wórld-sorrow; on an l. 8 fell.

l. 1. *Pitched past pitch*. Earlier drafts read: 'grief past pitch of grief', 'Grief past grief', and 'Grief tops grief'.

pitched: either 'thrown' or 'tuned by stretching a string' as with a violin.

l. 2. *forepangs*: earlier experiences of pain.

l. 3. *Comforter*: the Paraclete; see *S.* 70–1. Christ and the Holy Ghost are Paracletes, comforting and providing encouragement.

l. 6. *world-sorrow*: perhaps the world-weariness of ennui, perhaps part of the projected amplification of feeling found elsewhere in ll. 5 and 6, or an acknowledgement that all sorrow derives from the Fall.

l. 8. *force*: perforce.

l. 10. Earlier read: 'Frightful, sheer down, not fathomed.'

l. 12. *durance*: endurance. l. 13. Cf. *King Lear*, III. ii. 60–2.

To what serves Mortal Beauty? Marked 'common rhythm highly stressed'. Dated 'Aug. 23 1885'.

Metrical marks: l. 1 what serves l. 3 See: it . . . keeps warm l. 4 Men's wit . . . to what l. 5 more may l. 6 windfalls of war's storm l. 11 men's selves.

Hopkins explained that 'the mark (———) over two neighbouring syllables means that, though one has and the other has not the metrical stress, in the recitation-stress they are to be about equal' (*L.* II 129).

l. 2. *the O-seal-that-so feature*. Earlier read: 'face feature-perfect'.

ll. 3–4. *keeps warm|Men's wit*. Earlier read: 'keeps warm men's thoughts to what things be'.

ll. 4–5. Earlier read: 'One clear glance|May gather more than staring out of countenance' and 'where a glance|Gather more may than gaze me out of countenance'.

ll. 6–8. In the sixth century Pope Gregory saw a group of English boys (Angli) for sale as slaves in a Roman market. The fair-haired beauty of the lads allegedly caused Gregory to compare them to angels (angeli) and he decided that it would be worth trying to convert pagan England to Catholicism. This possibility of salvation is the good fortune that Hopkins calls 'that day's dear chance'.

153 ll. 9–11. Earlier read:

> Was man bid love, bid worship, block or barren stone?
> Our law is love what are world's loveliest, were all known,
> Most worth love, men's selves.

l. 12. *own*: acknowledge.

l. 13. *home at heart*: deep in your heart (?).

l. 14. *grace*. Refers to beauty of actions, the result of belief in God.

See *L.* I 95–6 on the different types of beauty (see above, note to 'The Handsome Heart', ll. 9–10), and *S.* 35–6.

153 (*Carrion Comfort*). Undated but the earliest draft extant (cancelled) follows a draft of 'To what serves Mortal Beauty' dated 'Aug. 23 '85'. A second draft precedes the only draft of (The Soldier), dated 'Clongowes Aug. 1885'. The final draft, which is probably from 1887 since it is written around an early draft of 'Tom's Garland', ends after l. 12. The last two lines are taken from the second draft.

Metrical marks: l. 1 comfort l. 5 terrible l. 8 O in . . . tempest . . . there . . . frantic to avoid l. 11 rather . . . lo . . . stole l. 12 The hero whose heaven-handling l. 13 him . . . which one . . . each one l. 14 wretch.

l. 1. *carrion comfort*: Despair, the false comfort of abandoning all effort.

l. 4. Earlier read: 'Can hold on, hope for comfort; not wish not to be.' Stop from earlier version.

ll. 5–6. Earlier read: 'Yet why, thou terrible, wouldst thou rock rude on me | ~~With~~ Thy wring-earth tread; launch lion-foot on me?' See Job 9: 6, God 'Which shaketh the earth out of her place, and the pillars thereof tremble'. In the final draft Hopkins wrote 'wring-world', adding as an alternative 'wring-earth' (which he had used in the earlier drafts) before completing the line.

lionlimb. See Job 10: 16: 'Thou huntest me as a fierce lion.'

l. 7. See Job 7: 8: 'thy eyes are upon me, and I shall be no more' (Douay).

fan: to separate the kernel or grain of wheat from the chaff or husk.

l. 8. See Job 9: 17: 'For he breaketh me with a tempest, and multiplieth my wounds without cause.'

l. 9. John the Baptist prophesied that Christ would divide mankind in a similar way. See Luke 3: 16, 17: 'John answered, saying unto *them* all, I indeed baptize you with water; but one mightier than I cometh, the latchet of whose shoes I am not worthy to unloose: he shall baptize you with the Holy Ghost and with fire: Whose fan *is* in his hand, and he will throughly purge his floor, and will gather the wheat into his garner; but the chaff he will burn with fire unquenchable.' See GMH's comments on the second passage in *S.* 267–8. Cf. Matt. 3: 12.

l. 10. Earlier read: 'because I kissed the rod'. 'Kissed the rod' may mean 'accepted depression, despair as a test set by God'. See *S.* 256, June 1884: 'Take it that weakness, ill-health, every cross is a help' towards greater spirituality (MacKenzie, *Reader's Guide*, 175).

l. 11. Earlier read: 'Nay from the storm my heart stole joy . . . '

l. 12. Earlier read: 'hero whose heavenforce'.

ll. 13–14. See Gen. 32: 24–30.

(*The Soldier*). Bridges' title. Dated 'Clongowes Aug. 1885'. Single stress-marks in the text represent double or strong stresses in the MS. See pp. xxii–xxiii, 167.

Metrical marks: l. 1 Why̋ . . . a̋ll, se̋eing . . . sóldier, bléss . . . ble̋ss l. 2 rédcoats, óur . . . Bóth thêse béing, the gréater párt l. 3 Here it is: the héart l. 5 ma̋kesbelieve l. 6 fáncies, féigns, déems, de̋ars . . . ártist áfter his árt l. 8 scárlet we̋ar . . . spírit of wár the̋re expréss l. 11 séeing somewhére some mán l. 12 lóve he le̋ans . . . néeds . . . néck . . . fáll . . . kíss.

l. 3. Hopkins had acted as confessor at the Cowley Barracks, Oxford.

154 l. 6. *dears . . . after*: values . . . as.

l. 9. See *S.* 70: 'he (Christ) led the way, went before his troops, was himself the vanguard, was the forlorn hope, bore the brunt of battle alone, died upon the field, on Calvary hill, and bought the victory by his blood. He cried men on . . . ' Cf. the Ignation prayer: 'To give and not to count the cost | To fight and not to heed the wounds | To toil and not to seek for rest | To labour and not to ask for any reward | Save that of knowing that I do thy holy will.'

l. 13. *Christ-done deed*: both a deed such as Christ would have done, and a deed that maintains Christ's presence on earth.

God-made-flesh: Christ incarnated.

'Thee, God, I come from'. Verso has cancelled drafts of 'To what serves Mortal Beauty?'. A hymn reminiscent of George Herbert. See N. White and T. Dunne, 'A Hopkins Discovery', *Library*, 24/1 (Mar. 1969), 56–8.

l. 6. See note to 'The Wreck of the Deutschland', l. 8.

155 *'Patience, hard thing'*.

Metrical marks: l. 8 Purple͡ eyes l. 11 do̎.

See *S.* 204, *Spiritual Exercises* VIII: 'Let him who is in desolation strive to remain in patience, which is the virtue contrary to the troubles which harass him; and let him think that he will shortly be consoled, making diligent efforts against the desolation . . . '

ll. 2–4. Patience is a quality that one develops in adversity.

ll. 6–7. Ivy is a vigorous plant that will grow over and hide the ruins of buildings.

155 l. 8. *Purple eyes*: berries.

ll. 9–11. 'During this retreat I have much and earnestly prayed that God will lift me above myself to a higher state of grace, in which I may have more union with him, be more zealous to do his will, and freer from sin . . . In meditating on the Crucifixion I saw how my asking to be raised to a higher degree of grace was asking also to be lifted on a higher cross' (*S.* 254, 8, 9 Sept. 1883, Retreat at Beaumont).

l. 10. *dearer*: both more severely, and spiritually more valuable; cf. note to ll. 9–11.

l. 14. *combs*: honeycomb.

156 *'My own heart'*.

Metrical marks: l. 13 you; unforseentimes rather.

ll. 6–7 are highly elliptical: comfortless (world) . . . (find) day or thirst can find (ease/drink).

l. 8. *all-in-all*: everything; cf. Coleridge's 'Rime of the Ancient Mariner', ll. 119–22.

l. 9. *Jackself*: everyday, working self. Perhaps an allusion to the saying, 'all work and no play makes Jack a dull boy.'

l. 11. *size*: grow. See 'The May Magnificat', l. 25.

l. 14. *Betweenpie*: probably a verb, suggesting either that the sky seen between mountains makes a pied or variegated pattern with them, or that sunlight falling into a valley changes the colour of those parts of the mountains it touches.

To his Watch. Undated. Hopkins transcribed into his commonplace book 'I pull'd my watch fr. out my fob' by HWC (Henry William Challis?), which, after describing the clock's mechanism, says:

So slowly roll the wheels and cogs
To move that transcendental clock
By wh. the acts of men are bound,
And regulate this dreary sound—
Alternate tick, alternate tock.

See C. Phillips, 'The Effects of Incompleteness in Three Hopkins Poems', *Renascence*, 42/1–2 (Fall 1989–Winter 1990), 26–9.

l. 2. Earlier read: 'With cold beat company, shall you, or I,'.

l. 3. Earlier read: 'Earlier, undone give o'er our work and lie'.

l. 4. *ruins*. Earlier read: 'wreck'.

l. 5. Earlier read: 'Telling of time our task is; yea ~~not~~ some part,'.

telling time. Perhaps, as applied to the poet, it means making time tell—making good use of time (perhaps see Col. 4: 5).

l. 6. *but we were*. Earlier read: 'time, being both' (cancelled).

l. 7. (We have) *One spell* (on earth) *and well* (must) *that one* (be used).

ah. Earlier read 'O'.

l. 8. Earlier alternative, uncancelled, read: 'Is comfort's carol of all or woe's worst smart.' Hopkins inserted 'sweetest' above 'comfort's', then cancelled it and rewrote the line as it now stands in the text.

l. 9. *Field-flown, the*. Earlier read: 'O see! The'. Cf. Isa. 39: 6.

157 *Spelt from Sibyl's Leaves*. Marked 'sprung rhythm: a rest of one stress in the first line'.

Metrical marks: l. 10 O͡ our.

Hopkins wrote to Bridges: 'I have at least completed but not quite finished the longest sonnet ever made and no doubt the longest making. It is in 8-foot lines and essays effects almost musical' (*L.* I 245). When he sent it to Bridges on 11 December 1886, he added that it should be read with 'loud, leisurely, poetical (not rhetorical) recitation, with long rests, long dwells on the rhyme and other marked syllables and so on. This sonnet shd. be almost sung: it is most carefully timed in *tempo-rubato*' (*L.* I 246). See Milroy, 232 ff., and Griffiths, 318–20.

Title. An allusion to the opening verse of the 'Dies irae' in the Catholic Mass for the Dead: 'Day of wrath, that day when the world is consumed to ash as David and the Sibyl testify.' Cf. also *Aeneid* vi. 11–12, 268–72, 539–43.

l. 1. *Earnest*: solemn. *stupendous*: terrifying.

l. 2. The evening darkens into night that seems to envelop everything from the creation of the earth to its end. See Matt. 24: 29.

ll. 2–3. 'First saw the Northern Lights. My eye was caught by beams of light and dark very like the crown of horny rays the sun makes behind a cloud. At first I thought of silvery cloud until I saw that these were more luminous and did not dim the clearness of the stars in the Bear. They rose slightly radiating thrown out from the earth-line. Then I saw soft pulses of light one after another rise and pass upwards arched in shape but waveringly and with the arch broken. They seemed to float, not following the warp of the sphere as falling stars look to do but free though concentrical with it. This busy working of nature wholly independent of the earth and seeming to go on in a strain of time not reckoned by our reckoning of days and years but simpler and as if correcting the preoccupation of the world by being preoccupied with and appealing to and dated to the day of judgment was like a new witness to God and filled me with delightful fear' (*J.* 200, 24 Sept. 1870).

157 l. 3. *hornlight*: the yellow glow like the light emitted through a lantern's horn window.

hoarlight. See *J.* 199: 'the burnished or embossed forehead of sky over the sundown; of beautiful "clear" | Perhaps the zodiacal light'.

l. 4. *waste*: fade away.

l. 6. *throughther*. I am grateful to Mr Myrddin Jones for pointing out that this dialect word, 'through-other', means confused, disorderly. (See *EDD*.)

pashed: crushed by blows. l. 7. *disremembering*: forgetting.

dismembering. See *J.* 236: 'darkness and despair. In fact being unwell I was quite downcast: nature in all her parcels and faculties gaped and fell apart, *fatiscebat*, like a clod cleaving and holding only by strings of root.'

round: rebuke.

l. 9. *dragonish*. See *S.* 199 and 243.

damask: make a pattern like that on ornate metal swords.

ll. 11–12. See Matt. 25: 31–3.

ll. 13–14. *ware of*. Remember that there will be a 'world' in the Day of Judgement when the behaviour of all men will be judged to be either right or wrong and those condemned to hell will suffer; see *S.* 243, 'the worm of conscience, which is the mind gnawing and feeding on its own most miserable self' (Meditation on Hell).

On the Portrait, &c. Dated 'Monasterevan, Co. Kildare. Christmas 1886'. Hopkins wrote to Dixon, 'I was at Xmas and New Year down with some kind people in Co. Kildare, where I happened to see the portrait of two beautiful young persons, a brother and sister, living in the neighbourhood. It so much struck me that I began an elegy in Gray's metre, but being back here I cannot go on with it' (*L.* II 150). See C. Phillips, 'The Mixed Emotions of Hopkins's "Portrait of Two Beautiful Young People"', *Hopkins Quarterly*, 16/4 (Jan. 1990), 137–46, and 'The Effects of Incompleteness in Three Hopkins Poems', *Renascence*, 42/1–2 (Fall 1989–Winter 1990), 29–33.

l. 3. Earlier read: 'Rich runs the juice in violets and fresh leaves'.

158 l. 7. *time's aftercast*. Earlier read: 'fate's afterthrow'.

ll. 7–8. Perhaps 'as for the future, the children will be (for their parents) a source of effort, hope, risk, and interest'.

l. 8. Earlier read: 'Things all of care, heft, hazard, interest.'

l. 12. *Barrow*: The river that runs through Monasterevan (see *L.* I 306).

ll. 23–4. See Matt. 19: 16–24.

Before l. 25 one draft read:

> Who yet was inward-lovely, bravèd well
> That world-breath's ransack nor wrestling nor stealth
> The least foil. How then? Rise he would not; fell
> Rather; he wore that millstone you wear, wealth.
>
> Ah, life, what's like it?—Booth at Fairlop Fair;
> Men/boys brought in to have each our shy there, one
> Shot, mark or miss, no more. I miss; and 'There!—
> Another time I' . . . 'Time' says Death 'is done'.

l. 29. *eye*: (verb) 'see'. l. 30. *banes*: 'cause of trouble' (OED).

ll. 29–31. Earlier read:

> feast of
> your ~~lovely~~ youth and that most earnest air,
> They do but call your banes to more carouse;
> Worst ~~will~~ batten on best: (cancelled)

There are two additional stanzas that alter the direction of the poem. They read:

> Two men wrestle who shall ride a mare, bestrid
> By one this long while. Look now, the other one—
> What else?—will but do what his brother did—
> Once saddled, override his mother's son.
>
> See where a lighthouse lifts above the world.
> Across the mouthing of the million foam
> Its bright eye broke but now, my heart, and hurled
> The deep, not dark nor Delphic, rede of Rome.

159 *Harry Ploughman*. Dated 'Dromore Sept. 1887'. Single stress-marks in the text represent double stresses in the MS. See pp. xxii–xxiii, 167.

Metrical marks: l. 1 hurdle arms l. 4 shōuldĕ̋r . . . shánk l. 6 Stand l. 8 Sōãred ő̆r sánk l. 9 Though as a . . . finds his, as at a l. 10 ín . . . whát . . . he each . . . do l. 11 His l. 12 to it, Harry l. 13 In him . . . quail . . . wallowing o'the . . . crîmsons l. 14 wînd liftẹd wind-lạced l. 16 Chũrlsgrace . . . chîld . . . Amansstrength . . . hângs or hũrls l. 17 Them—broad ín . . . híde . . . frówning féet . . . ráced l. 18 cold fũrls. Hopkins wrote: 'Marks used:

(1) ^ strong stress; which does not differ much from

(2) ⌒ pause or dwell on a syllable, which need not however have the metrical stress;
(3) ´ the metrical stress, marked in doubtful cases only;
(4) ˜ quiver or circumflexion, making one syllable nearly two, most used with diphthongs and liquids;
(5) ⁀ between syllables slurs them into one;
(6) ⁀ over three or more syllables gives them the time of one half foot
(7) ‿ the outride; under one or more syllables makes them extra-metrical: a slight pause follows as if the voice were silently making its way back to the highroad of the verse.'

Hopkins wrote to Bridges on 28 September 1887 that he had done the whole of one sonnet ('Harry Ploughman') and most of another ('Tom's Garland'). 'The one finished is', he said, 'a direct picture of a ploughman, without afterthought.' On 11 October 1887 Hopkins wrote to Bridges that he would enclose the sonnet on Harry Ploughman 'in which burden-lines [indented] (they might be recited by a chorus) are freely used: there is in this very heavily loaded sprung rhythm a call for their employment. The rhythm of this sonnet, which is altogether for recital, not for perusal (as by nature verse should be) is very highly studied' (*L.* I 263). He remarked that he wanted the ploughman 'to be a vivid figure before the mind's eye; if he is not that the sonnet fails' (*L.* I 265). See G. Storey, 'Hopkins as a Mannerist', *Studies in the Literary Imagination*, 21/1 (spring 1988), 81–4.

159 l. 1. *hurdle*: willow twigs twisted together.

flue: 'a woolly or downy substance' (OED), here 'hair'.

l. 2. *rack*: (technical) ribcage (MacKenzie, *Reader's Guide*, 194).

l. 3. *knee-nave*. Earlier read: 'knee-bank' = knee-cap.

l. 7. *curded*: bulged.

l. 9. *beechbole*. Beech trees are known for their strength and straightness. Beech trunks were used for ship's masts.

l. 14. *crossbridle*: tangle.

l. 16. *Churlsgrace*: hardy, peasant gracefulness.

ll. 16–17. *Churlsgrace . . . how it hangs or hurls | Them*. Grammatically: his churlsgrace controls his frowning feet broad-lashed in bluff hide as they race against the clods of earth turned by the plough.

frowning: moving forward aggressively? Gardner suggested that it referred to wrinkles in the leather of Harry's boots (*Poems*, 292).

l. 17. Hopkins wrote to Bridges (*L.* I 265, 6 Nov. 1887): 'dividing a compound word by a clause sandwiched into it was a desperate deed, I feel, and I do not feel that it was an unquestionable success.'

l. 18. *cold furls*. Earlier read: 'flame-furls'.

l. 19. Earlier read: 'With-a-wet-sheen-shot furls.' and 'With-a-wet-fire-flushed furls.'

(*Ashboughs*). Bridges' title. 1887? (OET 483). Written first as a curtal sonnet. A fair copy of this is written above drafts of 'To seem the stranger' and 'I wake and feel'. A second version, written on another sheet below the final lines of 'My own heart', has an additional revision that expands the poem to thirteen lines. Of 'Tom's Garland' Hopkins noted: 'Heavy stresses marked double, thus ʺ and stresses of sense, independent of the natural stress of the verse, thus ̏.'

Single stress-marks in the text represent double stresses in the MS; see pp. xxii–xxiii, 167.

Metrical marks: l. 1 Not of . . . wa̋ndering on l. 2 ánything . . . mílk . . . mínd . . . ső sȉghs de̋ep l. 3 Poetry tó it, as a . . . brȅak l. 4 Say it is a̋shboughs: whether on a December l. 5 ór . . . la̋shtender cȍmbs l. 13 Heaven . . . childs things by.

See *L.* III 202 for Hopkins's early enthusiasm for ash trees.

ll. 5–6. See *J.* 154, 177; *J.* 222: 'The ashes thrive and the combs are not wiry and straight but rich and beautifully curved'; *J.* 23: ' . . . in wind. Noticed also frequent partings of ash-boughs.'

l. 7. Earlier read: 'They touch: their wild weather-swung talons sweep'.

tabour: play on it as on a small drum.

l. 9. *mells*: mixes. *Eye*: MacKenzie suggests Hopkins meant 'Ay' (OET, 194).

ll. 9–11. Earlier read:

. . . a thousand fing-
Ers: then they are old Earth groping towards that steep
Heaven once Earth childed by.

160 *Tom's Garland*. Dated 'Dromore Sept. 1887'.

Numerous metrical marks. Hopkins noted that it is a 'sonnet common rhythm, but with hurried feet: two codas . . . Heavy stresses marked double, thus ʺ . . . ' Hyphen l. 16 editorial.

Metrical marks: l. 3 By him and l. 5 lustily he his l. 7 Seldomer l. 10 honour enough in l. 12 nő l. 14 nó l. 15 beyond l. 16 glory, earth's.

Hopkins asked Bridges how to construct codas: 'it is', he remarked, 'the only time I have felt forced to exceed the beaten bounds' (*L.* I 263). Neither Dixon nor Bridges found the poem's meaning easy to untangle and on 10 February 1888 Hopkins sent Bridges a crib: 'it means . . . that . . . the commonwealth or well ordered human society is like one man; a body with many members and each its function; some higher, some lower, but all honourable, from the honour which belongs to the whole. The head is the sovereign, who has no superior but God and from heaven receives his or her authority: we must then imagine this head as bare . . . and covered, so to say, only with the sun and stars, of which the crown is a symbol. . . . The foot is the daylabourer, and this is armed with hobnail boots, because it has to wear and be worn by the ground; which again is symbolical; for it is navvies or daylabourers who . . . in gangs and millions, mainly trench, tunnel, blast, and in other ways disfigure, "mammock" the earth and . . . stamp it with their footprints. And the "garlands" of nails they wear are therefore the visible badge of the place they fill, the lowest in the commonwealth. But this place still shares the common honour, and if it wants [lacks] one advantage, glory or public fame, makes up for it by another, ease of mind, absence of care; and these things are symbolized by the gold and the iron garlands. . . . Therefore the scene of the poem is laid at evening, when they are giving over work and one after another pile their picks, with which they earn their living, and swing off home, knocking sparks out of mother earth not now by labour and of choice but by the mere footing, being strongshod and making no hardship of hardness, taking all easy. And so to supper and bed . . . the labourer—surveys his lot, low but free from care; then by a sudden strong act . . . tosses it away as a light matter. The witnessing of which lightheartedness makes me indignant with the fools of Radical Levellers. But presently I remember that this is all very well for those who are in, however low in, the Commonwealth and share in any way the Common weal [goods]; but that the curse of our times is that many do not share it, that they are outcasts from it and have neither security nor splendour; that they share care with the high and obscurity with the low, but wealth or comfort with neither. And this state of things, I say, is the origin of Loafers, Tramps, Cornerboys, Roughs, Socialists and other pests of society' (*L.* I 272–4).

Hopkins remarked that the poem resembled 'Harry Ploughman', the result of their having been conceived at the same time (*L.* I 271).

160 l. 2. *fallowbootfellow*. Earlier read: 'The fallow booted navvy'.

fallow: no longer at work once the day's toil is over.

bootfellow: workmate.

161 *Epithalamion*. Unfinished drafts. Hopkins intended the poem for his brother, Everard, who married in April 1888 (*L.* I 277). The drafts are written on examination paper of the Royal University of Ireland, suggesting that Hopkins began it while invigilating. However, he found himself without the inspiration to complete it. See N. White, *Hopkins: A Literary Biography*, 425–8.

Metrical mark: l. 37 hōăr-huskèd.

162 l. 37. *selfquainèd*. See 'quoin'—an architectural term for an exterior angle or interior corner in a building.

l. 38. *shivès*: splinters; see 'That Nature is a Heraclitean Fire', l. 4.

'The sea took pity'. Undated fragment.

163 *That Nature is a Heraclitean Fire, &c.* Dated 'July 26 1888 | Co. Dublin' and marked 'sprung rhythm, with many outrides and hurried feet: sonnet with two codas'. It actually has three codas. Hopkins wrote that the sonnet was 'provisional only'.

The single stress marked in the text is a double stress in the MS. See pp. xxii–xxiii.

Metrical marks: l. 1 Cloud-puffball . . . pillows l. 2 thoroughfare: heaven-roysterers, in gay-gangs . . . marches l. 3 roughcast . . . whitewash l. 4 Shivelights . . . ín . . . lashes l. 5 boisterous l. 6 creases l. 7 crúst . . . stánches, stárches l. 9 Fóotfretted in it. Million-fuelèd . . . bonfire l. 10 to her, her l. 11 Mán . . . fást . . . firedint l. 12 Bóth are in an ű́nfáthomable, áll is in enórmous dárk l. 13 indignation l. 15 ány of him at áll so stárk l. 16 the Resurrection l. 17 héart's-clarion! Awáy . . . gásping l. 20 Fáll to the resíduary l. 23 Thís . . . jóke . . . pótsherd.

Heraclitus: a Greek philosopher (*c.*500 BC). It is difficult to establish the text and interpretation of Heraclitus' work since it has survived only in fragments and quotations. However, he seems to have suggested that the underlying substance of the universe is fire, understood not as flame but as a hot wind that was thought to exist in a pure form outside the earth's atmosphere, where it composed the sun and stars, and in a less pure, moist form close to the earth. (Fire is the material part of the world order or Logos.) Similar qualities were accorded the soul. Heraclitus suggested that the overall quantities of earth, water, and 'fire' were constant but that a continuous, cyclic process operated whereby some water evaporated to form 'fire', and other bits dried leaving behind earth while elsewhere earth and 'fire' dissolved or condensed to water. I am indebted to W. K. C. Guthrie, *A History of Greek Philosophy* (Cambridge, 1969), and G. S. Kirk, *Heraclitus: The Cosmic Fragments* (Cambridge, 1954).

163 ll. 1–2. Clouds show the world's constant flux, as 'fire' becomes moist and water dries. See *J.* 203–4, 207.

l. 3. *roughcast*: a mixture of lime and gravel used to coat walls.

l. 4. *shivelights*: splinters of light.

shadowtackle. Perhaps the shadows form a net-like pattern on the wall.

l. 5. *bright wind*: a term used by Diogenes Laertius to describe 'fire', the air rising to form the celestial bodies (Fr. 9.9).

l. 7. *squeezed dough, crust, dust*: stages in the drying-out of the mud to dust.

stanches: stops the flow.

starches: stiffens. See *Richard*, iv ll. 2–3.

l. 9. *Million-fuelèd, nature's bonfire burns on*. Fr. 30: the cosmos is compared to a huge bonfire, part of it already 'fire' while earth and water are potentially 'fire'.

l. 10. According to Macrobius, Heraclitus called the soul 'a spark of the substance of the stars' (Guthrie, 481).

ll. 13–14. *that shone | Sheer off, disseveral*: individual and unlike any other.

l. 14. Heraclitus spoke of the soul as being like 'fire', which could be destroyed by sin as 'fire' by water.

l. 19. Perhaps influenced by Fr. 96 (Heraclitus): 'Corpses are more fit to be cast out than dung.'

ll. 21–2. By allowing himself to be incarnated and crucified, Christ won for believers eternal life in a perfect body; see 1 Cor. 15: 52.

Hopkins wrote to Dixon: 'What a preposterous summer! It is raining now: when is it not? However there was one windy bright day between floods last week: fearing for my eyes, with my other rain of papers, I put work aside and went out for the day, and conceived a sonnet. Otherwise my muse has long put down her carriage and now for years "takes in washing" . . . ' (*L.* II 157, 29–30 July 1888). On 25 September Hopkins wrote to Bridges: 'lately I sent you a sonnet, on the Heraclitean Fire, in which a great deal of early Greek philosophical thought was distilled; but the liquor of distillation did not taste very Greek, did it?' (*L.* I 291).

164 *'What shall I do for the land that bred me?'* Bridges dated it August 1885, but Hopkins's letters suggest that most, if not all, of it must

have been written in 1888. On 8 September 1888, for instance, he wrote to Bridges: 'I had in my mind the first verse of a patriotic song for soldiers, the words I mean: heaven knows it is needed. I hope to make some 5 verses, but 3 would do for singing: perhaps you will contribute a verse. In the Park I hit on a tune, very flowing and spirited . . . I find I have made 4 verses, rough at present, but I send them . . . I hope you may approve what I have done, for it is worth doing and yet it is a task of great delicacy and hazard to write a patriotic song that shall breathe true feeling without spoon or brag' (*L.* I 283). He sent a revised version on 25 September 1888. See *L.* I 289–90, 292, and 301–2. An accompaniment was written by W. S. Rockstro.

St. Alphonsus Rodriguez.

Metrical marks: l. 1 Glory⁀is l. 13 by⁀of l. 14 Majorca⁀Alfonso.

Hopkins sent a draft to Bridges on 3 October 1888, saying 'I ask your opinion of a sonnet written to order on the occasion of the first feast since his canonisation proper of St. Alphonsus Rodriguez, a lay-brother of our Order, who for 40 years acted as hall-porter to the College of Palma in Majorca: he was, it is believed, much favoured by God with heavenly lights and much persecuted by evil spirits. The sonnet (I say it snorting) aims at being intelligible.' The penultimate version read:

> Honour is flashed off exploit, so we say;
> And those strokes once that gashed flesh or galled shield
> Should tongue that time now, trumpet now that field,
> And, on the fighter, forge his glorious day.
> On Christ they do and on the martyr may;
> But be the war within, the brand we wield
> Unseen, the heroic breast not outward-steeled,
> Earth hears no hurtle then from fiercest fray.
> Yet God (that hews mountain and continent,
> Earth, all, out; who, with trickling increment,
> Veins violets and tall trees makes more and more)
> Could crowd career with conquest while there went
> Those years and years by of world without event
> That in Majorca Alfonso watched the door.

l. 1. *so we say.* 'I mean "This is what we commonly say, but we are wrong"' (*L.* I 297).

165 l. 10. To an objection made by Bridges, Hopkins conceded, 'it is true continents are partly made by "trickling increment"; but', he added, 'what is on the whole truest and most strikes us about them and mountains is that they are made what now we see them by trickling *de*crements, by detrition, weathering and the like . . . And at any rate

naturally said to be hewn, and to *shape*, itself, means in old English to hew and the Hebrew *bara/* to create, even, properly means to hew. But life and living things are not naturally said to be hewn: they grow, and their growth is by trickling increment' (*L.* I 296–7).

165 *'Thou art indeed just'*. Dated 'March 17 1889'.

Metrical marks: l. 3 Why do sinners' l. 4 Disappointment l. 7 me? Oh l. 10 they are.

Hopkins wrote to Bridges that 'it must be read *adagio molto* and with great stress' (*L.* I 303, 21 Mar. 1889).

l. 9. *brakes*: thickets.

l. 11. *fretty chervil*: cow parsley, whose flowers are delicate, white, and lacy; Hopkins recorded its flowering in March 1868 (*J.* 162).

ll. 12–13. 'It is now years that I have had no inspiration of longer jet than makes a sonnet, except only in that fortnight in Wales: it is what, far more than direct want of time, I find most against poetry and production in the life I lead. Unhappily I cannot produce anything at all, not only the luxuries like poetry, but the duties almost of my position, its natural outcome—like scientific works . . . All impulse fails me: I can give myself no sufficient reason for going on. Nothing comes: I am a eunuch—but it is for the kingdom of heaven's sake' (to Bridges, 12 Jan. 1888, *L.* I 270). See too *S.* 262 (quoted in note to ll. 8 and 11–14 of 'To seem the stranger').

166 *'The shepherd's brow'*. Dated 'April 3 1889'.

Metrical marks: l. 3 they are.

l. 1. Earlier read: 'The shepherd fronting heaven's fork-lightning owns' and 'The shepherd's eye, fronting forked lightning owns'.

ll. 1–2. Hopkins describes the 'forked' appearance of lightning in *J.* 212 and its effect in *J.* 221 (19 July) and *J.* 233–4 (22 July). The shepherd has been variously identified as Christ, Moses, or even Michael; all acknowledge (*own*) the power and glory of God, represented by lightning (cf. 'The Wreck of the Deutschland', stanzas 2 and 9).

l. 3. *towers*. See Milton, *Paradise Lost*, v. 907, where the rebellious angels are described as 'those proud towers to swift destruction doomed'.

l. 8. Earlier read: 'What bass can his lute bear to tragic tones?'

viol. The translation sometimes used for *nēbel*, a kind of harp or lyre probably used to supply the bass when played with other instruments. It was played by David (*New Bible Dict.*, ed. J. D. Douglas). Milton in 'The Passion' declared 'softer strings | of lute, or viol still, more apt for mournful things' (ll. 27–8) were appropriate to his poem on Christ's crucifixion ('still' = quiet).

l. 11. Cf. *King Lear*, III. iv. 109–10, 'unaccommodated man is no more but such a poor, bare, forked animal'.

ll. 13–14. Earlier read:

> In spoons have seen my masque played and how tame
> My tempest and my spitfire freaks how fussy.

To R. B. Dated 'April 22 1889'.

Metrical marks: l. 4 mother of l. 7 widow of l. 10 rapture of.

l. 2. *blowpipe flame*. Cf. *S.* 242, 'You have seen a glassblower breathe on a flame; at once it darts out into a jet taper as a lance head and as piercing too.'

l. 5. *nine years*. Horace, in *The Art of Poetry* (ll. 386–9), suggested that a poem should be kept for nine years before publication so that it could be revised (MacKenzie, *Reader's Guide*, 208). See *L.* II 135, where in talking about music Hopkins remarked to Dixon 'the disproportion is wonderful between the momentary conception of an air and the long gestation of its setting'.

l. 6. *combs*: straightens out, grooms for presentation.

l. 12. Earlier read: 'The fire, the fall, the courage, the creation' and 'The wild wing, waft, cry, carol, and creation'.

ll. 13–14. Earlier read:

> Believe my withered world knows no such bliss
> Rebuke no more, but read my explanation.

Further Reading

BIBLIOGRAPHY

Cohen, Edward H., *Works and Criticism of Gerard Manley Hopkins: A Comprehensive Bibliography* (Washington, 1969).

Dunne, Tom, *Gerard Manley Hopkins: A Comprehensive Bibliography* (Oxford, 1976), This covers work up to 1970–1.

Bibliographical surveys can also be found in *Hopkins Quarterly*, and E. Hollahan, *Gerard Manley Hopkins and Critical Discourse* (New York, 1993).

MAJOR EDITIONS

The Poems of Gerard Manley Hopkins, ed. W. H. Gardner and N. H. MacKenzie (Oxford, 1967, 1984) and *Gerard Manley Hopkins*, ed. Catherine Phillips (Oxford Authors series; Oxford, 1986, 1991) both contain all the poems. (The latter also includes a selection of Hopkins's prose.) The best edition of Hopkins's poetry is Norman H. MacKenzie's *Poetical Works of Gerard Manley Hopkins* (Oxford English Texts; Oxford, 1990). There are also two volumes of facsimilies of the manuscripts edited by Norman H. MacKenzie: vol. i, *Early Poetic Manuscripts and Notebooks*; vol. ii, *The Later Poetic Manuscripts* (New York, 1989, 1991).

The Journals and Papers were edited by Humphry House (London, 1959, reprinted 1966) and completed after his death by Graham Storey. Christopher Devlin, SJ, prepared the edition of Hopkins's *Sermons and Devotional Writings* (London, 1959, reprinted 1967) while C. C. Abbott produced three volumes of letters; those of *Gerard Manley Hopkins to Robert Bridges*, second edition revised (London, 1955, repr. 1970); *The Correspondence of Gerard Manley Hopkins and Richard Watson Dixon*, second edition revised (London, 1955, repr. 1970); and *Further Letters of Gerard Manley Hopkins*, second edition revised and enlarged (London, 1956, repr. 1970). A number of additional letters were published in *The Hopkins Research Bulletin*. These were included in an edition of the *Selected Letters of Gerard Manley Hopkins*, ed. Catherine Phillips (Oxford, 1990, with corrections 1992).

BIOGRAPHY

Norman White, *Hopkins: A Literary Biography* (Oxford, 1992) and Robert Bernard Martin, *Gerard Manley Hopkins: A Very Private Life* (London, 1991).

CRITICAL BOOKS

Allsopp, Michael E., and Sundermeier, Michael W. (eds.), *Gerard Manley Hopkins: New Essays on His Life, Writing and Place in English Literature* (Lampeter, 1989).

Ball, Patricia M., *The Science of Aspects: The Changing Role of Fact in the Work of Coleridge, Ruskin and Hopkins* (London, 1971).

Bender, Todd K., *Gerard Manley Hopkins: The Classical Background and Critical Reception of his Work* (Baltimore, 1966).

Bottrall, Margaret (ed.), *Gerard Manley Hopkins: Poems—A Casebook* (London, 1975).

Boyle, Robert, SJ, *Metaphor in Hopkins* (Chapel Hill, 1960, 1961).

Bremer, Rudolf, 'Gerard Manley Hopkins: The Sonnets of 1865.' Ph.D. thesis, State University of Groningen, 1978.

Cotter, James Finn, *Inscape: The Christology and Poetry of Gerard Manley Hopkins* (Pittsburgh, 1972).

Downes, David A., *Gerard Manley Hopkins: A Study of his Ignatian Spirit* (London, 1960).

——— *Victorian Portraits: Hopkins and Pater* (New York, 1965).

Ellis, Virginia Ridley, *Gerard Manley Hopkins and the Language of Mystery* (London, 1991).

Fulweiler, Howard, *Letters from the Darkling Plain: Language and the Grounds of Knowledge in the Poetry of Arnold and Hopkins* (Columbia, 1972).

Gardner, W. H., *Gerard Manley Hopkins, 1844–89: A Study of Poetic Idiosyncrasy in Relation to Poetic Tradition*, 2 vols. (London, 1944, 1949; repr. London, 1966).

Giles, Richard (ed.), *Hopkins Among the Poets: Studies in Modern Responses to Gerard Manley Hopkins* (International Hopkins Association Monograph, 3; Hamilton, 1985).

Griffiths, Eric, *The Printed Voice of Victorian Poetry* (Oxford, 1989).

Hartman, Geoffrey, *The Unmediated Vision: An Interpretation of Wordsworth, Hopkins, Rilke, and Valery* (New Haven, 1954; repr. New York, 1966).

——— (ed.), *Hopkins: A Collection of Critical Essays* (Englewood Cliffs, 1966).

Heuser, Alan, *The Shaping Vision of Gerard Manley Hopkins* (London, 1958; repr. New York, 1968).

Hollahan, Eugene (ed.), *Gerard Manley Hopkins and Critical Discourse* (New York, 1993).

Holloway, Sister Marcella M., *The Prosodic Theory of Gerard Manley Hopkins* (Washington, 1947; repr. 1964).

Johnson, Wendell Stacy, *Gerard Manley Hopkins: The Poet as Victorian* (Ithaca, 1968).

Keating, John E., SJ, *'The Wreck of the Deutschland': An Essay and Commentary* (Kent, Ohio, 1963).

Kenyon Critics, The, *Gerard Manley Hopkins* (New York, 1945; repr. London, 1975).

Lees, Francis, N., *Gerard Manley Hopkins* (New York, 1966).

McChesney, Donald, *A Hopkins Commentary* (London, 1968).

MacKenzie, Norman H., *A Reader's Guide to Gerard Manley Hopkins* (London, 1981).

——— *Hopkins* (Writers and Critics series; Edinburgh, 1968).

Mariani, Paul, *Commentary on the Complete Poems of Gerard Manley Hopkins* (London, 1970).

Milroy, James, *The Language of Gerard Manley Hopkins* (London, 1977).

Milward, Peter, SJ, *Commentary on G. M. Hopkins' 'The Wreck of the Deutschland'* (Tokyo, 1968).

——— *A Commentary on the Sonnets of G. M. Hopkins* (Tokyo, 1969).

——— and Schoder, Raymond V., SJ, *Landscape and Inscape: Vision and Inspiration in Hopkins's Poetry* (London, 1975).

——— and ——— (eds.), *Readings of 'The Wreck': Essays in Commemoration of the Centenary of G. M. Hopkins' 'The Wreck of the Deutschland'* (Chicago, 1976).

North, John S., and Moore, Michael D. (eds.), *Vital Candle: Victorian and Modern Bearings in Gerard Manley Hopkins* (Waterloo, 1984).

Peters, W. A. M., SJ, *Gerard Manley Hopkins: A Critical Essay towards the Understanding of his Poetry* (London, 1948; repr. Oxford, 1970).

Phare, E. E., *Gerard Manley Hopkins* (Cambridge, 1933; reprinted New York, 1967).

Phillips, Catherine, *Robert Bridges: A Biography* (Oxford, 1992).

Pick, John, *Gerard Manley Hopkins: Priest and Poet*, second edition (London, 1966).

——— (ed.), *Gerard Manley Hopkins: 'The Windhover'* (Columbus, 1969).

Plotkin, Cary H., *The Tenth Muse: Victorian Philology and the Genesis of the Poetic Language of Gerard Manley Hopkins* (Carbondale, 1989).

Ritz, Jean-Georges, *Robert Bridges and Gerard Manley Hopkins, 1863–1889: A Literary Friendship* (London, 1960).

——— *Le Poète Gérard Manley Hopkins, S.J.: L'Homme et l'œuvre* (Paris, 1963).

Schneider, Elisabeth, *The Dragon in the Gate: Studies in the Poetry of G. M. Hopkins* (Berkeley and Los Angeles, 1968).

Shimane, Kunio, *The Poetry of G. M. Hopkins: The Fusing Point of Sound and Sense* (Tokyo, 1983).

Stephenson, Edward, *What Sprung Rhythm Really Is* (International Hopkins Association Monograph, 4; Hamilton, 1987).

Sulloway, Alison G., *Gerard Manley Hopkins and the Victorian Temper* (London, 1972).

Thomas, Alfred, SJ, *Hopkins the Jesuit: The Years of Training* (London, 1969).

Thornton, R. K. R., *All My Eyes See: The Visual World of Gerard Manley Hopkins* (Sunderland, 1975).

——— *Gerard Manley Hopkins: The Poems* (London, 1973).

Weyand, Norman, SJ, and Schoder, Raymond V., SJ (eds.), *Immortal Diamond: Studies in Gerard Manley Hopkins* (London, 1949).

Zanniello, Tom, *Hopkins in the Age of Darwin* (Iowa City, 1988).

Index of Short Titles and First Lines

(Titles are set in italic, first lines in roman)

GENERAL EDITOR: FRANK KERMODE

THE OXFORD POETRY LIBRARY

GENERAL EDITOR: FRANK KERMODE

Matthew Arnold	*Miriam Allott*
William Blake	*Michael Mason*
Lord Byron	*Jerome McGann*
Samuel Taylor Coleridge	*Heather Jackson*
John Dryden	*Keith Walker*
Thomas Hardy	*Samuel Hynes*
George Herbert	*Louis Martz*
Gerard Manley Hopkins	*Catherine Phillips*
Ben Jonson	*Ian Donaldson*
John Keats	*Elizabeth Cook*
Andrew Marvell	*Frank Kermode and Keith Walker*
John Milton	*Jonathan Goldberg and Stephen Orgel*
Alexander Pope	*Pat Rogers*
Sir Philip Sidney	*Katherine Duncan-Jones*
Henry Vaughan	*Louis Martz*
William Wordsworth	*Stephen Gill and Duncan Wu*